Missouri & North Arkansas Railroad: History Through the Miles

Barton Jennings

Missouri & North Arkansas Railroad: History Through the Miles
Copyright © 2019 by Barton Jennings

All rights reserved. This book may not be duplicated or transmitted in any way, or stored in an information retrieval system, without the express written consent of the publisher, except in the form of brief excerpts or quotations for the purpose of review. Making copies of this book, or any portion, for any purpose other than your own, is a violation of United States copyright laws.

Publisher's Cataloging-in-Publication Data
Jennings, Barton

Missouri & North Arkansas Railroad: History Through the Miles
440p.; 21cm.
ISBN: 978-1-7327888-2-4

Library of Congress Control Number: 2019904819

First Edition

Front cover photos all by Barton Jennings
From top: M&NA depot, St. Joe, Arkansas, 2018; M&NA depot, Wheaton, Missouri, 2014; M&NA depot, Rondo, Arkansas, 1986; Railroad tracks through warehouses, Helena, Arkansas, 2018.

Back cover photo by Sarah Jennings

Please send comments or corrections to sarah@techscribes.com

TechScribes, Inc.
PO Box 620
Avon, IL 61415
www.techscribes.com

Printed in the United States of America

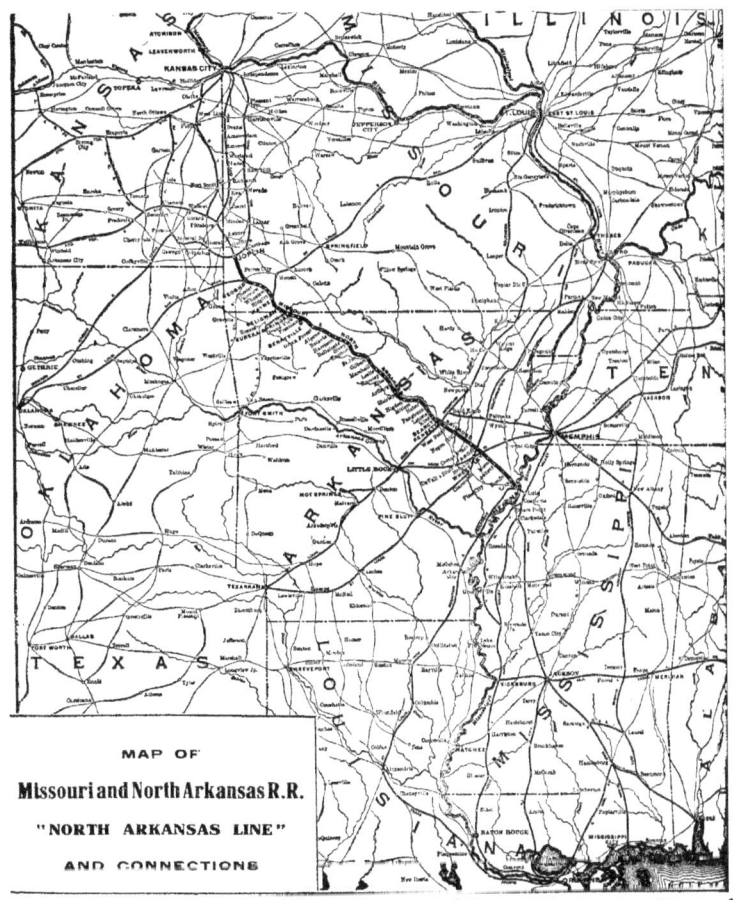

From *The Official Guide of the Railways and Steam Navigation Lines of the United States*, January 1910, page 950.

Other books by this author:

Arkansas & Missouri Railroad: History Through the Miles
Alaska Railroad: History Through the Miles
Iowa Interstate Railroad: History Through the Miles
Everett Railroad: History Through the Miles
Tennessee Central Railway: History Through the Miles
Whitewater Valley Railroad: History Through the Miles
Oregon's Joseph Branch: History Through the Miles

Contents

History of the Railroad 9
Characteristics of the Railroad 39
The Missouri & North Arkansas Railroad Depots 43
Missouri & North Arkansas Route Guide
   First District – Joplin (MO) to Harrison (AR) 47
   Joplin (MO) to Neosho (MO) 51
   Neosho (MO) to Wayne (MO) 79
   Wayne (MO) to Seligman (MO) 97
   Seligman (MO) to Harrison (AR) 105
   Eureka Springs Branch 179
   Berryville Branch 193
   Second District – Harrison (AR) to Heber
      Springs (AR) 201
   Harrison (AR) to Heber Springs (AR) 205
   Third District – Heber Springs (AR) to Helena
      (AR) 297
   Heber Springs (AR) to Helena (AR) 303
About the Author 439

Missouri and North Arkansas R. R.
NORTH ARKANSAS LINE.

SELIGMAN, Mo.,
TO
GRAND VIEW, Ark.
Good for One Continuous Passage.
Gen'l Pass. Agt

2270

Missouri and North Arkansas
Railroad

JOPLIN, Mo.,
TO
ALPENA, Ark.
Good for One Continuous Passage, commencing not later than one day after date of sale. Subject to tariff regulations.
Traffic Mgr

2734

Missouri and North Arkansas
Railway Company

BERRYVILLE, Ark.,
TO
EUREKA SPRINGS, Ark.
Good for One Continuous Passage, commencing not later than one day after date of sale. Subject to tariff regulations.
Asst. Gen'l Pass. Agt.

9739

Missouri and North Arkansas
Railway Company

JOPLIN, Mo.
TO
BERRYVILLE, Ark.
Good for One Continuous Passage, commencing not later than one day after date of sale. Subject to tariff regulations.
Genl Pass Agt

A 535

Missouri and North Arkansas
RAILWAY COMPANY
W. Stephenson, Receiver

HARRISON, Ark.
—TO—
JOPLIN, Mo.
Good for One Continuous Passage, commencing not later than one day after date of sale. Subject to tariff regulations.
Genl. Pass. Agt

A 2401

Missouri and Arkansas
RAILWAY COMPANY

BERRYVILLE, Ark.
—TO—
FREEMAN, Ark.
Good for One Continuous Passage. Subject to tariff regulations.
Gen. Frt. & Pass. Agt.

621

Tickets from the collection of Barton Jennings.

Creating a Missouri & North Arkansas Route Guide

This book is designed to provide a guide to the now-abandoned Missouri & North Arkansas Railroad Company and some of the history that can be found along its route. Even with the changes that time has allowed, those who follow the route can easily relive some of the railroad's history. There is a tourist railroad that can be ridden, a museum at Harrison, and several structures listed on the National Register of Historic Places.

The Missouri & Arkansas Railway shut down in 1946, and the last parts of the railroad operated as the Arkansas & Ozarks (abandoned 1961) and the Cotton Plant-Fargo Railway (abandoned 1977). This means that most of the railroad has been gone for more than seventy years, with the last parts abandoned for more than forty years. During this time, much of the route has been flooded, turned into roadways, plowed under, or just left to erode away. However, an amazing amount of the railroad can still be found and followed, and a number of bridges and structures still exist.

A challenge with describing the railroad is that the Missouri & Arkansas and the Missouri & North Arkansas both showed that the railroad operated north-south, even though much of the route was actually east-west. The route description will use the north-south railroad directions, but will often use the real directions when describing certain features along the route. Additionally, the tracks were often described by their car-lengths. These car-lengths varied over the years, but were generally around 45 feet per car. Therefore, a track listed as being 20 cars in length could hold about 900 feet of train.

Another help in following the railroad are the many maps available on the internet. County road maps, topographic (topo) maps, and many other maps from the era can be found. Comparing these older maps with newer maps can often make finding the railroad easier. One map site that I found very helpful while following the railroad is TopoZone (www.topozone.com), whose maps generally clearly showed the railroad grade.

Finally, materials from The Missouri and North Arkansas Research Group and the Boone County Historical & Railroad Society can also be used to study and follow the route. The organization has an entire room dedicated to the railroad, and they sell a number of books related to the line.

A final issue deals with all of the names that were used to represent the railroad over its sixty years. To simplify the issue, the name Missouri & North Arkansas will generally be used, even when another railroad originally built the line. Please forgive this simplification.

History of the Railroad

Like many railroads, it took a number of companies to create the Missouri & North Arkansas Railroad. There were just as many, if not more, that operated parts of the railroad after its failure. The railroad started in 1880 with the creation of the Missouri & Arkansas Railroad Company of Missouri and the Eureka Springs Railway Company of Arkansas, and then their merger to create the Eureka Springs Railway Company by 1883. This railroad operated from Seligman, Missouri, to Eureka Springs, Arkansas.

In 1899, plans were underway to expand the railroad to the east, and the railroad became the St. Louis & North Arkansas Railway Company, completed to Harrison, Arkansas, by 1901. By 1903, the line had been extended further to the south to Leslie, Arkansas, but the railroad failed financially. The Southeastern Railroad Company had surveyed from Leslie to Pangburn, and the company was acquired and then the Missouri & North Arkansas Railroad Company was created to complete the job in 1906. It became the Missouri & North Arkansas Railway Company in 1922. Following the failure of this railroad, it became the Missouri & Arkansas Railway Company in 1935. The company then closed in 1946 and was sold off, creating several short line railroads. Even these smaller parts of the railroad system could not survive, and today only the several miles of the Eureka Springs Branch still exist, rebuilt and operating as a tourist railroad. A bit of track at Neosho, Searcy, and Helena also survived as industrial or yard trackage.

A brief history of each of the railroad companies is provided here. However, anyone interested in the full history should read *The North Arkansas Line* by James R. Fair,

Jr. The book *Shortline Railroads of Arkansas*, by Clifton E. Hull, is also a good source of information. The Missouri and North Arkansas Research Group, which works with the Boone County Historical and Railroad Society, publishes a regular newsletter on the railroad's history, and is highly recommended to anyone wanting to stay up-to-date on information about the railroad. The website *North Arkansas Line* once hosted large amounts of information about the railroad, including photos and documents. Area newspapers also contain large, but sometimes questionable reports about the railroad. David Hoge is a master of these newspaper resources and is due a thank you for his research in this area.

Eureka Springs Railway Company of Arkansas (1880 – 1882)

The Eureka Springs Railway Company of Arkansas was incorporated on June 26, 1880, as part of the planning process to build a railroad from the new Frisco line (St. Louis & San Francisco Railway at the time) through Seligman, Missouri, to the booming resort town of Eureka Springs, Arkansas. The company was organized by former Arkansas Governor Powell Clayton as a way to attract financing for the construction of the railroad. By early 1882, he had sold enough stock subscriptions to start construction. On February 27, 1882, the Eureka Springs Railway Company of Arkansas was merged with the Missouri & Arkansas Railroad Company of Missouri, creating the Eureka Springs Railway Company, the actual builder of the railroad.

Missouri & Arkansas Railroad Company of Missouri (1880 – 1882)

The Missouri & Arkansas Railroad Company of Missouri was the sister company of the Eureka Springs Railway Company of Arkansas and was incorporated on September 21, 1880. Like the Arkansas corporation, it was created to demonstrate the ability to raise funds and to build a railroad from Seligman to Eureka Springs. The two railroads were merged on February 27, 1882, before any construction began.

Eureka Springs Railway Company (1882 – 1899)

The Eureka Springs Railway Company was created by the merger of the Eureka Springs Railway Company of Arkansas and the Missouri & Arkansas Railroad Company of Missouri on February 27, 1882. The Western Construction Company of Little Rock, Arkansas, was awarded the contract to build the railroad, and a small group of stockholders funded the company. Most of these investors were long-time associates of Powell Clayton. These included Richard Kerens, an investor in a number of railroads who had served with Clayton and who would later be the U.S. ambassador to Austria. Kerens was elected the first president of the company. Another investor was Logan Roots, another military veteran with Clayton. Roots handled the tasks of company treasurer and much of the work with the construction company. Powell Clayton was elected company vice-president and was the third largest individual stockholder.

The Frisco Railroad was the second largest stockholder of the Eureka Springs Railway. The *Sixth Annual Report of the President of the St. Louis and San Francisco Railway*

Company for the Year 1882 announced some of the details of the relationship.

> "The railroad to Eureka Springs, Arkansas, referred to in my last Annual Report, has just been completed and put in operation. The line of that road now extends from Seligman on our Main Line to Eureka Springs, a distance of about 20 miles. The road was built by the Eureka Springs Railway Co. under and in accordance with an Agreement and Traffic Contract with this Company by the terms of which this Company agrees to devote a limited percentage of its earnings derived from the traffic interchanged therewith towards the payment of the interest of the First Mortgage Bonds of the Eureka Springs Railway Co., should the same be necessary for that purpose. In consideration of this Agreement this Company receives a portion of the Capital Stock and of the Second Mortgage Income Bonds of the Eureka Springs Railway Company.
>
> With this new road in operation and with first class day and sleeping coaches running to and from St Louis, without change, a large increase of passenger and freight traffic for our lines may be expected."

By May 1882, survey crews were determining the route of the new railroad, and the actual bids for construction were opened on July 10, 1882. The firm Jones and Cowen, a major railroad contractor in Texas, was awarded the bid. The process of clearing the route and grading the line started almost immediately. The rugged terrain and desire to

History of the Railroad

avoid the large costs of major fills, cuts and bridges made the line steep, with grades of 1.75% being common, and some measuring 2.60%. Grading was basically completed by November 1882. Tracks reached Eureka Springs on January 24, 1883, and according to Interstate Commerce Commission records, the full line opened for operation on February 1, 1883.

The railroad was primarily a passenger carrier, hauling visitors to and from the resorts in Eureka Springs. Many of these passengers rode on passenger cars from St. Louis and other major Frisco communities, operating through to Eureka Springs over the Eureka Springs Railway. Freight did move over the railroad, often ties and other timber products, fruits and vegetables, and many consumer products heading to the Eureka Springs market, which at the time was the sixth largest city in Arkansas. The railroad was profitable in 1883, even after the debt payments, a very unusual situation as the company grew.

The next several years saw the railroad develop a pattern of operations as Eureka Springs grew and modernized. During this time a number of proposals were made to extend the line through Harrison to reach the zinc and lead mines along the Buffalo River, or to Little Rock, Arkansas. By the late 1890s, the railroad began to face financial troubles as the debt was not being paid down, and freight and passenger levels had peaked and were starting to decline. The solution was to extend the line to the south and east to reach new markets, and hopefully new profits.

St. Louis & North Arkansas Railroad (1899 – 1906)

With plans to extend the line to the east and south, the Eureka Springs Railway Company was deeded to the new St. Louis & North Arkansas Railway Company (StL&NA), chartered on May 25, 1899. At the same time, the Allegheny Improvement Company was created as an affiliated company to manage the construction. The new company looked to the east with plans to connect to several existing towns such as Berryville and Harrison. The challenge was that there was no major stream or river to follow, meaning the grade would have to cross a number of ridges along the route. This led to a number of sharp curves and steep grades, with a reported five grades of 1.75% eastbound to Harrison, and six 1.75% grades westbound. These curves and grades would limit the speeds and capacities of trains for the entire history of the railroad.

By early 1900, J. B. Colt & Son was grading the line eastward from what became known as Junction, Arkansas. Colt & Son had earlier graded the Iron Mountain (Missouri Pacific) line from Newport to Batesville, a line that in some way forced the hands of the owners of the Eureka Springs Railway. The immediate challenge was the tunnel under Charcoal Gap, not far east of Junction. There were also the bridges over the Kings River and Long Creek, projects that required large amounts of masonry work and the erection of steel deck truss spans.

North of Berryville, the grade followed Clabber Creek, and a 3-mile branch line was required to reach Berryville. With a promised bonus from Harrison, the track reached there on March 22, 1901, with regular service beginning on April 15th after final surfacing and other work was completed. The branch to Berryville was completed on June 15, 1901, and the line from Seligman to Eureka Springs was rebuilt with heavier rail and new ties. At about the same time, the White River Railroad was granted a charter to build from Batesville to the northwest along the White River, just north of the St. Louis & North Arkansas Railway. *The Lead and Zinc News* produced numerous reports on the construction of these two railroads, with a detailed

History of the Railroad

report about the St. Louis & North Arkansas plans in the August 7, 1901, issue.

With the railroad at Harrison, routes to Little Rock and to the mines to the southeast were compared. In a decision that set the future of the railroad, the zinc and lead mines around St. Joe and the Buffalo River, known as the Rush Creek mining district, became the target of construction. The decision to build toward the mines was probably influenced by the announcement of the creation of the Morning Star Railroad with plans to connect Newport with the Rush Creek mining district. Construction by the Allegheny Improvement Company began in October 1901, and ten miles of grade was completed by January 1902. March saw the completion of the Crooked Creek bridge outside Harrison and the start of track construction. By summer, grading had reached St. Joe and rail was at Olvey.

Much of the construction of the M&NA used traditional techniques. For example, this stone culvert near Gilbert, Arkansas, shows the use of local stone, stacked to form the culvert's sides and top. Photo by Barton Jennings.

The large bridge over the Buffalo River was the next major project, and track construction halted at the new town of Gilbert, located on the north bank, for the year. This meant that 35 miles of track was opened in 1902 and that the zinc and lead mines in the area now had rail service as the Morning Star Railroad was never built. Construction of the concrete piers and the installation of the large through truss spans were delayed by high water and cold temperatures, and it wasn't until early summer that the bridge was completed. Grading had been completed and the track reached Leslie and regular service began on September 11, 1903.

Over the next several years, there were additional plans to extend the railroad, including the creation of the Leslie & Southern Railway Company and the Southeastern Railroad Company. There were other plans to extend the line west from Seligman. However, the company was also unable to pay off its debt, and on July 1, 1905, the railroad defaulted on its bond interest payments. By the end of the year, the St. Louis Union Trust arranged for a foreclosure on the railroad. With that, the railroad was sold at foreclosure, and on June 18, 1906, the route became the Missouri & North Arkansas Railroad Company.

Leslie & Southern Railway Company (1902 – 1905)

On December 18, 1902, backers and investors in the St. Louis & North Arkansas Railway Company chartered the Leslie & Southern Railway Company to build a railroad between Leslie and Little Rock, Arkansas. The formation of the company was reported in the December 24, 1902, *New York Times*. The article stated that the railroad had a capital stock of $3 million. *The Manual of Statistics: Stock Exchange Hand-Book* (1905) stated that an "extension to Little Rock, under the charter of the Leslie & Southern

Railway Co., was planned in 1903." A number of surveys were made and communities along the various proposed routes campaigned for the construction. The primary route was southeast to near Heber Springs, and then south to Conway and on to Little Rock. However, by 1905, the plans of the St. Louis & North Arkansas seemed to have changed and efforts to build toward Little Rock through the Leslie & Southern Railway ended and the Leslie & Southern Railway was heard of no more.

Southeastern Railroad Company (1905 – 1906)

The second railroad chartered to expand the St. Louis & North Arkansas was the Southeastern Railroad Company, chartered on July 17, 1905. It had much of the same management as the St. Louis & North Arkansas Railway. This included president George L. Sands (StL&NA vice-president), vice president John Scullin (StL&NA president), and treasurer Charles Gilbert, a major StL&NA investor. The *Arkansas Biennial Report of Secretary of State* (1906) had a route description for the planned railroad. It stated that the charter was to "build a railroad from the southern terminus of the St. Louis and North Arkansas Railroad" to Bagley Creek and on to a junction with the "St. Louis, Iron Mountain and Southern Railroad" in White County, then to the southwest to Pulaski County, "a total distance of one hundred and forty four miles." It was obvious that Little Rock was still in the plans.

The Railway Age (July 21, 1905) described the route as being from Leslie "to Garner, a point on the Iron Mountain Railroad about 40 miles north of Little Rock. The charter includes also a branch line to Little Rock, and states that the company contemplates building through to a point on the Mississippi River, either Helena or Arkansas City." The report stated that the capital stock was $3.5 million and had been "subscribed almost entirely by Saint Louis capitalists." The *Railroad Gazette* (July 28, 1905) had a similar article that mentioned Garner, but also Lonoke, Arkansas. Lonoke was also mentioned in a followup article in *The Railway Age* (July 28, 1905).

As rough surveys were made, a route was considered that ran from Leslie to Garner in White County with grades limited to 0.6% and curves of eight degrees. From there it turned south to Lonoke, Arkansas. The plan was for Lonoke to be a junction town with a line being built west to Little Rock, plus one to the southeast to the Mississippi River. There was even talk about the railroad being extended to the Gulf of Mexico.

On February 15, 1906, the destination of the railroad was changed from Little Rock to Helena, Arkansas. The company's owners voted on November 23, 1906, to transfer their assets, essentially a railroad survey from Leslie to Pangburn, to the Missouri & North Arkansas Railroad Company. The Southeastern Railroad Company officially ended on December 1, 1906.

Missouri & North Arkansas Railroad Company (1906 – 1922)

The St. Louis & North Arkansas Railway Company was sold to a committee established by the railroad bondholders on May 29, 1906, and the property became the Missouri & North Arkansas Railroad Company. The new incorporation was finally filed with the State of Arkansas on August 6, 1906, and Missouri on October 22, 1906. The August 17, 1906, issue of *The Railway Age* stated that "official notice is given to connecting lines that the Missouri & North Arkansas railroad company has purchased the St. Louis & North Arkansas railroad and that all balances and earnings after June 17, 1906, are payable to the Missouri & North

Arkansas company. The circular is signed by John Scullin, president of both companies." The December 28, 1906, issue provided more information by reporting that "the St. Louis & North Arkansas, 126 miles, was promptly reorganized with new capital as the Missouri & North Arkansas Railroad, and is constructing 328 miles of extensions east and west which will make it an important line."

A report by the Interstate Commerce Commission described the new Missouri & North Arkansas Railroad Company as including 19 miles of track originally built by the Eureka Springs Railway Company, and 106 miles of track built by the St. Louis & North Arkansas Railway Company. The new company planned to extend the railroad, and on August 15, 1906, an agreement was reached with the Allegheny Improvement Company to extend the line 178 miles from Leslie to Helena, and to also build a 32-mile route from Seligman west to Neosho and Joplin. The original cost estimate was $4,750,000, but the cost quickly surpassed this amount. Burke and Jones of Cape Girardeau, Missouri, won the contract on October 20th for clearing and grading the route to Searcy, while the Wisconsin Bridge & Iron Company got the contract for the steel bridges. On December 27th, a contract for grading between Wayne and Neosho was issued to Scott and Dalhoff, a combination of firms from St. Louis and Little Rock. Almost immediately, construction was again underway.

Throughout 1907, crews were building grades and track west of Wayne, Missouri, and east of Leslie, Arkansas. Meanwhile, a number of survey crews were attempting to find a route through the White River and Cache River bottoms. A shortage of funds and high costs slowed the work, but the northern extension was completed on January 25, 1908. By the middle of June, mixed train service was operating as far as Shirley, and soon Searcy-Heber Springs trains began to move. Construction was underway all along the railroad, and track was being built north from Helena by September. The December 1, 1908, M&NA timetable showed the line in service from Neosho to Kensett, and Cotton Plant to Helena. The White and Cache River bottoms were the challenges that were keeping the railroad from being finished. This was finally conquered on March 1, 1909, when the railroad began Joplin to Helena service. At the railroad's peak, there were a reported 92 stations along the line. Today, fewer than ten of the buildings survive.

Missouri and North Arkansas Railroad Party Ticket. From the collection of Barton Jennings.

The construction cost far more than the $4.75 million estimate, and according to several newspaper articles, much of this construction was the most expensive ever in Arkansas. By the time it was all done, 32 new miles of track was built between Neosho and Wayne, and 178 miles from Leslie to Helena. As described by the Interstate Commerce Commission, the "railroad of Missouri and North Arkansas Railroad Company, hereinafter called the carrier, is a single-track standard-gauge steam railroad, located in the States of Missouri and Arkansas. The owned main line consists of two disconnected sections of road, extending southeastwardly from Neosho to Wayne, Mo., and from Seligman, Mo., to Helena, Ark., with short branches from Junction to Eureka Springs and Freeman to Berryville, Ark., a total of 335.211 miles. The carrier operates a through line by means of trackage rights from Joplin, Mo., to Helena, Ark."

With some construction and bond interest payments not made, the St. Louis Union Trust Company again asked for a receiver to straighten out the company's finances. Federal Judge Jacob Trieber handled the case. Trieber was the first Jew to serve as a federal judge in the United States. He was well known for being an early civil rights leader who also was a leader in the women's suffrage movement. The Jacob Trieber Federal Building in Helena, Arkansas, listed on the National Register of Historic Places, is named for him. Judge Trieber appointed W. S. Holt, George Sands and Jesse McDonald as receivers for the railroad. Judge Treiber was later involved with the Missouri & North Arkansas several more times. For example, in April 1921, Trieber sentenced a striker to prison for the abuse of a strikebreaker, and ordered a deputy marshal to protect the M&NA rail yard in Helena from strikers.

Receivers operated the railroad from April 1, 1912, until the United States Railroad Administration (USRA) took over the railroad on January 1, 1918. The receivers arranged for better Pullman service, new train schedules, improvements in the railroad's shops, and new freight equipment. One of the biggest changes was the centralization of the shops at Harrison, Arkansas, and smaller shops being built at Heber Springs, replacing the shops at Eureka Springs and Leslie. This change was in response to the regulatory creation of the eight-hour workday and 100-mile crew runs. There was obviously some success, as on June 30, 1913, the Interstate Commerce Commission reclassified the Missouri & North Arkansas Railroad from a Class II railroad to a Class I railroad.

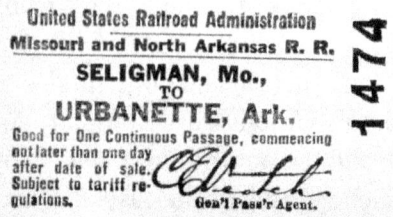

This circa 1918 ticket for passage from Seligman, Missouri, to Urbanette, Arkansas, on the Missouri and North Arkansas R. R. clearly shows that the United States Railroad Administration was operating the railroad. From the collection of Barton Jennings.

To prevent any labor issues during World War I, the wage scale was raised by the USRA to the standard paid on the large roads, or about double the previous pay, in April 1918. The railroad was returned to the receiver on June 29, 1918. During early September, the railroad began lowering the pay and the shopmen went on strike, shutting the railroad down. On September 24, 1918, the railroad owners again lost their railroad as part of the nationalization of the railroad system during World War I, and the higher pay was reinstated. Meanwhile, the lease by the federal government paid the railroad $175,000 per year, barely enough to cover the interest on the receiver's certificates. After losing a reported $875,121.62 operating the M&NA, the United States Railroad Administration returned the railroads to their owners starting on February 28, 1920, and the M&NA was faced with a reduction in war traffic and higher wages approved during the war to prevent strikes. The M&NA began to cut back workers, and then wages, leading to a series of strikes. On July 31, 1921, the company ended regular service and the railroad shut down. Multiple studies were conducted on what to do with the line, and a loan was applied for from the Interstate Commerce Commission. As a part of the application, a study of the line was conducted. What may be the most fitting description of the railroad ever written was put together by William Z. Ripley, a consultant for the Interstate Commerce Commission. In his report, he wrote:

> "It is evident from the map that the road neither begins nor ends anywhere, and it is difficult to see how it could perform any useful function except to serve the towns locally along the line. Whether they can afford sufficient business to keep it alive is open to question."

With the failure of the loan request, in January and February of 1922, steps were taken to foreclose on the railroad and to sell it at auction. On February 28, 1922, the Missouri & North Arkansas Railway Company was organized, which bought the railroad on April 10, 1922. However, the new company issued $5,000,000 in securities as collateral for the government loan, and the railroad stayed in debt.

Missouri & North Arkansas Railway Company (1922 – 1935)

The Missouri & North Arkansas Railway Company was organized on February 28, 1922, with the purpose of acquiring the Missouri & North Arkansas Railroad Company during its receivership. The new Railway acquired the old Railroad on April 10, 1922. To pay off the existing debt, a loan was obtained through the Interstate Commerce Commission, and the new M&NA issued $5,000,000 in first mortgage bonds that was used as collateral. After more than eight months, the railroad started the slow process of starting operations again. New employees were hired and the first mixed train began service between Seligman and Kensett on May 15, 1922. However, the existing American Federation of Labor (AFL) union employees made their displeasure known. For example, George W. Anderson, Vice President of the Order of Railway Trainmen, stated that: "This road has no right to live if it cannot pay a living wage." With what appeared to be a fight for the life or death of the railroad, the next year featured a number of burned bridges and sabotaged trains. January 1923 was the peak of activity as at least eight bridges were burned in one week, the Harrison depot safe was blown up and its contents taken, and several trains were derailed. The railroad soon announced that it would close again if the violence didn't end. With that announcement, citizens and businessmen from along the line armed themselves and organized an effort to protect the railroad. By mid-January, more than 1000 armed men were in Harrison to send the strikers packing. Led by what was known as the "Committee of Twelve," the force interviewed strikers and escorted many out of the north Arkansas area, all with the knowledge of local courts who had convicted several strikers of violence and theft against the railroad.

The peak of the anti-union actions took place on January 16, 1923, when Ed C. Gregor, a union activist who had shot at the vigilantes and was then arrested, was taken from the Harrison jail and hanged from the Crooked Creek railroad bridge. The Committee and its supporters also rounded up other union leaders across the railroad, beat some, and escorted most out of Arkansas. Documents showing the union's participation in some of the violence were found and turned over to local courts, and soon the violence ended and the citizens returned home. As stated in several reports, this was the first union strike to force a railroad to abandon operations and the first where the public rose up against a union to force the end of a strike. For more information on the strike, check out the report *The Missouri and North Arkansas Railroad Strike* by Orville Thrasher Gooden, or *An Industrial War: History of the Mis-*

souri and North Arkansas Railroad Strike and a Study of the Tremendous Issues Involved, published in 1923 by Bradley & Russell Publishers of Harrison, Arkansas.

Over the next several years the railroad returned to normal operations, and even made some operating improvements. However, the railroad couldn't return to profitability. As a result of several changes at the Frisco, the M&NA, still being called the May Never Arrive, acquired Wellington Stephenson, who became the president and general manager on January 1, 1926. Stephenson, who had previously been with the St. Louis Southwestern (Cotton Belt) and then the Jonesboro, Lake City & Eastern, would be with the company until June 22, 1933. Wellington, who always used "W" and never his full name, immediately hit the road to see the condition of the railroad. Although the Missouri & North Arkansas Railroad Company had invested heavily, leading to its failure, Stephenson wanted to start another infrastructure campaign. This included track and bridge work, and even the construction of a new three-story office building in Harrison. Many of the announcements appeared to be an effort to show a modern and capable railroad, although 250,000 new ties were installed and heavier rail was replacing older rail from the line's construction. Even new freight cars were built in the Harrison shops.

With most work completed, the M&NA started to show a profit in early 1927, but then spring flooding set records across the region, and railroads were under water by mid-April. At first the Missouri & North Arkansas benefitted as Missouri Pacific trains detoured from Kensett north to the Joplin area. However, the shops at Harrison were flooded by April 22, and soon the entire White and Cache River bottoms were flooded and towns like Cotton Plant were isolated. What became known as The Great Mississippi River Flood of 1927 was the most destructive river flood in the history of the United States, and the railroad was impacted until Fall 1927.

After the flood, Stephenson continued to spend money, acting like the railroad was part of a major operation. He bought a series of steam locomotives that were too heavy, forcing the rebuilding of bridges between Seligman and Kensett. During this time, Stephenson raised some funds by selling Receiver's Certificates, and Frank Kell of Texas began buying into the railroad. Kell had earlier built the Wichita Falls & Northwestern and the Wichita Falls & Southern railroads. He had also made money owning a milling company with multiple locations across the country.

An interesting announcement about the Missouri & North Arkansas was reported in the September 22, 1928, issue of *The Railway Age*. The news article, entitled "Asks to be included in merger," reported that "Federal Judge Martineau of Little Rock, Ark., on September 17 authorized W. Stephenson of Harrison, Arkansas, receiver of the Missouri and North Arkansas, to intervene before the Interstate Commerce Commission and request that the railroad be included in the proposed merger of the Missouri-Kansas-Texas, the St. Louis Southwestern and the Kansas City Southern." The merger talk went nowhere and the M&NA continued to operate on its own.

During the summer of 1929, Kell made an offer to buy all shares of the railroad, obtaining more than 80% of them just days before the Great Depression began in August 1929. However, the Depression took some time to hit the M&NA as revenues were up due to new oil train movements from Oklahoma to Helena. Business on the railroad dropped significantly in 1930, especially on the passenger side, and cost savings began again. With the poor history of the railroad, the company was turned down for various government loans and the railroad again spiraled quickly to failure with even employees not being paid. By June 1933, the employees, though not unionized, were almost in open revolt. After a meeting with a number of employees, much of the M&NA management departed.

A new management team seemed to calm things down, and the railroad began operating in the black except for its government debt payments. With the potential of saving his investment, Frank Kell petitioned the Federal Judge for the Western Division of the Eastern District of Arkansas, John E. Martineau, to foreclose on the property and to order its sale. The request was granted and the railroad was sold again on March 12, 1935. The minimum bid price was $350,000, far short of the almost $7 million of debt the Missouri & North Arkansas Railway Company had at its death.

Missouri & Arkansas Railway Company (1935 – 1949)

On April 16, 1935, the Missouri & Arkansas Railway Company was established and assumed the previous M&NA property. Frank Kell was now in charge of the railroad, having paid $350,000 for the company and getting most of that money back as the holder of the Receiver's Certificates. The Kell family owned 3495 of the 3500 shares of the company, and Joe, the son of Frank Kell, was made president.

Things began as new operations often did, and improvements such as new paint were underway. Kell also had management looking for new shipments, and unneeded assets such as old steam locomotives were scrapped for cash. A unique attempt to support new business was the creation of the Manda Corporation. Manda was formed to make investments in new businesses along the railroad, and to buy their products. A major success of Manda was the creation of the Everton Silica Sand Company in Everton, Arkansas.

The railroad turned a profit in 1936, and a dividend was actually paid.

The positive news and the desire to further cut costs led to the purchase of a new Brill gasoline-powered motor car (#605) in 1937 for the Kensett to Helena passenger train. The next year, the railroad bought two streamlined motorcars from American Car & Foundry (ACF), ending the steam-pulled passenger trains. These cars, #705 – Thomas C. McRae, and #706 – John L. Martineau, began operating on June 26, 1938. McRae was the governor of Arkansas during the strike of the early 1920s and Martineau was the federal judge involved with the creation of the Missouri & Arkansas Railway. The success of the ACF motorcars was the subject of an article in *The Railway Age* of December 10, 1938.

While the motorcars were good news for 1938, most of the rest of the news was bad. Several miles and more than a dozen bridges near Beaver were washed out by flooding in May. The economy turned worse in 1938 as another recession extended the Great Depression. On November 21, 1939, Joe Kell was killed in an auto accident, leaving no clear successor for Frank Kell, who was already losing interest in his questionable investment. Attempts to sell the railroad were again underway when Frank Kell died on September 17, 1941. Soon, World War II brought more changes to the railroad, which was now owned by the many members of the Kell family. To keep the family involved, Malcolm Putty, the husband of one of Frank Kell's daughters, became executive vice president. Another son-in-law, Orville Bullington, was the railroad's general counsel. Finally, daughter Willie May Kell was named chairman of the board. A dividend for their stock was soon issued as the company started to make some money during the beginning of World War II.

During the next few years, railroad labor unions started calling for substantial pay raises to make up for the stagnant pay during the Great Depression. Although the Missouri & Arkansas was primarily non-union, the call for higher wages was also made by the local employees. To prevent a national strike, President Roosevelt nationalized the railroads on December 27, 1943, raised the pay rate for railroaders retroactively to April 1, and then returned the railroads to their owners on January 22, 1944. The M&A did not recognize the pay raise as it would cost more than the total profits the railroad was making, and workers voted to go on strike. The strike was stopped by the National Mediation Board until an investigation of the railroad's finances could be made.

The study was conducted by Kansas City Southern executive Samuel W. Fordyce, possibly the most detailed report in the railroad's history. The report called for the elimination of many business units, including the passenger trains, as well as a reduction in management and overtime expenses. It also clearly stated that the railroad could not afford the new wages. However, a labor walkout occurred on July 28, 1944, leading to some significant pay raises.

Just as things seemed to have settled down, much of the backshop in Harrison burned down. After announcing another dividend, the Kell family set about selling the railroad. However, March of 1945 was another wet month and the railroad was flooded and washed out in the Georgetown area. Even after the war in Europe had ended, the railroad was still forced to detour trains south of Kensett. The end of the war also meant a reduction in freight traffic.

By 1946, assets of the railroad were being sold off to pay bills, and labor was again calling for higher wages. Also, years of minimal track work was causing an increase in derailments, costing the company even more money. Over the weekend of September 6th and 7th, the crews walked off the job. For the next week, a few employees, aided by management, cleaned up the railroad by moving foreign freight cars to interchange locations. By the end of the month, all equipment was parked and the railroad was closed. On September 21, 1946, the railroad applied to the Interstate Commerce Commission to abandon the property.

By November, the railroad had been sold to the Salzberg Interests. The Salzbergs had been buying small railroads across the region, often abandoning them for the scrap value. Attempts were made to prevent the railroad's abandonment, but the use of a receiver and a federal abandonment hearing kept the efforts from being successful. Also helping was a proposal to abandon only part of the railroad while selling the rest for operations by shortline railroads. The abandonment became official on April 6, 1949, and plans were made to operate parts of the railroad under the names of the Arkansas & Ozarks, and the Helena & Northwestern. The Missouri & Arkansas completely folded up on July 14, 1949, and most of its property was scrapped over the next year. This was the largest railroad abandonment in the United States up until that time, and remained the largest until the abandonment of the New York, Ontario & Western Railroad in 1957.

The abandonment of the Missouri & Arkansas Railway resulted in the creation of several new smaller railroads, each designed to protect clusters of shippers. The Arkansas & Ozarks saved the line between Seligman and Harrison, while the Helena Northwestern saved the line between Helena and Cotton Plant. However, eight of the fifteen largest sources of traffic in 1945 saw the end of railroad service. These included Heber Springs (1120 carloads), Red River (734), Everton (627), Shirley (459), Pangburn (393), Marshall (228), Leslie (188) and Letona (149). Fortunately, the Doniphan, Kensett & Searcy continued to serve many of the shippers at Searcy (308 carloads).

History of the Railroad

Arkansas & Ozarks Railway Company (1949 – 1961)

The Salzberg plan to abandon much of the line, but save the most valuable parts, led to the creation of the Arkansas & Ozarks Railway between Seligman, Missouri, and Harrison, Arkansas. This route served three of the top twelve sources of 1945 traffic on the Missouri & Arkansas. This included Eureka Springs (463 carloads), Berryville (219), and Harrison (679).

The charter for the railroad was approved on March 4, 1949, with the Salzbergs the primary owners, but also with a number of local stockholders. The Interstate Commerce Commission delayed operations until the Missouri & Arkansas was officially abandoned, but a great deal of work was begun to repair the three years of damage that occurred while the railroad was shut down. Initial work trains were pulled by steam – primarily former Missouri & Arkansas 4-6-0 #20. Sidings were pulled so the rail could be used elsewhere, and used ties from across the system were brought in to upgrade the line. Reportedly, the biggest challenge was reopening the tunnel south of Eureka Springs.

Two 70-ton diesel locomotives from General Electric were acquired, and the first arrived on the railroad on November 30, 1949. Operations began on February 1, 1950, with a grand celebration held at Harrison a week later. Trains typically operated Harrison to Seligman on Monday-Wednesday-Friday, and then back the next day. The shops in Harrison were sold off and a new small two-stall engine house was opened. By 1953, the railroad was making money and the first mortgage was actually paid off. Inbound freight consisted of animal feed, building materials, petroleum products and other similar materials. Outbound shipments continued to be wood products such as railroad ties, cedar fence posts and lumber; canned and fresh fruit from several canning facilities; grain; Ozarka drinking water from Eureka Springs; and poultry from Berryville. However, the railroad soon began to lose money again, and some have pointed out that the owners had stopped promoting the railroad and were looking to make their money by scrapping the railroad.

On January 19, 1959, the Corps of Engineers announced that almost three miles of the railroad would be flooded by the new Table Rock Lake, and that the land was to be condemned. Instead of forcing the grade to be raised, the railroad was happy to sell out, if it could find a buyer. The railroad continued to operate until much of the line in the area was damaged by floods on May 5, 1960. No repairs were attempted and the ICC was contacted on June 9, 1960, with an application to abandon the railroad. On April 7, 1961, permission to abandon was received. However, the St. Louis-San Francisco Railway (Frisco) filed suit against the Arkansas & Ozarks Railway to stop the abandonment because $30,594 in interchange services had not been paid. Apparently the payment was made, and by the end of summer, the railroad, which included the first grades built, was gone. According to Railroad Retirement Board reports, the Arkansas & Ozarks had an official life from February 1, 1950, to September 30, 1962.

Helena & Northwestern Railway (1948 – 1952)

The Missouri & Arkansas Railway ended service in 1946, but the line between Helena and Cotton Plant was sold to the Helena & Northwestern Railway (H&NW). When the M&A shut down, a plan for saving parts of the route included the Cotton Plant to Helena territory, primarily because of the Helena timber industry and the suppliers along the line. The area also had a history of shipping agricultural products such as cotton and rice. West Helena (431 carloads), Cotton Plant (268) and Helena (163) were all in the top fifteen of sources of freight traffic for the Missouri & Arkansas in 1945. To protect this business, the Helena & Northwestern was created by a number of local businessmen, including Ben C. White, the traffic manager of the Southwest Veneer Company at Cotton Plant. The railroad was officially incorporated on October 8, 1948, and soon the line was purchased.

The cost of the 55 miles of track was $300,000, and included the ability to salvage an estimated 30,000 treated ties from the abandoned line from Cotton Plant to Kensett. The H&NW immediately began to rebuild their railroad and bought several steam locomotives from the Apalachicola Northern in St. Joe, Florida. Company officials also started working to attract overhead traffic between the Illinois Central at Helena, and the Rock Island at Wheatley and the Cotton Belt at Fargo.

The railroad began service late in 1949 (September 14th according to Interstate Commerce Commission records, but the 15th according to the *Arkansas Gazette*). James R. Fair, Jr., also stated that service started on the 15th after the Illinois Central *Pelican* delivered the two steam locomotives on the previous day. Locomotive #200, a coal burning 4-6-0 built in 1922 by Cooke (#63283), immediately went into service. The second locomotive (#201) was almost identical except that it burned oil.

The immediate service was in response to a strike on the Missouri Pacific, switching industries in the Helena and West Helena area. The first train to Cotton Plant was on October 11, 1949, and it operated far behind the planned schedule. For the next few months, trains ran slowly, unexpected repairs to the line had to be made, and the company lost money. Interest payments on the railroad's debt were not being paid, and by early 1950 the owners were already considering abandonment. Some efficiencies were made, such as the purchase of a 70-ton General Electric diesel locomotive. However, on April 27, 1951, the Salzbergs filed suit against the Helena & Northwestern Railway for the unpaid mortgage. There was immediately a change in management, and the owners voted to abandon the line on July 11, 1951. A series of hearings were held by the Interstate Commerce Commission, and the abandonment was approved on November 2, 1951, and service ended on December 1, 1951. According to the Railroad Retirement Board, the Helena & Northwestern existed from October 11, 1949, to May 31, 1952.

The railroad was quickly abandoned. The route between Cotton Plant and Fargo was sold in January 1952 for $50,725. A few miles of industry tracks were also saved in Helena. However, the investors in the Helena & Northwestern walked away with nothing for all of their work and money. Actually, that is not entirely true. For several years, the owners faced a series of lawsuits by local farmers and landowners who claimed the railroad's right-of-way. For example, the case *Daugherty et al. v. Helena & Northwestern Railway* (November 1952) argued that the right-of-way was an easement that should go back to the original landowner, while the railroad stated that the land was a purchase, and thus could be sold. This specific case involved a "1.32-acre tract of land that was formerly occupied by the company's tracks."

The court case released a copy of the contracts, which stated:

> *"In consideration of the sum of five dollars....and of the benefits to accrue to us from the construction of the Missouri & North Arkansas Railroad, we do hereby grant, bargain, sell and convey unto the Missouri & North Arkansas Railroad Company, and unto its*

successors and assigns forever, a strip of land 100 feet in width for a right of way, over and upon the following described [a description of the original landowners land], said strip of land being fifty feet in width on each side of the center of the main track of said railroad as the same is now, or may hereafter be, located and constructed on and across said tract of land, with the right to change watercourses, and to take stone, gravel and timber, and to borrow earth on said right of way for the construction and maintenance of said railroad."

Eventually, the Supreme Court of Arkansas determined that such agreements created an easement, so the railroad owners didn't even have much of the land the abandoned railroad once sat on. The key to the ruling was that the agreement granted the railroad "the right to change watercourses, and to take stone, gravel and timber, and to borrow earth on said right of way for the construction and maintenance of said railroad." It was determined that a purchase would not need to provide these rights, while an easement did. It should be noted that the case *Daugherty et al. v. Helena & Northwestern Railway* has been used nationwide as a precedent for similar legal issues.

Cotton Plant-Fargo Railway (1952 – 1977)

This line was opened in 1952 after the Helena & Northwestern was abandoned in November 1951. The Cotton Plant-Fargo Railway was created by the Southwest Veneer Company to protect service to its Cotton Plant facility on December 11, 1951. Service began on April 1, 1952, and was operated as needed for Southwest Veneer and the few other shippers on the line, using a 20-ton Plymouth switcher. A statement in their *Official Guide* listing made it clear that the railroad was "operated for carload freight service only."

The purchase agreement stated that the railroad was from "1815 feet northwest of Milepost 306" to "3020 feet southeast of Milepost 311." This basically made the railroad extend from Arkansas Highway 38 south to the St. Louis Southwestern at Fargo, plus the short spur tracks at Cotton Plant required to serve several area industries. The purchase price was $50,725, reportedly paid in cash by David D. Bush, Trustee for the Southwest Veneer Company. Along with the railroad, the Cotton Plant-Fargo Railway acquired some land in Cotton Plant in what was identified as the M&NA Addition. There was also a "triangular piece of land" located to the southwest of the former Rock Island diamond location.

For years, the railroad office was in a former Missouri & Arkansas caboose. Traffic slowly went away over the next two decades, and Southwest Veneer eventually started closing their operations. The line applied to the Interstate Commerce Commission in 1976 to abandon the railroad. The ICC granted authority to the Cotton Plant-Fargo Railway to abandon its entire railroad on November 22, 1976, and it finally closed in 1977. The Railroad Retirement Board stated that the Cotton Plant-Fargo started on April 1, 1952, and "ceased to be an employer on December 31, 1978, date of final report received." This made the Cotton Plant-Fargo Railway the last significant portion of the M&NA in use for freight service.

Eureka Springs Railroad (1976 – 1986)

During the late 1970s and early 1980s, steam-powered passenger trains operated in the Beaver area. The railroad was created by Dreat and Reat Younger, sons of Bob Younger, an M&NA telegrapher and dispatcher. Dreat actually worked as a fireman for the railroad. The Youngers obtained a lease from the U.S. Army Corps of Engineers, allowing them to operate trains along Poker Bluff and across the White River bridge. The railroad operated until the mid-1980s before being shut down, with the collection of M&NA artifacts being donated to the Boone County Heritage Museum in Harrison. The small steam locomotive was sold to a steam tractor association near Harrison, and the passenger cars went to a planned excursion railroad that never operated.

Eureka Springs & North Arkansas Railway (1981 – present)

The last significant part of the railroad that still operates is the Eureka Springs Branch. This branch was abandoned by the Arkansas & Ozarks, and the grade was left unused, remaining this way until Robert Dortch, Jr. and his wife Mary Jane decided to move their Scott & Bearskin Lake Railroad from Scott, Arkansas, to Eureka Springs. The railroad opened in 1981 as a for-profit passenger tourist railway, restoring 2½ miles of track to service.

The railroad operates out of the historic Eureka Springs depot, and the yard area features a steel water tank, the former Fort Smith, Arkansas, Frisco turntable, a number of machinery displays, and a siding. The line runs to Junction, where the wye was rebuilt to turn the trains. Steam was originally used, but today an old diesel locomotive pulls the trains, which can be either a traditional excursion train or a full dinner train. A fascinating part of the excursion train's history is that the name Eureka Springs & North Arkansas Railway has lasted longer than any of the original names used by the freight railroad.

CONNECTIONS

NEOSHO, MO.
K. C. S. Southbound Ar. Neosho 12:25 AM.
K. C. S. Northbound Lv. Neosho 5:20 AM.
Frisco to Muskogee, Ft. Worth and Dallas
Lv. Neosho 11:33 PM.
Frisco to Vinita, Tulsa and Oklahoma City,
Lv. Neosho 2:36 AM
Frisco from Muskogee, Ft. Worth and Dallas
Ar. Neosho 2:00 AM

SELIGMAN, MO.
Frisco to Springfield, St. Louis, etc.
Lv. Seligman 9:15 PM.
Frisco from Springfield, St. Louis, etc.,
Ar. Sligman 4:39 A. M.
Frisco from Paris, Dallas, Ft. Worth, etc.,
Ar. Seligman 9:15 PM.
Frisco to Paris, Dallas, Ft. Worth, etc.,
Lv. Seligman 4:39 AM.

KENSETT, ARK.
Mo. Pac. to St. Louis, Lv. Kensett 10:10 PM.
Ar. St. Louis 7:28 AM.
Mo. Pac. to Memphis, Lv. Kensett 3:30 A. M.
Ar. Memphis 6:45 AM.
Mo. Pac. to Little Rock and beyond,
Lv. Kensett 8:45 AM, Ar. Little Rock 9:40 PM,
Ar. Dallas 8:45 AM, Ar. Ft. Worth 10:00 AM.
Mo. Pac. from St. Louis, Ar. Kensett 6:40 AM.

FARGO, ARK.
S. S. W. to St. Louis, Jonesboro, etc.,
Lv. Fargo 8:02 PM.
S. S. W. to Pine Bluff, Texarkana and Texas
Lv. Fargo 9:19 AM.

WHEATLEY, ARK.
C. R. I. & P. to Memphis
Lv. Wheatley 9:44 AM.
C. R. I. & P. to Little Rock,
Lv. Wheatley 7:54 PM.

MISSOURI and ARKANSAS RAILWAY COMPANY

Time Table

SHOWING

Local Passenger Schedules

ALSO

Connections

TO POINTS

ON CONNECTING LINES

Trains 1 and 2

Are Streamlined Rail Motor Cars

Corrected to February 25, 1945

CORRECTED TO FEBRUARY 25, 1945

Read Down 5 DAILY		STATIONS		Read Up 6 DAILY
6:30am	Lv.	Neosho,	Mo. Ar.	7:05pm
6:55		Stark City,		6:39
7:10		Fairview,		6:24
7:20		Wheaton,		6:14
7:45		Wayne,		5:49
8:03	Ar.	Seligman,	Lv.	5:31
8:13	Lv.	Seligman,	Mo. Ar	5:21
f 8:45		Beaver,	Ark.	f 4:49
9:08		Eureka Springs,		4:26
9:36		Grandview,		3:59
9:58		Berryville,		3:38
f10:18		Urbanette,		f 3:18
10:41		Green Forest,		2:58
11:04		Alpena,		2:34
11:44	Ar.	Harrison,	Lv	1:56
11:59am	Lv.	Harrison,	Ar.	1:41
f12:11pm		Bellefonte,		f 1:30
f12:24		Olvey,		f 1:17
12:36		Everton,		1:06
12:51		Findall,		12:51
1:03		St. Joe,		12:34
1:23		Gilbert,		12:19
f 1:40		Zack,		f12:02pm
1:53		Marshall,		11:49am
f 1:59		Baker,		11:43
2:14	*Ar.Leslie,		Lv.	11:28
2:34	*Lv.Leslie,		Ar	11:08
2:59		Elba,		10:43
3:19		Arlberg,		10:28
3:50		Shirley,		9:53
4:21		Edgemont,		9:22
4:27		Hirden,		9:16
4:42		Miller,		9:01
4:57	Ar.	Heber Springs,	Lv.	8:46
5:12	Lv.	Heber Springs,	Ar.	8:31
—Motor— 5:40		Pangburn,		8:03 —Motor—
DAILY, 5:52		Letona,		7:51 DAILY,
EXCEPT 6:18		Searcy,		7:25 EXCEPT
SUNDAY 6:30pm	Ar.	Kensett,	Lv.	7:15am SUNDAY
7:30am	Lv.	Kensett,	Ar.	4:10pm
7:40		West Point,		4:01
8:10		Georgetown,		3:30
8:20		McClelland,		3:20
8:29		Dixie,		3:11
8:49		Cotton Plant,		2:50
9:04		Fargo,		2:34
9:16		Wheatley,		2:21
9:45		Moro,		1:54
10:05		Aubrey,		1:34
10:21		Rondo,		1:20
10:57		West Helena,		12:45
11:20am	Ar.	Helena,	Ark. Lv.	12:20pm

General Information

CHILDREN under five years of age, when accompanied by parent or guardian, will be transported free of charge. Children five years of age and under twelve years of age will be charged one-half fare.

ADJUSTMENT OF FARES—In case of dispute with Conductors or Agents, pay the fare required, take receipt and communicate with General Passenger Agent, Harrison, Ark.

REDEMPTION OF TICKETS—Tickets unused or partially used will be redeemed under tariff regulations at proper value.

BAGGAGE MAXIMUMS—No single piece of baggage exceeding 300 pounds in weight or 72 inches in greatest dimension, or exceeding $2,500 in value will be checked. Free allowance subject to tariff stipulations as to contents, weight, size and value.

LIABILITY LIMITED—Excess value should be declared and paid for at time of checking. This company will not be responsible for unchecked articles left in stations or cars.

Address all communications relative to adjustment of fares, lost articles, etc., to General Passenger Department, Harrison, Arkansas.

For further information consult local agent or write

H. P. MITCHELL
General Passenger Agent
Harrison, Arkansas

* Lunch Stop—Restaurant in Station.
f Flag Stop.

(For Connections See Page 4)

Missouri and Arkansas Railway Company Passenger Time Table, February 25, 1945. From the collection of Barton Jennings.

Characteristics of the Railroad

The Missouri & North Arkansas was never the best built or most modern railroad. It was built across mostly rugged country, or lowlands that regularly flooded. With the shortage of cash and the construction techniques available, the line was built to avoid deep cuts and tall fills. The line often jumped across ridges to follow small mountain streams from town to town, using steep grades and sharp curves. A report entitled *Physical Characteristics Missouri and Arkansas Railway Company* that was dated December 31, 1940, provided a significant amount of information about the physical characteristics of the railroad. Some of this information is provided here.

The railroad was shown to have 405.756 miles of track. They were divided as follows

	Missouri	Arkansas	Total
Main Track – Owned	40.428	295.116	335.544
Main Track – Trackage Rights	29.146	0.320	29.466
Yard and Side Tracks – Owned	3.097	37.649	40.746
Total Miles	72.671	333.085	405.756

Of the mainline, 236.83 miles was straight, or tangent track, while 98.71 miles was curved track. This means that almost 30% of the track was curved, an amazingly high number considering that the track from Kensett to Helena was almost all straight. The curves were often sharp and the grades steep. Compare these numbers to the standard practice of attempting to keep mainline curves to five degrees or less and grades less than 1.2%.

Territory	Maximum Curves	Maximum Grades
Neosho to Wayne	3 degrees	0.8%
Seligman to Harrison	10 degrees	2.6%
Freeman to Berryville	12 degrees	1.75%
Harrison to Leslie	10 degrees	1.75%
Leslie to Heber Springs	9 degrees	0.6%
Heber Springs to Helena	6 degrees	0.6%

When the Missouri & Arkansas closed, the Interstate Commerce Commission investigated some of the reasons for the failure. One of the causes noted was the extremely slow speeds of trains due to the poor track conditions. Testimony by assistant to the chief operating officer J. E. Halter demonstrated that the average speed of trains on the railroad had been 9.9 to 11.6 miles per hour. This meant that it could take several days for a train to cross the railroad. The slow speeds also cost the railroad enormously in car rental and demurrage. Halter stated that foreign owned cars stayed on the railroad an average of 5.37 to 7.19 days, an indication of the slow speeds and infrequent train service.

The practice of following streams and crossing ridges also led to a number of bridges. According to the report, the railroad had 37 steel bridges measuring a total of 4543 feet long, and 292 wooden bridges measuring a total of 36,637 feet, or a total of 7.8 miles of bridges. This was 2.3% of the entire railroad. The report noted that the steel bridges included 1808 feet of truss spans and 2735 feet of plate girder spans.

Of the 335.5 miles of mainline track owned by the railroad, only 69%, or 232.96 miles, was ballasted. Only 17% of the track used tie plates. The rail was also small, all weighing between 65 and 90 pounds per yard (the current mainline standard is 141 pounds per yard).

65# ASCE	301.380 miles	89.8%
70# ASCE	7.115 miles	2.1%
75# ASCE	3.972 miles	1.2%
80# ASCE	1.030 miles	0.3%
85# ASCE	11.420 miles	3.4%
90# ASCE	6.550 miles	2.0%
90# ARA	4.080 miles	1.2%

At the time of the 1940 report, the railroad had 1 stone and 34 frame combination passenger-freight stations, 1 stone and 3 frame passenger stations, 4 frame freight stations, 5 passenger shelters, 2 combination passenger and freight shelters, and used 4 frame stations jointly with other railroads. The railroad's right-of-way was normally 100 feet wide, except around where stations stood, which was 200 feet wide. The track between the Cache River and the White River also generally had a 200-foot right-of-way.

The territory that the Missouri & North Arkansas passed through was never heavily settled, and even today is considered to be very rural. The largest town served in 1920 was Joplin (population 29,902), and that town was served by four other major railroads, all larger than the M&NA. The next largest town that year was Helena, with 9112 residents and two other railroads. Neosho was next with 3968 residents and two other railroads, and then Harrison had 3477 residents. No other town along the line had more than 3000 residents, with Searcy having 2836 and Eureka Springs having 2429. Among the rest of the "major" stations were Leslie (1472), Heber Springs (1675), and Berryville (1474). Much of the freight that was moved over the railroad for the first several decades was based upon this undeveloped nature of the route – timber, crossties, fence posts, and stone. Later, the products were based upon farming – canned goods, cotton, fresh strawberries, and rice. Manufactured goods were not a major source of revenue, and most such products were inbound to serve local markets such as flour and petroleum.

Much of the M&NA was also closely followed by other railroads, often in far better shape. Between Joplin and Seligman, a majority of the line was actually on someone else's railroad. From that area south to Kensett, the Missouri Pacific had their White River line to the north. The Rock Island had a route from Searcy to Wheatley that was once proposed to be used so the M&NA line through the White River bottoms could be abandoned. South of there to Helena, the Missouri Pacific had much of the territory covered. The situation has been compared to other railroads with similar histories such as the Tennessee Central and the New York, Ontario & Western.

The Missouri & North Arkansas Railroad Depots

The various railroads related to the Missouri & North Arkansas built a surprising number of depots of different designs. Stations such as Joplin, Eureka Springs, Leslie and Cotton Plant were different from many of the other stations. Additionally, even where stations were of the same design, small changes such as having the freight section on the opposite end or having larger or smaller waiting rooms made many unique. Window and door locations, the location of station signs, and a number of other details also made a number of stations unique. Additionally, many "stations" were little more than a simple shelter or small shed, while others used retired freight car or passenger car bodies. Some were even nothing more than a cinder platform or a road crossing.

Probably the most detailed analysis of the many railroad stations along the Missouri & North Arkansas Railway was created by Tim Kubat and published in the Fall 1982 issue of *Oak Leaves*, the newsletter of the Missouri & Arkansas Railroad Museum. Kubat defined four basic designs. Station designs #1 and #2 were built between 1901 and 1908 and only north of Marshall. Station designs #3 and #4 were built in 1908 and 1909 from Arlburg south. These latter stations were generally smaller than the earlier buildings.

The stations were all built with brick chimneys for heat, and none initially had plumbing. Toilet facilities were provided in adjacent outhouses. Electricity was generally installed as it became available locally. Some of these depots also included small rooms for the agent to live in.

A Standard #1 depot normally measured 18' x 58', although some are shown to be 52 feet long. According to the National Park Service of the United States Department of the Interior, these depots featured "two partitions which created three rooms: a passenger waiting room, the station agent's office, and a freight and baggage area." The waiting room was about 22 feet long while the baggage area was about 24 feet long. These early buildings also included slightly flared eaves as a part of the roof design, as well as a bay window on the track side. The St. Louis & North Arkansas Railway Company (StL&NA) built a number of these in Arkansas, including Grand View, Batavia, Bellefonte, Olvey, and Gilbert.

A Standard #2 depot normally measured 18' x 72', although there were some slight variations. The building was very similar to the Standard #1 depots and also featured a bay window for the agent and the gable-on-hip roof. The Standard #2 depots were used at larger communities and often featured a "Colored Waiting Room" on the baggage side of the agent's office. These stations were generally built by the StL&NA, and were a majority of the depots built by that railroad. These include Freeman, Berryville, Green Forest, Alpena, Everton, St. Joe, and Marshall. The second depot built at Harrison also used this design.

A Standard #3 depot normally measured 22' x 40' and was built with four rooms. In the center was an agent's office with a bay window track side. The bay window added about four feet to the station's size, and the office was about twelve feet wide. On one side of the office was a freight and baggage room with a door facing the tracks and one at the back. On the other side of the agent's office were two waiting rooms. The trackside waiting room had a door to the tracks. The second waiting room had its door on the end of the building and was labeled as the "Colored Waiting Room." The baggage and waiting room ends were sometimes swapped based upon local needs. Additionally, some of these stations apparently had another room that the agent lived in.

A Standard #4 depot measured 20' x 40', the smallest of the standard depots used on the line. The Standard #4 was also the least used of the standard depot designs. These stations included small freight areas to allow the building to house two waiting rooms.

Besides the four standard designs, several stations were always unique. Eureka Springs was initially the headquarters and destination of the railroad and it received a large two-story building which was later replaced by a stone building. Leslie also received a stone depot. Other stations, such as those at Helena, Seligman, and Joplin, were shared with other railroads and used their designs.

Jim Wakefield has also researched the subject, including information on the telegraph station status of the various stations. Much of this information was included in issues of *Oak Leaves* in 2015 and 2016. He also provided a number of reports over the years about the restoration projects involving Green Forest and St. Joe, and the removal of several other stations.

Information from these studies is included here, but those who want the articles should consult the Boone County Historical & Railroad Society for the availability of back issues. Additionally, in the more than 35 years since the Kubat study, some changes have naturally taken place and additional details have also come to light. This is especially true for stations like St. Joe, Green Forest, Marshall, and others that have been rebuilt or torn down.

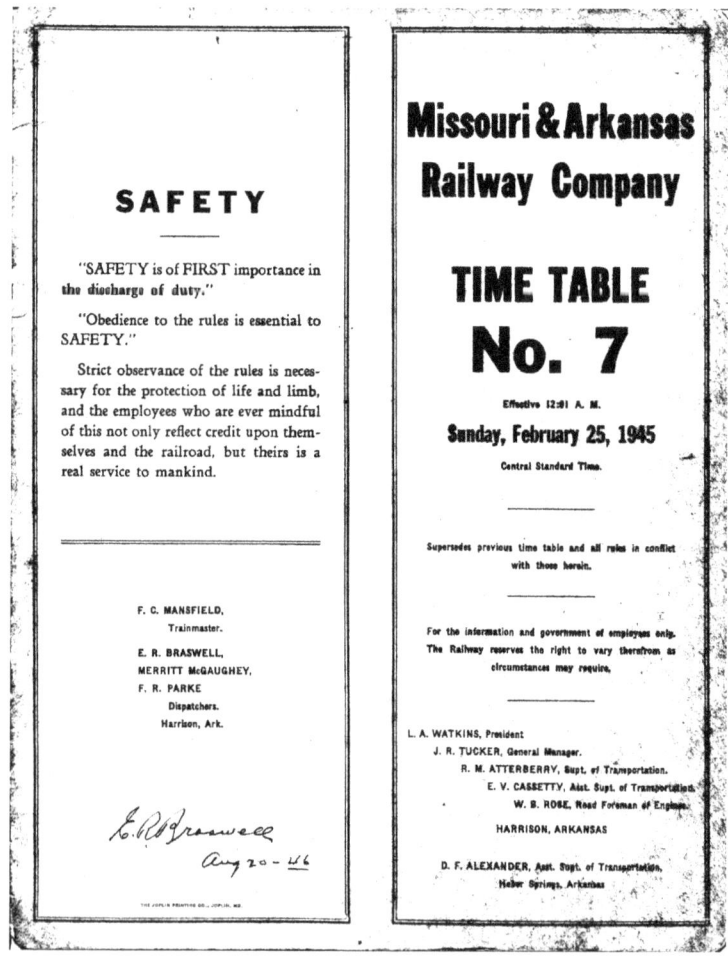

Front and back covers of the *Missouri & North Arkansas Railway Company Time Table No. 7,* Sunday, February 25, 1945. Courtesy Boone County Historical & Railroad Society.

Missouri & North Arkansas Route Guide
First District –
Joplin (MO) to Harrison (AR)

The First District of the Missouri & North Arkansas/Missouri & Arkansas, defined as being Joplin to the company's headquarters at Harrison, included both the oldest and the newest track on the railroad. It also included trackage rights over the Kansas City Southern and the Frisco railroads. The M&NA started with the Eureka Springs Railway between Seligman, Missouri, and Eureka Springs, Arkansas, and was completed with the line between Wayne and Neosho, Missouri. The District's route also included the highest point on the entire railroad – Wayne, Missouri – and the railroad's only tunnel. It also included some of the sharpest curves and steepest grades on the line. Today, the First District is still represented by a tourist railroad that operates over several miles of the original line into Eureka Springs.

The mileposts presented are from *Missouri & Arkansas Railway Company Time Table No. 7*, dated Sunday, February 25, 1945, and a June 28, 1925, timetable of the Missouri & North Arkansas. However, it should be noted that mileposts for many of the station locations have changed slightly over the years. A significant issue with the mileposts is that during the early years, the milepost distances included the Eureka Springs and Berryville branches. However, during the later years, the mileposts only included the mainline distances. The exact station mileposts also changed as depots were built and then later replaced with passenger shelters.

SOUTHWARD

THIRD CLASS 323 Local Freight Tues. Thurs. Sat.	SECOND CLASS 11 Manifest Freight Daily	FIRST CLASS 1 Passenger Daily	Siding Capacity		Distance from Joplin	Maximum Grade	TIME TABLE No. 7 Effective 12.01 A. M. SUNDAY February 25, 1945 STATIONS	
			Pass.	Other				
Lv 8.00AM	Lv 9.30AM				1.17		DN...⎛..JOPLIN..CTWX⎞	
							$\quad$ 19.70	
8.40 / 8.50	10.20 / 10.35	Lv 6.30AM	18B	23	19.70	0.80	D...Via KCS Ry.⎝..NEOSHO....WY⎠ 6.54	(
9.11	11.00	f 6.45	20B	2	26.24	0.80	............AROMA............ 4.16	(
9.26	11.15	s 6.55		23N	30.40	0.80	.STARK CITY...... 6.71	(
9.46	11.35	s 7.10	.44B		37.10	0.80	...........FAIRVIEW........... 4.18	(
10.01	11.50AM s	7.20	44B		41.29	0.80	D............WHEATON........W 4.96	(
10.15	12.04PM f	7.32	18B		46.25	0.80	............RIDGLEY............ 5.61	(
10.36	12.25	s 7.45	35B		51.86	1.10	D........⎛..WAYNE..⎞ 9.43	(
11.01 / 11.31	12.50 / 1.20 M-12 M324	8.03 / 8.13	Yd.		61.29	0.00	DN Via SL-SF⎝..SELIGMAN..TW⎠ 2.22	1
11.40AM	1.29	8.21	12B		63.51	0.50	............PENDER............ 7.85	2
12.05PM M12	1.50	f 8.38	42B		71.38	0.40	............WALDEN............ 2.29	1
12.10	1.55	f 8.45	18B		73.65	0.84	............BEAVER............* 3.79	1
12.20	2.05	f 8.57	27B	27	77.44	1.25	............JUNCTION.......CWY 1.81	0
12.30		s 9.08		51	79.25	0.00	D......EUREKA SPRINGS........ 1.81	0
12.45	2.30	f 9.18			77.44	1.75	............JUNCTION.......CWY 2.52	1
1.00	2.45	f 9.25		78	79.96	1.75	............TUNNEL............ 4.57	0
1.18	3.03	s 9.36	37B		84.53	1.50	............GRANDVIEW.......... 4.07	1
1.33		f 9.48 M324	17B		88.60	1.90	............FREEMAN........WY 2.58	1
1.45		s 9.58	32B	29	91.18	0.00	D........BERRYVILLE............ 2.52	0
2.08	3.28 M2	f 10.08			88.66	1.75	............FREEMAN........WY 3.09	1
2.23	3.40	f 10.18 M12	26B		91.75	1.75	............URBANETTE.........* 3.99	0
2.37	3.54	f 10.29	43B		95.74	1.75	............CISCO............* 4.82	1
2.58 M2	4.15	s 10.41	20B	25	100.56	1.49	D......GREEN FOREST.......... 5.81	1
3.23	4.40	f 10.54	21B		106.37	1.75	............COIN............ 4.65	1
3.43	5.00	s 11.04	32B	8	111.02	1.75	D............ALPENA..........W 6.40	1
4.18	5.35	f 11.21		4N	117.42	1.41	............BATAVIA............* 2.58	1
4.36	5.43	f 11.28	27B		120.00	0.00	............CAPPS............* 6.33	1
Ar 5.00PM	Ar 6.05PM	Ar 11.44AM	Yd.		126.33		DN........HARRISON.....CTWX	1
Tues. Thurs. Sat. 323	Daily 11	Daily 1	End Connected B—Both N—North S—South				126.33 135.05	

First District – Joplin (MO) to Harrison (AR)

TIME TABLE No. 7 Effective 12.01 A. M. SUNDAY February 25, 1945 STATIONS	Maximum Grade	Station Numbers	Telegraph Call	NORTHWARD		
				FIRST CLASS	SECOND CLASS	THIRD CLASS
				2 Passenger	12 Freight	324 Local Freight
				Daily	Daily	Mon. Weds. Fri.
DN {JOPLIN..CTWX} 19.70 Via KCSRy.	....	0	JO	lv 4.50PM	lv 4.05PM	
D {..NEOSHO....WY} 6.54	0.50	20	N	lv 7.05PM	4.10 3.35	3.25 3.15
....AROMA.......... 4.16	0.00	26	f	6.49	3.15	2.55
..STARK CITY...... 6.71	0.80	30	s	6.39	3.00	2.40
....FAIRVIEW....... 4.18	0.80	37	s	6.24	2.40	2.20
D......WHEATON......W 4.96	0.30	41	HN s	6.14	s 2.30	2.00
......RIDGLEY........ 5.61	0.72	46	f	6.02	2.05	1.35
D.. {....WAYNE......} 9.43 Via SLSF	0.60	52	WN s	5.49	1.50	1.20
DN {..SELIGMAN..TW} 2.22	1.14	61	SI	5.31 5.21	1.20 12.50 M11	12.50 12.20 M11
......PENDER...... 7.85	2.60	64		5.13	12.30	12.08PM
......WALDEN...... 2.29	1.58	71	f	4.56	12.05PM M323	11.35AM
......BEAVER...... * 3.79	1.04	74	f	4.49	11.52AM	11.22
.....JUNCTION......CWY 1.81	0.00	77	f	4.40	11.45	11.15
D......EUREKA SPRINGS......... 1.81	0.00	79	AW s	4.26		10.58
......JUNCTION......CWY 2.52	1.25	77		f 4.16	11.22	10.43
......TUNNEL...... 4.57	0.00	80	f	4.10	11.07	10.28
....GRANDVIEW...... 4.07	1.75	85	s	3.59	10.45	10.05
......FREEMAN......WY 2.58	1.75	89	f	3.48	10.30	9.48 M1
D......BERRYVILLE......... 2.52	0.00	91	B s	3.38		9.30
......FREEMAN......WY 3.09	1.90	89	f	3.28 M11		9.15
......URBANETTE...... * 3.99	0.00	92	f	3.18	10.18 M1	9.00
......CISCO...... * 4.82	1.75	96	f	3.09	10.00	8.45
D......GREEN FOREST......... 5.81	1.75	101	KN s	2.58 M323	f 9.45	8.30
......COIN...... 4.65	1.75	106	f	2.45	9.20	8.15
D......ALPENA......W 6.40	1.75	111	PA s	2.34	s 9.00	7.55
......BATAVIA...... * 2.58	1.40	117	f	2.18	8.35	7.40
......CAPPS...... * 6.33	1.75	120	f	2.11	8.25	7.25
DN......HARRISON.....CTWX	1.75	126	DS Lv	1.56PM	Lv 8.00AM	Lv 7.00AM
126.33 135.05	.			Daily	Daily	Mon. Wed. Fri.
				2	12	324

49

The Missouri & North Arkansas/Missouri & Arkansas included the distances over the Kansas City Southern and the St. Louis & San Francisco Railway in their mileposts. Because of this, the mileposts on the KCS and Frisco routes are also provided, and a description of these lines is included.

SIDINGS AND SPURS BETWEEN STATIONS—NOT SHOWN ON SCHEDULE PAGES

STATION	LOCATION	CAR CAPACITY	END CONNECTED
(FIRST DISTRICT)			
Norton	MP 99.06	4	South
(SECOND DISTRICT)			
Mercer	MP 153.93	7	Both
Karber	MP 225.76	6	North
(THIRD DISTRICT)			
Mt. Pisgah	MP 263.43	2	South
Miss. River Fuel	MP 282.00	5	South
Pryor	MP 285.54	9	North
Watkins	MP 289.15	8	South
Putty	MP 313.56	2	South
Little Prairie	MP 324.98	4	South
Airport No. 2	MP 351.28	8	South
Airport No. 1	MP 351.91	7	North

Timetable excerpts on this and preceeding pages are from *Missouri & Arkansas Railway Company Time Table No. 7,* dated Sunday, February 25, 1945. Courtesy Boone County Historical & Railroad Society.

Joplin (MO) to Neosho (MO)
Trackage Rights Over Kansas City Southern

The Missouri & North Arkansas Railroad, and later the Missouri & Arkansas Railway, used trackage rights over the Kansas City Southern (KCS) to travel between Joplin and Neosho, both in Missouri. Heading south from the Joplin Union Depot property, M&NA trains used the KCS mainline for both passenger and freight trains. The May 31, 1936, *KCS Northern Division Employee Timetable* included information on these rights. By this time, only M&A freights #211 and #212 used the route, listed as Third Class trains. A timetable note stated that Missouri & Arkansas trains leaving Neosho were required to obtain train orders with the information required in the KCS Book of Rules before departing.

The history of this line dates back to 1887 when Arthur E. Stilwell started building what he hoped to be a farmer-supported railroad from Kansas City to the Gulf of Mexico. Stilwell built some track, but also bought existing railroads to assemble the railroad. One of these was the Kansas City, Fort Smith & Southern Railroad, which had already been built between Joplin, Missouri, and Sulphur Springs, Arkansas. Owned by Mathias Splitlog, Stilwell's Kansas City, Pittsburg & Gulf Railroad Company bought it as a part of the construction plans on October 30, 1897. This part of the line was merged into the Kansas City Southern on April 1, 1900, as a part of an unfriendly takeover after the railroad entered receivership. Over the years, KCS has expanded beyond its Kansas City to the Gulf of Mexico plans, and now has lines to such places as Fort Worth, Texas; New Orleans, Louisiana; Springfield, Illinois; Meridian, Mississippi; and Mexico City, Mexico.

Trackage rights over the KCS from Neosho to Joplin were acquired by the Missouri & North Arkansas as part of their 1908 expansion plans. The rights included the use of KCS facilities at Neosho and Joplin, rights that were used until the Missouri & Arkansas Railway shut down in 1946, and abandoned the line to Neosho the following year.

In 1936, this was the Second District of the Northern Division, covering the KCS between Pittsburg, Kansas, and Watts, Oklahoma. By 1966, this was the Second Subdivision of the KCS. Today, it is the Heavener Subdivision – Pittsburg, Kansas, to Heavener, Oklahoma.

Sign on Joplin Union Depot Company building in Joplin, Missouri. Photo by Barton Jennings.

0.0 JOPLIN – The City of Joplin is split between southern Jasper County and northern Newton County, and is still the largest city in Jasper County, Missouri. Located at the junction of Interstates 44 and 49, Joplin is the home of several trucking companies and trucking service companies. It is located on the mainline of the Kansas City Southern (KCS) railroad, and is also served by branches of BNSF and the Missouri & Northern Arkansas Railroad. The population is approximately 50,000.

Joplin (MO) to Neosho (MO)

One of the first settlers in the area was Reverend Harris G. Joplin, who built near a spring and small stream about 1840, both of which soon took his name. The City of Joplin can trace its history back to the discovery of lead in the Joplin Creek Valley before the Civil War. However, the lack of good transportation prevented the development of the area. In 1871, after the Civil War, John C. Cox filed a plan for a city to serve the mines that were starting to develop. The town was soon named Joplin City.

With Cox's town being on the east side of the valley, Patrick Murphy created the town of Murphysburg on the western side. Almost immediately, the two towns merged to form Union City, but a court ruling declared the merger illegal. A new set of documents led to a legal merger on March 23, 1873, creating the City of Joplin. Joplin attracted railroads, businesses and other services needed to support the lead and zinc mining industries. Declaring itself the lead and zinc mining capital of the world, Joplin soon featured some of the finest saloons in the region. Probably the most famous was the House of Lords, a three-story complex with a bar and restaurant on the first floor, gambling rooms on the second floor, and a brothel on the third.

Mining methods included open pit and deep mining, resulting in huge spoil piles to the north and west of town, and almost 75% of Joplin sitting over underground mines. This didn't stop the town from growing or modernizing, quickly obtaining lights and electricity. However, there was still enough of the rough edge that Bonnie and Clyde spent several weeks in Joplin in 1933, even robbing several local businesses for spending money. When their apartment (3347½ Oak Ridge Drive) was raided by police, they were forced to leave behind many of their possessions. Included in these items was a camera. The film was quickly developed by the *Joplin Globe*, resulting in some of the most famous pictures of the outlaw couple. These included the picture of Bonnie with her foot on a car fender, posed with a pistol in her hand and cigar in her mouth, and Bonnie holding Clyde at mock gunpoint. The apartment is now on the National Register of Historic Places.

Route 66 was becoming a boom for Joplin by the mid-20th Century. However, most of the mines closed after World War II, and like most cities, residents moved to the suburbs. Much of downtown was destroyed by attempts at urban renewal, but some buildings from the era still stand. Many of these are listed on the National Register of Historic Places. Mother Nature has even been a challenge to Joplin, with a major tornado damaging much of the town on May 5, 1971, and another EF5 tornado on May 22, 2011, damaging almost every building in the area. A reported 8400 homes, 450 businesses, and 18,000 cars were damaged or destroyed by this storm. The 2011 storm kicked off the second phase to return Joplin to its boom times. Its location at the junction of two Interstate Highways had already led to new industry, and nearly $800 million in reconstruction spending continued the progress.

While many of the older buildings are gone, much of Joplin's history still exists. Pauline Starke, an early silent-film actress, was born in Joplin on January 10, 1901. On June 4, 1924, *Gunsmoke* and *McCloud* star Dennis Weaver was also born in Joplin. Sports stars Hale Irwin, 3-time U.S. Open golf champion, and NASCAR driver Jamie McMurray, have also called Joplin home. Finally, Blondie and

Dagwood Bumstead are from Joplin, according to their creator Chic Young in an interview with the *Joplin Globe* newspaper.

Joplin Union Depot Company

When the Missouri & North Arkansas first obtained trackage rights between Neosho and Joplin, the M&NA used the KCS facilities at both locations. The original KCS Joplin station was located on the west side of the tracks south of 4th Street. However, the Santa Fe and KCS were already discussing a new joint station and terminal, and the M&NA immediately proposed that they be included in the plans.

Located at Milepost 0.0 for the Missouri & North Arkansas Railroad, and Milepost 154.3 for the Kansas City Southern, is a major 300-foot-long and 80-foot-wide concrete union station that once served Joplin, Missouri, as well as a 7930-foot-long siding. The Joplin Union Depot Company was incorporated on June 23, 1908, to build a joint station to serve the Atchison, Topeka & Santa Fe Railway; Kansas City Southern Railway; Missouri, Kansas & Texas Railway; and the Missouri & North Arkansas Railroad. According to the *Missouri, Kansas & Texas Railway Company Report to the Stockholders for the Year Ended June 30th, 1910*, the company was created "to acquire suitable freight and passenger terminals in Joplin for the joint use of the four railroads named, each of which subscribed for $10,000 capital stock of the Depot Company. The construction of the terminals is financed by an issue of bonds which has been made and sold by the Depot Company, such bonds being guaranteed, both principal and interest, by the four proprietary railway companies above mentioned." Much of the land chosen had been the site of the William Brugger Custom Ore Crusher.

A later report stated that the Joplin Union Depot Company owned 0.740 miles of main track and 5.657 miles of sidings and yard tracks, 26 acres of land, plus the station buildings. These buildings included the Union Passenger Depot, Union Freight Depot, and assorted support structures. While few of the tracks remain, the shell of the station building still stands near downtown Joplin. Plans for the station started in the 1900s, and Canadian-born architect Louis Curtiss was chosen to head the design work. Curtiss had a long history designing railroad stations, including many for the AT&SF, the Fred Harvey Company, and the Union Terminal in Wichita, Kansas. Curtiss was also known for his many buildings in the Kansas City area. There, his Boley Clothing Company Building is considered to be "one of the first glass curtain wall structures in the world." He was sometimes known as "the Frank Lloyd Wright of Kansas City."

The design of Joplin Union Depot called for reinforced concrete, mixed with local mine waste. The buildings were considered to be absolutely fireproof, and the buildings all had walls designed to allow the construction of additional stories. The design was featured in the January 1912 edition of *Popular Mechanics*, as well as several other magazines of the time. On June 5, 1910, it was announced that the Manhattan Construction Company of New York, through their branch office in Fort Smith, Arkansas, had been awarded the contract to build the Union Depot. According to the *Joplin Daily Globe*, construction started on June 24th.

Joplin (MO) to Neosho (MO)

Almost immediately, construction on the complex was slowed as excavation work uncovered a major seam of zinc. Some of the workers organized a mining company and soon mined and sold off the zinc. However, once the zinc was gone, construction progressed rapidly, except for several weeks when winter cold halted work. The tracks were completed enough that a work train entered the property on May 19, 1911. During the evening of July 1, 1911, Missouri, Kansas & Texas passenger train #83 became the first train to use the station. Reportedly more than 2500 local residents met the train at 10:30pm, and fireworks and numerous railroad torpedoes made sure that the rest of Joplin's citizens knew that the first passenger train had arrived.

The Joplin Union depot still exists as a shell and any visitor can see the magnificent building that it once was. This view is of the trackside entrance to the station. Photo by Barton Jennings.

Multiple sources provided descriptions of the building. Some described it as being an "old Roman type, antedating the classic style." The building was made of concrete, with oak finish. The passenger depot consisted of three parts, the central section measuring 180 feet long, with 60-foot-long north and south wings. The two-story central section housed the ticket office; general, women's and men's waiting rooms; and related offices and rooms. The second floor featured office space for the various railroads. The south one-story wing housed the dining room, later converted into the Railway Express Agency office, while the north one-story wing featured the express and baggage rooms. The local newspaper stated that the "general arrangement of the depot is very much similar to that of the union depot in St. Louis, although the interior is more beautifully decorated than its larger counterpart." Outside, the complex included train sheds, a roundhouse, and a number of tracks.

According to the 1936 KCS employee timetable, rules of the Joplin Union Depot Company applied between the yard limit boards at Joplin. A train register, bulletin books, and a standard clock were all located in the Joplin Union Depot Telegraph Office.

The Missouri & North Arkansas, later the Missouri & Arkansas, used the Joplin Union terminal until the end for freight operations, with an agency in the Union Depot that used the telegraph call of "JO". In 1936, M&A Freight #211 was scheduled to depart daily at 9:30am as a Third Class train, and Freight #212 was scheduled to arrive at 5:05pm. The locomotive and caboose were serviced at the shops of the Union Depot. While M&A freight service lasted until the end of the railroad, passenger service ended in 1934, instead using Neosho, Missouri, as a connection with the Kansas City Southern trains.

The last passenger train, KCS' *Southern Belle*, served the station on November 4, 1969. The complex was soon abandoned, but with numerous proposals for museums, restaurants, and other businesses to fill the space. However, none of the proposals actually resulted in the building's use, and the station slowly deteriorated. The passenger depot was placed on the National Register of Historic Places on March 14, 1973. It is currently owned by the Missouri Department of Natural Resources and plans continue to pop up for its use. For those wanting more information about the Joplin Union Depot, the *Historic Joplin* website has a large article on its planning, construction, and possible future.

Other Joplin Railroads

While the Kansas City Southern, the route used by the Missouri & North Arkansas to reach Joplin, is the main north-south railroad that passes through Joplin, the large number of lead and zinc mines attracted other railroads. Today, many of these routes still exist, and some of their history is also still present. However, a majority of the rail lines that once reached Joplin are gone.

Reviewing these lines clockwise from the KCS line north to Kansas City, there were once more than a dozen lines out of town. The KCS line through Joplin is the Heavener Subdivision, the main route from Kansas City south to Shreveport, Louisiana, the original core of the company. Clockwise, the next line was the former Frisco line that ran northeast to the mainline at Oronogo, Missouri. This line was built by the Missouri & Western Railway Company and acquired by the Frisco in 1879. A few miles of this line still exists in the Joplin area and crosses the KCS south of Joplin Union Station. It is today operated by the Missouri & Northern Arkansas, a regional railroad owned by the Genesee & Wyoming.

Immediately to the east of the former Frisco line was the Southwest Missouri Electric Railway, an interurban that operated from Carthage to Webb City, then southwest to Joplin, and then west to Galena, Kansas. Created in 1892, this interurban railroad absorbed local routes in several cities, but was bankrupt and in receivership by 1927 and was selling off property and going to buses. It crossed the KCS just south of today's MNA Crossing, wandered through Joplin, and then headed west, following today's BNSF route to Galena.

The next two lines bridge over the KCS route. Using joint track in this immediate area, they include a short Frisco branchline to Webb City, and the former Missouri Pacific line from Carthage. The MP line is today operated by the Missouri & Northern Arkansas. Further south is another former line of the Southwest Missouri Electric Railway which curved around the southeast side of Joplin using 15th Street.

Continuing in a clockwise direction from the KCS line south toward Shreveport, there was once a short Missouri Pacific branch to Grand Falls. Grand Falls is a large waterfall on Shoal Creek where a hydroelectric plant and a park were built. The park included a theater, boat houses, a German Village and a dance pavilion, and Missouri Pacific used to run special excursion trains to and from the falls over this line. Next are Southwest Missouri Electric Railway and Frisco lines heading west to Galena, Kansas. The interurban line, acquired from the Joplin & Galena Electric Railway in 1896, is long gone. The Frisco line, once known as the Joplin & Galena Branch,

Joplin (MO) to Neosho (MO)

still exists and is operated by BNSF. Two other lines also headed west toward Galena. One was another Frisco line that reached Galena via Horn (all now abandoned), and the other was the Missouri-Kansas-Texas (MKT) line, now partly operated by BNSF. The MKT (Katy) Joplin Line was built from the Kansas City-Texas mainline at Oswego, Kansas, by the Walsh-List-Gifford Construction Company to serve the various mines in the area. Katy abandoned much of their own route to Joplin in the early 1980s, using trackage rights over BN's line from Galena.

Heading west from downtown, and then north from Schiffendecker Park, was the Joplin & Pittsburg Railway, another interurban company. This line was a combination of several electric lines and was built to Joplin from Pittsburg to the north. Finally, between the Joplin & Pittsburg Railway and the KCS line was another Frisco line, this one also heading north to Pittsburg. This was originally the Joplin Railroad, built between Joplin and Girard (just west of Pittsburg, Kansas), and acquired by the Frisco in 1879. The Joplin Railroad, built by local mine owners, has the claim of being the first railroad to serve Joplin. To serve this and other lines in the area was a turntable and small roundhouse, located south of 11th Street and east of Byers Avenue. It sat in the middle of a large wye just north of the Galena Branch. All of the Frisco lines in this area are now gone.

Existing Joplin Railroad Facilities

Probably the most documented railroad structure in town besides Joplin Union Depot is the **St. Louis-San Francisco Railroad Building**, also known as the Frisco Building. Located at 601 South Main Street, this was the second Frisco station in Joplin. The first was a small wooden structure a block to the east, but this building is a nine-story, "L"-shaped, brick and stone trimmed station, built under contract for the local Odd Fellows Lodge Hall. Spending approximately $1 million on what was described as Joplin's first modern, high-rise, fireproof office building, the Odd Fellows agreed upon a fifty-year lease with the Frisco for the first two floors, and then leased office space on the upper levels, mostly to doctors. The railroad used the first floor as the station, and the second floor featured company offices and a public café. The station opened to rail service on November 30, 1913, and construction on the platforms, tracks, and train shed were completed by the end of the year. At its peak, the station served as many as fifty-two passenger trains a day, using tracks that came in from the east. However, the last train departed in 1955, and a new medical building caused most of the doctors to depart the same year. The building then went through multiple owners and uses.

The building was added to the National Register of Historic Places on October 22, 2002. Among some of its historic features is its design in what was known as the "Chicago Style" by the St. Louis architectural firm of Mauran, Russell and Crowell. The firm was noted for its many St. Louis buildings, including the Railway Exchange Building, the Federal Reserve Bank Building, the St. Louis Globe-Democrat Building, and the Missouri Pacific Building. The firm also designed a number of the Carnegie libraries across the Midwest. Today, the building is

Joplin (MO) to Neosho (MO)

known as the Frisco Station Apartments, and provides affordable housing for senior citizens.

The Frisco station certainly doesn't look like a typical railroad station, as it is actually located within an office building. However, it still stands downtown and is listed on the National Register. Photo by Barton Jennings.

There are also several former **Missouri Pacific** (MP or MoPac) structures still standing in Joplin. The most recognizable one is the former 8-stall roundhouse at 1070 S. Missouri Street. The railroad long ago sold off the building, and it no longer includes tracks or a turntable, but it is used by a local business for storage and manufacturing. The original MoPac brick depot once stood nearby on the southwest corner of Main and Tenth Streets. In 1916, a new cut stone station opened on the east side of Main Street. This station has since been torn down and then rebuilt at 29th and Rangeline as a restaurant. While not restored fully to its original design, the beautiful stone building now stands next to the KCS mainline.

Several of the interurban railroad facilities also still exist at Joplin. The **Joplin & Pittsburg Railway**'s brick carbarn still stands on the northwest corner of 4th Street and Maiden Lane, just west of downtown. Further west on 4th Street is Schifferdecker Park. This large park today includes golf, swimming, trails, and about anything else a park should have. During the early 1900s, the park, known as Electric Park, was built by the Joplin & Pittsburg Railway as a destination for the trolley and interurban system.

The interurban carbarn for the **Southwest Missouri Electric Railway** also still stands, today a part of the Tamko Building Products manufacturing complex on North High Avenue. Tamko is one of the largest roofing manufacturers in the nation, and the carbarn is almost surrounded by additions and new buildings.

0.5 **MNA RAILROAD CROSSING** – This diamond, located at KCS Milepost 154.8, is for the former Missouri & Western Railway Company line from Oronogo, now used by the Missouri & Northern Arkansas to reach the Tamko Building Products manufacturing complex just northeast of town. Timetables from the 1960s show this to be a St.L.&S.F. Crossing. There was also a St.L.&S.F. Crossing at Milepost 154.9.

0.8 **MNA CONNECTION** – Located at KCS Milepost 155.1, this connecting track serves as an interchange track between KCS and the Missouri & Northern

Joplin (MO) to Neosho (MO)

Arkansas. The line connects to the former Missouri Pacific line from Carthage, as well as the abandoned Frisco Webb City branch. Just south of the switch, the former MoPac line bridges over the KCS.

South of here at KCS Milepost 156 (M&NA 1.7) was the Joplin Buff Brick Company, located to the east of the tracks. The firm sold brick across the region, and a number of buildings in Kansas City were built using the company's brick.

3.3 REX – This station was listed at KCS Milepost 157.6 in the *Thirty-Fourth Annual Report of the Railroad and Warehouse Commissioners of the State of Missouri, Year Ending June 30, 1909*. Documents from the time show that the area was known as Rex City. The area is still known as the Rex Voting District of Jasper County. Several area histories state that this planned mining suburb of Joplin was thought to be so well located that it would boom and be the "king" of the mining camps. Therefore, it was named Rex (Latin for king) by its founders. The Rex Mine, a lead and zinc mine, was once located here.

3.7 COUNTY LINE – Leaving Joplin, the KCS line heads to the southeast and goes from **Jasper County** and into **Newton County** at the 32nd Street grade crossing, KCS Milepost 158.0. **Jasper County** was created on January 29, 1841, with the first government organized on February 25, 1841. A new town, Carthage, was created as the new county seat on March 28, 1842. At the time, Jasper County also included what eventually became Barton County. Like many area counties, it was mostly abandoned during the guerilla wars of the Civil War. Later, the county boomed due to lead and zinc mining.

The county honors Sergeant William Jasper, a Revolutionary War hero. During the battle of Sullivan's Island in June 1776, the British pounded the American fort, eventually shooting down the flagpole bearing the Fort Moultrie Flag – a blue flag with a white crescent used by South Carolina forces. William Jasper, a member of the Second South Carolina Regiment, jumped out of the fort, walked the entire length in full view of the British, and then cut the flag from its pole. Climbing the wall, he fastened the flag to a cannon sponge-staff and planted it in the wall, all while in the face of deadly fire. For this feat, South Carolina President John Rutledge presented Jasper with his dress sword at a review held soon after the battle and offered him a commission. Jasper turned this down, instead preferring to serve as a scout for the American forces. Jasper was also recognized later for his scouting efforts against the British until he was killed at Savannah in 1779 while planting the colors of the Second South Carolina Regiment on the British lines. He was buried somewhere near the scene of the battle in a mass grave with many of his comrades.

Newton County dates to December 31, 1838, and is today the eighteenth most populous county in Missouri, with about 60,000 residents. Neosho is the county seat. The county's name has an interesting history, as it is often used along with Jasper as a county name. The name Newton comes from John Newton, a somewhat fictional hero who fought in the Revolutionary War. Newton served in the forces of Brigadier General Francis Marion, the famous and legendary "Swamp Fox." While officers who served with Newton called him a "thief and villain," he was made famous in the early 19th century schoolbooks

Joplin (MO) to Neosho (MO)

written by Parson Weems. Weems claimed many great achievements for Newton, a number of which seem almost identical to those of William Jasper. With the fame created from the schoolbooks, many western states have a county or town named for John Newton.

Not far to the southeast, the railroad passes under Interstate 44 at KCS Milepost 158.6. The railroad continues to the southeast until reaching Thurman Creek, where it turns to the southwest and follows the creek to Shoal Creek. The area from here south also has a number of cuts, and much of the dirt (more than 125,000 yards) was moved to Joplin as fill for the Joplin Union Depot project.

5.7   **SAGINAW** – The KCS has a short 2450-foot siding to the east at KCS Milepost 160.0. The grade of an old quarry spur track can be made out in the woods. The community of Saginaw started with a country store operated by a Mr. Thurman, giving the community the name of Thurman. A post office with that name opened here in 1873. The post office was renamed Saginaw in 1889, reportedly named after Saginaw, Michigan. During the 1930s, a railroad mail crane was located at Milepost 160.7 to serve the post office. This allowed mail to be picked up by trains without stopping. Today, the population of Saginaw is approximately 300.

The May 31, 1936, KCS employee timetable showed that M. & A. Freight #211 was scheduled to pass through here southbound at 9:45am. Northbound M. & A. Freight #212 was scheduled for Saginaw at 4:50pm.

Just south of Saginaw, the railroad turns to the southeast and follows Shoal Creek uphill to Neosho, Missouri. The railroad crosses a number of bridges over small streams flowing in off the hillside to the east.

10.8 TIPTON FORD – Look for the grade crossing with Old Highway 71 and the Undercliff Grill and Bar to the east at KCS Milepost 165.1. There was once a short siding here. The name Tipton Ford comes from a ford across Shoal Creek to the west that was once near the home of the Tipton family. A post office opened here in 1890, but the town never grew very large and the post office closed in 1923. Today, the community is unincorporated and the railroad has no side tracks here. Just north of Tipton Ford, the railroad passes under the new Interstate 49 at KCS Milepost 164.8. Heading south, the railroad closely follows Shoal Creek.

On August 5, 1914, just before 6:00pm, Tipton Ford became the center of attention of the Kansas City Southern and the Missouri & North Arkansas. KCS Pacific-type locomotive 805 pulling a northbound passenger train (Train First #56, actually a much delayed #2) had just hit southbound M&NA gasoline motorcar No. 103 (Train #209), apparently after the M&NA crew misinterpreted their orders to meet the KCS train at Tipton Ford. The M&NA motorcar telescoped more than twenty feet and was thrown back 650 feet by the impact. The collision and resultant fire from the fuel tank killed 43 of the 77 persons onboard. Many of those killed were buried in the Neosho cemetery, all victims of the worst accident ever on the KCS and the M&NA.

The Interstate Commerce Commission (ICC) conducted a detailed study of the accident, spending much of their time examining the handling of

Joplin (MO) to Neosho (MO)

train orders for the two trains. The report produced a description of M&NA operations on the line, stating that "(T)he 20 miles of track between Joplin and Neosho is used jointly by trains of the Kansas City Southern and Missouri & North Arkansas Railroads. Four first-class and two third-class trains of the latter road are, scheduled to pass over this section of track daily, subject to the operating rules of the Kansas City Southern Railway."

The accident was also a historic one for the ICC, as indicated by part of their report. "This is the first accident investigated by the commission wherein a gasoline motor car was involved. On account of the fire caused by ignition of this highly inflammable substance, the casualty list in this accident was much larger than it otherwise would have been. The rapidly increasing use of these motor cars, carrying large quantities of gasoline, introduces such an additional element of danger as to demand extraordinary precautions against the possibility of collisions wherever such cars are used."

M&NA passenger service ended through Tipton Ford in 1934, but their freight trains continued to run until the end of the company. In 1936, M. & A. Freight #211 was scheduled to pass through here southbound at 9:55am. Northbound M. & A. Freight #212 was scheduled here at 4:40pm.

15.8 **DALBY** – This is a siding to the east that KCS documents show to be 8900 feet long in 2012 after being extended in 2007. Timetables from the 1930s show it to be at KCS Milepost 170.5. Later, the siding was extended and Dalby was located at 170.1, with North Dalby at Milepost 168.9 and South Dalby at Milepost 170.8. D. B. Dalby was the Freight Claims

Agent for Kansas City Southern in 1915, but there is no clear record of the history of the siding's name.

Southbound M. & A. Freight #211 passed through here at 10:07am, and northbound M. & A. Freight #212 at 4:28pm, in 1936.

17.8 OZARK TERMINAL SPUR – While gone today, there was once a steep spur track to the east at KCS Milepost 172.1. This facility began as a series of limestone caverns, mined since at least the 1930s for the production of calcium oxide. In 1936, the Southwest Lime Company had a 40-car spur track here.

The road that serves the facility is still named Lime Kiln Road. According to the July 15, 1956, issue of the *Neosho News*, the limestone company was turning their underground facilities into a series of warehouses, operated by a new company known as Ozark Terminal, Inc. The article also stated that the "Kansas City Southern Railroad will lay a 4030-foot spur track from its main line, which passes just west of the lime plant, into the warehouse to permit underground loading and unloading of entire trainloads of materials to be stored."

The 1966 KCS employee timetable provided instructions on using the spur track. It stated: "All movements on the Ozark Terminal Spur Mile 172.1, are restricted to 6 mph and because of the heavy grades in this track no movement will be made until the automatic brakes are cut in and operative."

18.1 SHOAL CREEK BRIDGE – Located at KCS Milepost 172.4, this bridge includes a through truss span on the north end, and eleven relatively new precast concrete ballast deck spans. Shoal Creek is more than 80 miles long and is one of the largest tributaries of the Spring River. Shoal Creek begins near Cassville, Missouri, and flows to the southwest to here, where it turns to the northwest to near Joplin, and then west to the Spring River. Shoal Creek reportedly gets its name from its fast, rocky ledges and falls. The Missouri Department of Conservation reports that the stream is great for fishing, including "all three species of black bass, black and white crappie, a variety of sunfish, rock bass, and both flathead and channel catfish."

18.4 BNSF RAILROAD CROSSING – Located at KCS Milepost 172.7, this is the BNSF mainline between St. Louis, Missouri, and Tulsa, Oklahoma, and on to Avard, Oklahoma, and a connection with the BNSF Transcontinental Line between Chicago and Los Angeles. There is an interchange track between the two railroads in the southeast quadrant of the diamond. The BNSF route has a somewhat complicated history, going through the hands of a number of companies in the period of late 1860s - late 1870s.

Planning and construction on the line dates back to July 27, 1866, when the Atlantic & Pacific Railroad Company (A&P) was chartered to build a railroad from Springfield, Missouri, to the Pacific Ocean. As the years passed and track was built, the line was divided into several divisions. The Missouri Division extended from Franklin (now Pacific, near St. Louis), Missouri, to Seneca (west of Neosho), Missouri, about 292 miles. On October 26, 1870, the route was described as being in service as a "standard-gage, single-track railroad" from Franklin to Pierce City, Missouri. West of Pierce City, there were 39 miles of graded roadbed to Seneca, Missouri.

On October 23, 1875, a suit was filed against the A&P due to unpaid interest on certain Missouri Division bonds, and receivers were soon assigned. The Missouri Division was sold by auction on September 8, 1876, to a representative of the St. Louis & San Francisco Railway Company. On June 30, 1896, the railroad was sold to the St. Louis & San Francisco Railroad Company, which was sold to the St. Louis-San Francisco Railway Company (Frisco) on September 15, 1916. The Frisco became a part of the Burlington Northern Railroad on November 21, 1980, and then the Burlington Northern & Santa Fe Railway (BNSF) with the merger with the Atchison, Topeka & Santa Fe Railway on December 31, 1996.

19.8 NEOSHO – Neosho has a population of approximately 12,000, making it the largest city in Newton County, Missouri. It is also the county seat. White settlers began to move into the area during the 1820s and 1830s, generally of English, Scottish, Welsh, Scots-Irish and German ancestry. The area was open prairie on the top of the Ozark Plateau. The first communities were to the east, but John W. McCord and Levie Lee located near Walbridge Spring in an area known as "Six Bulls" for the six roaring streams in the area ("Six Boils").

Walbridge Spring, also known as Bell's Iron Spring, indirectly provided the name of Neosho, an Osage word that means "clear, cold water," generally from a spring. Besides Walbridge Spring, the largest spring in the area – Clark or Big Spring – became the center of the community and is now located in Big Spring Park. Both were used for many purposes, including industrial and residential, giving Neosho the nickname of "City of Springs." The town was

Joplin (MO) to Neosho (MO)

platted in 1833, incorporated on August 20, 1847, and incorporated as a city in 1878. Part of the initial growth of Neosho was due to the discovery of lead and zinc. Much of the ore was shallow, and miners could mine it and move it to the Arkansas River in Indian Territory (Oklahoma) for water shipment to New Orleans. This attracted stores, taverns, and other industries to Neosho to support the needs of the miners and their mines.

The town's importance can be seen by the creation of a monthly Pony Express mail route from Neosho to Albuquerque, New Mexico, on August 3, 1854. However, the Civil War ended the region's importance with four years of guerilla warfare and multiple military campaigns. The courthouse was burned, as was much of the town as it changed hands on a regular basis. The decade after the Civil War saw Neosho regrow, with many buildings constructed using brick. A new courthouse opened in 1878, and the population surpassed 2000 by 1890. Much of the boom during the late 1800s was due to the improved transportation available when the Atlantic & Pacific Railroad (Frisco) reached Neosho in 1870. A second railroad arrived in 1887 – the Kansas City, Fort Smith & Southern Railroad, later the Kansas City Southern Railroad. A third railroad, the Missouri & North Arkansas, arrived in 1908.

A unique and historic event links Neosho to the great vineyards of Europe. In 1882, vineyards across France, Spain and Portugal died from the deadly phylloxera louse, a small pale yellow sap-sucking insect. After searching for answers, it was discovered that Neosho winemaker Hermann Jaeger was growing a new grape that was resistant to the phylloxera louse. Cuttings from Jaeger's vineyards near Monark

Springs were shipped to Europe, ending the destruction of the wine industry. Because of his assistance, Jaeger was awarded the French Legion of Honour, the highest award that France can bestow on a civilian.

A unique facility at Neosho is the Neosho National Fish Hatchery, the oldest Federal Fish Hatchery still operating today. This facility opened in 1888 next to the Kansas City Southern Railroad on East McKinney Street. The hatchery at first used water from Hearrell Spring, and expanded to using McMahon Spring in 1907, giving the facility 1000 gallons of water a minute. Since then, the hatchery has raised more than 130 different species of fish, with rainbow trout, pallid sturgeon, and Topeka shiners the primary species currently being raised.

The Neosho National Fish Hatchery is hard to miss, and is certainly worth the time for a tour. Photo by Barton Jennings.

On August 7, 1914, a funeral was held at the Newton County courthouse for the victims of the M&NA-KCS accident at Tipton Ford. Many of the victims were not identified, and more than 30 were buried in a mass grave in the Neosho Independent Order of Odd Fellows cemetery, located southeast of downtown.

The monument to those who lost their lives in the Tipton Ford wreck still stands in the Neosho IOOF cemetery. Photo by Barton Jennings.

While the Tipton Ford Memorial lists the names of many who lost their lives, not all of the names were known. Therefore, it includes the statement "and others who lost their lives." Photo by Barton Jennings.

Neosho was also once the home of Camp Crowder, built south of town in 1941 as an armored training center. It was converted by 1943 to be a U.S. Army Signal Corps training center. It was also used as an infantry replacement center and as a German prisoner-of-war detention facility. The name Crowder came from General Enoch Crowder, who developed the draft during World War I. One of the famous alumni of Camp Crowder was Dick Van Dyke. In *The Dick Van Dyke Show*, Camp Crowder was where Rob (Dick Van Dyke) and Laura (Mary Tyler Moore) met. The plot had Rob as a sergeant in Special Services and Laura was a USO dancer. Camp Crowder was also the model for Camp Swampy, the base of the comic strip *Beetle Bailey*. This was due to the well-known nature of the facility, and cartoonist Mort Walker's assignment there during WWII. The camp was deactivated in 1951, with much of the base sold off. The location is now an industrial park, the home of Crowder College, and the Fort Crowder Conservation Area.

The 1950s and 1960s saw a growth in local industry, and national recognition. For example, Neosho won the 1957 All-America City Award from *Look* magazine and the National Municipal League for its beautification efforts, making it "The Flower Box City." Much of downtown Neosho is known as the Neosho Commercial Historic District and is listed in the National Register of Historic Places.

In 1872, Missouri law required a school for African Americans. The small wooden school at Neosho was known as the Lincoln School. One of the students was an orphan with the name of George Washington Carver. Carver had been born nearby as a slave in 1864, and after the Civil War moved as a child to attend school. He was known as Carver's George at the time for his one-time owner, Moses Carver, but had his name changed to George Carver by a teacher at the school. He attended school at Neosho for about five years before moving for more advanced education.

Another student educated in Neosho was humorist Will Rogers. Rogers was born in 1879 in the Cherokee Nation of Indian Territory. His parents were both of mixed-race and Cherokee ancestry, and identified as Cherokee. His father was a Confederate veteran, an attorney and Cherokee judge, and a successful rancher. To help with his education Will Rogers attended the Willow Hassel School at Neosho, where he claimed that he "studied the Fourth Reader for ten years."

Railroads

The railroad era at Neosho began in 1870 when the Atlantic & Pacific Railroad arrived. This line later became part of the Frisco Railroad's St. Louis to Tulsa route, and is today operated by BNSF. The line loops around the north and west side of Neosho. The stucco Frisco passenger and freight depot was at Benham Avenue and Commercial on the north side of town. Today, a modern metal office building and a communications tower stands where the old station once was.

The second railroad to reach Neosho was the Kansas City, Fort Smith & Southern Railroad, later the Kansas City Southern Railroad. It arrived in 1887 and runs north-south on the east side of downtown. The large brick station, located at KCS Milepost 174.1, was once where the large communications tower now stands between East Coler and East Brook on the west side of the mainline along North Washington. At one time it housed Bulletin Books, a Train Register, and a Standard Clock. In 1938, the movie *Jesse James* starring Tyrone Power and Henry Fonda was filmed in the area, and several scenes were filmed at the KCS depot.

In 1908, the Missouri & North Arkansas reached Neosho and shared the KCS facilities for many years, before building their own basic facilities in 1933, and then abandoning the line in 1947. In 1936, M. & A. Freight #211 was scheduled to arrive here at 10:20am to meet KCS northbound Second Class Manifest Freight #42. The railroad's own northbound was scheduled to depart daily at 4:20pm as Freight #212.

Missouri and North Arkansas R. R. Receipt for Fare. From the collection of Barton Jennings.

Neosho (MO) to Wayne (MO)

This part of the First District was built by the Allegheny Improvement Company, with help on land acquisition by the MonArk Townsite Company, for the Missouri & North Arkansas Railroad Company. MonArk Townsite was created by Truman and Mary Lou Elmore, and Lee D. Bell. The firm bought farmland and subdivided it for several townsites as well as small farms for new settlers. The firm included a depot site, a public park and a public well at each townsite. They also laid out and graded streets. Eventually, the towns of Aroma, Chester, Fairview, Ridgley and Wheaton were created.

The route between Neosho and Wayne was designed with a maximum grade of 1%, with few curves. Reportedly, the route between Neosho and Wayne is 80% straight and the sharpest curve is only four degrees. The route passed through few towns, but the railroad and the MonArk Townsite Company created several towns of their own. Construction on this part of the railroad didn't start until April 1907, and it was completed from Wayne to Neosho on January 25, 1908.

19.8 NEOSHO – Neosho was the connection with the Kansas City Southern line north to Joplin. Construction on the line from Wayne to Neosho started in April 1907, and was completed to Neosho on January 25, 1908. Regular service between Neosho and Helena, Arkansas, began March 1, 1908. Initially the M&NA used the KCS facilities at Neosho. This included the passenger station, located where the large communications tower now stands between

East Coler and East Brook on the west side of the mainline along North Washington. For the M&NA officials who worked in Neosho, the telegraph call was a simple "N".

The railroad connected with the KCS just south of today's East Spring Street, just south of the location of the KCS passenger station. The M&NA initially had a small yard and a spur track that crossed East Spring Street. As the Missouri & North Arkansas failed financially, efforts were made to cut expenses. One of these efforts was to close joint facilities where the railroad could operate them cheaper. In November 1933, the M&NA opened up a small stucco Neosho depot on their line east of the KCS depot. There was also an 18-car siding to the east. To store the gasoline motorcars used in passenger service, the railroad built a small shed. The railroad had a section house here, as well as a small 6000-gallon water tower made up of an old railroad tank car body, set on a wood frame. The facility was used to store equipment and materials when the railroad shut down in 1946.

Heading toward Harrison, the M&NA crossed both legs of a KCS wye. The grade can still be found. At the former McKinney Street grade crossing, note that the convenience store is centered on the old railroad. Starting at Neosho at an elevation of 1039 feet, the railroad climbed a steady grade to Wayne, except for a small dip into Stark City. Heading southeast from Neosho, the M&NA followed Hickory Creek to where the Elm Spring Branch flows in from the south near a location once known as Possum Trot School. The stone schoolhouse still stands, and was used until 1959 when the school, officially known as the Pleasant Valley School but shown as Possum

Neosho (MO) to Wayne (MO)

Trot on many maps and in many area histories, was consolidated with the Neosho School District. The school was first known as McMahan after a local land owner, but took the name Pleasant Valley when the new building was built. The schoolhouse has since been rebuilt into a rental home. Near there, the railroad turned to the northeast to reach Monark Springs, spelled Monarch Springs by the railroad.

The former M&NA grade can easily be found as it heads southwest out of Neosho at McKinney Street. Photo by Barton Jennings.

22.4 **HICKORY CREEK BRIDGE** – The railroad turned to the northeast and crossed Hickory Creek near the site of the Possum Trot School. This bridge was built in 1907 and consisted of three 40-foot deck plate girder spans. It was built to Cooper E-50 rating, which means that the largest axle load would be 50,000 pounds.

Theodore Cooper was a civil engineer who published numerous articles on railroad and highway bridge design. He was very interested in the live loads placed on bridges as traffic moved across them, and created what became known as the Cooper E-rating for railroad bridges. In 1894 when his design recommendations came out, he created what was called a Cooper E-10 design. This design assumed a pair of 2-8-0 type steam locomotives, pulling an infinite number of rail cars. Each locomotive was assigned an axle loading of 10,000 pounds for the driving axles, 5000 pounds for the leading truck, and 6500 pounds for each tender truck. Each railcar was assigned an axle loading of 1000 pounds per foot of track involved. Higher ratings simply multiplied the weight limits, thus an E-20 was twice these weights, and an E-30 was three times the base weights.

Cooper recommend in 1894 that bridges be built to E-40 ratings, the original design for bridges on the Eureka Springs Railway Company, and the St. Louis & North Arkansas Railway as far as the Buffalo River bridge at Gilbert. However, a standard of E-60 was recommended by 1914, so even more modern bridges using E-50 were out of date within a decade. During the 1920s, the Missouri & North Arkansas installed many extra steel girders and wood stringers on bridges to attempt to raise their Cooper ratings. For those who are curious, the American Railway Engineering and Maintenance-of-Way Association (AREMA) now recommends at least an E-72 rating for concrete bridges and E-80 for steel bridges.

According to the website *Missouri Trout Hunter*, Hickory Creek is the newest of Missouri's managed trout areas. They describe the stream as having "plenty of character, with a variety of fair sized rif-

Neosho (MO) to Wayne (MO)

fles, nice deep pools, and plenty of obstructions like downed trees and strategically placed boulders." The stream starts southeast of Aroma and the railroad followed it almost to its headwaters.

24.7 **MONARCH SPRINGS** – Monark Springs, spelled Monarch Springs by the railroad, was not listed as a station in the June 18, 1911, timetable. However, the small community was shown on topographical maps from 1914. In the Missouri & Arkansas 1945 timetable, Monarch Springs was shown as a flag stop, but there were no side tracks.

Monark Springs was created in early 1913 when Truman Elmore of the MonArk Townsite Company bought the Scotch Ranch and subdivided it into a number of home lots and small farms. A general store was built and operated by the company to attract people to the property. By 1914, the land was sold and the railroad started to stop here when flagged, and a passenger shelter was built.

The online history of the Monarch Springs Church of God Campground covers the community that developed due to the church campmeetings that were routinely held here. The website starts with a painting of a steam train delivering passengers to the stone station shelter, reportedly in 1905 even though construction on the railroad didn't even start until April 1907. However, reports from the early 1900s make it clear that many of those attending the campmeetings did arrive and depart by train. A large wooden tabernacle was built here in 1940 for the Church of God events, increasing the importance of the location.

In August 1956, a national Church of God campmeeting became the source for a national outbreak of typhoid fever. A carrier of the disease was attending the meeting and somehow contaminated the drinking water well. The illness spread beyond the camp as people returned home, resulting in a Center for Disease Control (CDC) response.

Today, some sources call Monark Springs a ghost town, but there are a few homes in the area and the Monark Springs Community Park is a popular attraction. The park features the original 14' x 35' stone flag stop shelter, restored in 1994. There is also a bay window caboose that is painted as M&NA #311. The caboose was never used or operated by the M&NA/M&A, but instead is former Kansas City Southern caboose #300. The park also features a brick community center built to resemble a railroad station.

Heading east, the railroad stayed south of today's Springs Road to the station of Aroma.

The stone passenger shelter at Monark Springs, Missouri, has been restored and is used as part of a community park. Photo by Barton Jennings.

26.2 AROMA – For the railroad, Aroma was a passenger train flag stop in 1945, but there was never a station or shelter here. There was a 20-car siding on the north side of the mainline, used to load cars from a lead ore tipple. There was also a short 2-car long spur track. The February 28, 1920, issue of the *Engineering and Mining Journal* reported on the construction of a lead mine, as well as the development of "Aroma, the new camp" associated with the mine. The 1922 *International Edition of The Mines Handbook* listed the St. George Mining Company as being at Aroma. The facility was described as being on 40 acres, with a "274-foot shaft sunk in 1919, and another sunk in 1920. Equipment includes a 500-ton mill erected in 1920." The lead ore was described as being under 200 feet of limestone.

The St. George Mining Company was not the only working mine in the area. Just northeast of the St. George mine was the Oriental Mining Company. The Dallas Zinc & Lead Mining Company was a short distance north of the St. George property. The Lone Star Mining Company was north and east of the St. George operation. A report in *The Neosho Times* (April 22, 1920) stated that all were hitting water below the limestone and had installed large pumps to allow mining.

Today, the unincorporated community, located on County Road H, is simply two blocks of scattered homes. The railroad was located on the south side of Aroma along Front Street. While *The Neosho Times* commented that Aroma was a camp town for the mines, a post office opened at Aroma in 1910, but stayed open for only one year. The name Aroma reportedly comes from the Aromas strawberry, an early crop planted by area farmers. According to several gardening sources, "the Aromas Strawberry is a patented variety characterized by its exceptional fruit quality, crop and fruit size. Aromas Strawberry has a very broad environmental tolerance and is resistant to mildew and spider mites making it a very easy strawberry to grow in many climates." In 1913, 30 rail car loads of strawberries were shipped from Aroma. However, the berry shed at Aroma was retired in 1926 by the railroad.

The elevation at Aroma is shown as 1228 feet. Heading east toward Stark City, the railroad remained a short distance south of Mulberry Road. It crossed a low ridge, part of the Olivers Prairie, peaking at an elevation of 1255 feet between Aroma and Stark City. According to the M.A. thesis of Robert Lee Meyers entitled "Place Names In The Southwest Counties Of Missouri" (University of Missouri-Columbia, 1930), Olivers Prairie was named for the Olivers family, reportedly the first settlers on the prairie.

27.0 **ST. GEORGE** – St. George was a spur track named for the St. George Mining Company. The mine opened in 1919-1920 and a track was built here soon after. It was removed when the mine closed in 1929.

30.4 **STARK CITY** – Stark City is another town that once shipped lead and zinc ore by rail. Maps show a spur track to the north side of town to serve the Dungy Mine. Early on, this was the Dungy & Shinn Mines, and by the 1940s was known as the Dale Mining Company Dungy mine. Also nearby was the Pioneer Mine. In both 1942 and 1948, the mines were tested for beryllium by the U.S. Geological Survey. Beryllium is a silvery-white soft metal that is used in alloys with copper or nickel to make items more electrical and thermal conductive. In particular, items such as gyroscopes, springs, spot-welding electrodes, high-speed aircraft, missiles, spacecraft and communication satellites all use beryllium alloys. According to the *Miami Daily News-Record* from Miami, Oklahoma, the Dungy Mine was the only lead and zinc mine in southwestern Missouri to operate all of 1949.

In the first timetables of the Missouri & North Arkansas, this station was known as Chester. However, this soon changed and the Stark City post office opened in 1912. The name change started when William P. Stark purchased 700 acres of land north of Chester in 1907. He established a nursery for fruit trees on the land, creating the William P. Stark Nurseries. He was not the first Stark to do this, as his father had established a commercial orchard in 1835 at Louisiana, Missouri, claimed to be the first nursery west of the Mississippi River – the Stark Brothers Nurseries.

Stark made an offer to the community of Chester to have its name changed, and it soon paid off as the nursery brought jobs and national fame to the community. The company shipped many products across the country, including fruit and ornamental trees and bushes, grape vines, strawberries, and even bulbs. The company was particularly known for its Delicious apple and J. H. Hale peach trees.

The main office and packing house was relocated to Neosho, but the Stark City area still had hundreds of acres in nursery stock. Much of this was shipped on the M&NA from a station that developed the nicknames of Stark Station or Starkdale. The company was known for the "William P. Stark 3000-mile package," used with sphagnum moss and rye straw to safely ship trees around the country. For a while, shipment volumes were so heavy that the company had their own private switch engine to move freight cars at the packing house.

Unfortunately, William P. Stark had come to southwestern Missouri after a quarrel with his family, and the original Stark Brothers Nurseries was not happy about his use of the Stark name. The name "Stark Trees" was a name trademarked by Stark Brothers in 1913, and William's use of Stark in his advertisement led to a series of court cases starting in 1917, ending with a 1921 Supreme Court ruling by Justice Oliver Wendell Holmes. The ruling prevented William from using the name Stark, and he couldn't even mention Stark City. A nervous Stark City wondered if it needed to again change its name, but William P. Stark sold the company to the Neosho Nursery Company in 1919, saving the town from the change.

According to Kubat, the station here was a Standard #1 building measuring 18' x 58'. The station was located on the south side of the mainline and there was a 23-car spur track to the north, according to several track diagrams. Kubat stated that the station building was sold on November 15, 1945, and replaced by a small 6' x 12' shelter. Initially, this station used the telegraph call "RH" but later changed to "SC". Stark City apparently lost its telegraph station listing in 1934. The M&NA annual report for 1926 stated that the berry shed at Stark City was retired.

In 2010, the population of Stark City was 139. The post office is still open and the Barry County Co-op has a facility here. However, the lead and zinc mines are gone, as are the acres of nurseries. Heading from

Neosho (MO) to Wayne (MO)

Stark City (1225 feet of elevation) to Fairview (1246 feet of elevation), the railroad continued due east until it turned to the southeast and closely followed Missouri Highway 86 to Fairview.

37.1 **FAIRVIEW** – Fairview was a town created for the railroad and was named for the setting of the town with its great views of rich farmland. A post office opened at Fairview in 1907. The next year, the Horner Institute, a private school offering courses of study for eighth grade through high school, opened at Fairview. It closed in 1912 when it moved to Stella, Missouri, and merged with the Stella Academy. The population of Fairview peaked in 1920 with 378 residents. It experienced a steady decline to 250 in 1960, but has grown back to about 400 today.

For a few years, Fairview was part of the strawberry boom of the area. Most stations between Neosho and Wayne had at least one berry shed, and many also had canning and packing plants. There was a berry shed at Fairview for the shipping of fresh strawberries. However, the business ended by the early 1920s and the shed was retired in 1926, along with many others in the area. Stock was also loaded here, but the stock pens were retired in 1930.

The railroad's route through town is still easy to identify. The railroad had a 44-car siding on the southwest side of the mainline, with a Standard #1 depot measuring 18' x 58' on the northeast side near downtown. Fairview was telegraph call "FA" and was listed into 1933 as a telegraph station. While the station was a scheduled stop for passenger trains until the end of the railroad, Kubat stated that the station building was sold on November 15, 1945, and replaced by a small 6' x 12' shelter.

At Fairview, the M&NA railroad grade continues to the southeast across fields and pasture to Wheaton. The railroad gained 141 feet in just over four miles, grades averaging 0.65%, a challenge for the smaller locomotives used on the M&NA.

39.6 **COUNTY LINE** – **Newton County** is to the west while **Barry County** is to the east. **Barry County** was organized in 1835 (the first meeting of the Barry County Court was on February 4, 1835) and named after William Taylor Barry from Kentucky, the United States Postmaster General during most of the President Andrew Jackson administration. Barry was the only Cabinet member to not resign in 1831 as a result of the Petticoat Affair. The Petticoat Affair (also known as the Eaton Affair) was a move by many of the wives of Cabinet members to criticize the Secretary of War John Eaton and his wife Peggy about the circumstances surrounding their marriage. It was an embarrassment to Jackson, giving his opponents an excuse to attack him. Eventually all but Barry resigned, earning him much favor among Jackson supporters.

41.3 **WHEATON** – Wheaton is another town created by the construction of the Missouri & North Arkansas. As the railroad was being planned and built in 1907, Truman Elmore's MonArk Townsite Company was hired to acquire land. With the railroad being planned, land around existing communities like Rocky and Stella skyrocketed in price, and the company looked at a new route several miles away from the existing towns. Wheaton was one of these towns located on the new route. The town was almost immediately platted and lots sold by the MonArk

Townsite Company. One of the first structures built was the Wheaton Milling Company's elevator and mill, served once trains started running in August 1908. The mill was soon operating at full capacity, attracting other businesses. The Duncan and Reed general store was also soon in business. By the 1920s, the Wheaton Canning Company was also in operation. For many years, Wheaton has declared itself to be the newest town in Barry County. Its population peaked at 721 in 2000, and has stayed at just below 700 ever since.

Wheaton is still the home of a wooden M&NA train station, designated as a "Standard No. 1 Frame Structure" in the town's original plans. The railroad had a siding on the east side of the mainline with the station on the west side of the tracks at the end of Main Street. The station used telegraph call "HN" and was placed on the National Register of Historic Places on February 10, 2000. The application includes a great deal of information about the station building. It states that the station was built in 1908 and measures 18 feet by 58 feet, featuring a three-sided bay window where the agent and ticket office were located. The building was sold when the railroad closed down in 1947. The building still stands on its original lot at the northeast corner of Main and Barnett Streets in downtown Wheaton.

When placed on the National Register, the depot was painted in a faded orange with plans to return it to the dark brown and beige that the railroad used for many years. The interior had been removed over the years so the building could be used as a warehouse. However, it originally included a passenger waiting room, the station agent's office, and a freight and baggage area. The roof has also been changed from the unique flared eave design initially used by the M&NA to a straight design.

Mostly restored, the station is now a project of the Wheaton Depot and Historical Society Museum. Next to the station is former Frisco caboose 115. This caboose was built in 1946 by the Frisco at their West Shops in Springfield. It was one of twenty cabooses (SLSF 100-119) built as part of that order. The caboose had wood sides and featured a straight side steel cupola, a design created in 1938. The caboose had been in Webb City, Missouri, and then sold to Jane Ballard of Joplin and made part of her County Caboose store. When the store closed, Jane Ballard donated it to the Wheaton Depot in 2009. It was moved here on December 3, 2009, and has since been restored.

The Wheaton depot is one of several along the M&NA to have been restored, shown here freshly painted in 2014. Photo by Barton Jennings.

In 1940, Wheaton was also a source of water for steam locomotives. There was a standard 16' x 24' wooden 50,000-gallon water tank set on a wood frame, supported by a railroad well and pump house. The water station was a topic of the railroad improvement efforts of 1927.

The railroad continued to the southeast, passing Wheaton City Park, donated by the Missouri & North Arkansas. It then left Wheaton (1387 feet), again crossing open fields, before rejoining Missouri Highway 86, which it followed to Ridgley (1479 feet). The steady climb continued all the way to Wayne, the highest point on the entire railroad.

46.3 **RIDGLEY** – Coming into Ridgley from the northwest, the terrain gets much rougher as a number of streams flow off to the southwest. Ridgley is a small unincorporated community in Barry County, and another community established on the new Missouri & North Arkansas. The Ridgley post office opened in 1909, but with the town not growing, it closed in 1919. While the post office was open, the railroad had a mail crane on the west side of the tracks, just north of the station platform. Kubat noted that the station was a frame building measuring 18' x 40', but did not list a design.

The name Ridgley reportedly came from the ridge that the community was built on at 1497 feet. The town was platted and built in 1907 on land that was once the hay field of Joe Stamps. The first building was the Coolie general store. The railroad depot and a water tower were built later that year. Stock pens were also built by the railroad. A second store and a doctor's office opened about 1910. Other businesses included the Calvin Stamps tie and timber yard, the Ridgley Tomato Canning Factory, and a grist mill. A school opened in 1913.

A 1909 map showed an 18-car siding to the northeast with the train depot on the southwest side of the mainline at the north end of Main Street. The water tower was located at the south end of the station. A shed was also built by the railroad for the loading of strawberries, a popular regional crop during the early 1900s.

Heading southeast toward Wayne, the railroad grade continues to follow Missouri Highway 86 until the road curves to the east near the location of the former Independence School (1495 feet). Photos of the school show that it was a wooden building until about 1940, after that photos show a building built of field stone. From the school, the grade cuts cross country to the southeast, following Farm Road 1057 the last mile to Wayne.

At the location where Highway 86 turns east, the railroad once bridged across the highway at Milepost 48.8. Little of this overpass can be found except for the railroad fill on each side of the road, however it once consisted of a 40-foot through plate girder span, installed in 1927.

51.9 WAYNE – Between 1908 and 1949, Wayne was a junction between the St. Louis-San Francisco and the Missouri & North Arkansas. There was a 35-car siding on the east side of the mainline just north of the junction. Construction on the railroad between Wayne and Neosho began here in April 1907.

Early records indicate that the community was officially created when William S. Erwin and his wife F. N. Erwin, recorded a plat for the town of East Woodruff on February 29, 1908. It was surveyed by early June of 1909. East Woodruff soon changed its name to Wayne and both railroads built various facilities at the junction. The early railroad history here is confusing, with some reports stating that the

Neosho (MO) to Wayne (MO)

M&NA used the original Frisco station. In 1912, the M&NA proposed a new station, which was built between a spur and the M&NA siding just west of the junction. Some reports state that the station and the attached freight transfer shed were 233 feet long and 16 feet wide. North of the depot was a set of stock pens. The station reportedly was torn down in 1946 and the lumber used to build a house.

Missouri and Arkansas Railway Company Ticket. From the collection of Barton Jennings.

Form 546　　　　　　　　　　　　　　　　Invoice No._____

Missouri and Arkansas Railway Company
INVOICE
Harrison, Ark., _____ 19____

Agent

_____ Conductor

Immediately upon receipt of the supplies shown below, check this Invoice with the supplies, fill in station name and date, sign the Invoice, and return it by first train.

G. M. TONEY
Audr. Frt. & Pass. Accts.

Destination	Form	INCLUSIVE	
		Com. No.	Closing No.

_____ Station, _____ 19____

I hereby acknowledge receipt of supplies enumerated above.

_____

Missouri and Arkansas Railway Company Invoice. From the collection of Barton Jennings.

Wayne (MO) to Seligman (MO)
Trackage Rights Over
St. Louis-San Francisco

To reach the new route between Wayne and Neosho, and then on to Joplin, the Missouri & North Arkansas used trackage rights over the Frisco to travel between Seligman and Wayne, both in Missouri. The St. Louis & San Francisco Railway Co. (StL&SF, or SL-SF), better known as the Frisco, was organized in 1876 in Missouri. The Frisco's first line into Arkansas came south from Monett, Missouri. As was typical at the time, the construction involved a number of paper companies coming together to build and initially operate the railroad. The first of these companies was the St. Louis, Arkansas & Texas Railway Company of Missouri, incorporated June 4, 1880. By summer 1881, the company owned and operated 32 miles of track from Monett to the Missouri-Arkansas state line. It is part of this trackage that the Missouri & North Arkansas operated over.

The Frisco used several different companies to build on south, and on June 28, 1881, they were merged to create the St. Louis, Arkansas & Texas Railway Company. On January 21, 1882, this railway was sold to the St. Louis & San Francisco Railway Company (which became the St. Louis & San Francisco Railroad Company on June 30, 1896). Several other railroads extended the line on south to Paris, Texas, and connections to Dallas and Fort Worth. After the Frisco's improved mainline was built to the west across Oklahoma during the late 1890s and early 1900s, the line between Monett and Fort Smith, and on south to Paris, Texas, took on the role of a secondary line mostly serving local businesses. By the early 1910s, the railroad became the St.

Louis–San Francisco Railway Company. On November 21, 1980, the Frisco merged into the Burlington Northern Railroad, and the line south of Monett was turned over to the Arkansas & Missouri Railroad in 1986.

Looking at various St. Louis–San Francisco Railway Company employee timetables from the 1930s, it is interesting that they did not include schedules for the Missouri & Arkansas trains.

51.9 **WAYNE** – Between 1908 and 1949, Wayne was a junction between the St. Louis–San Francisco (Milepost 303.6) and the Missouri & North Arkansas line towards Neosho, and eventually Joplin, Missouri. The M&NA operated over the Frisco from here southward to Seligman. Originally called Woodruff, some maps show that it was also known as East Woodruff, or Woodruff Station in 1909. At the time, it was shown as a 13-block town platted to the east of the Frisco mainline at the new junction.

Sometime after the junction was created, the location was renamed Wayne. Wayne (telegraph code "WN") was the highest station elevation on the M&NA at 1571 feet. Local sources state that the small 20' x 40' three-room depot (Kubat stated that it was a 16' x 40' "Frisco Style" building) was built in 1913 and located just north of the junction with the M&NA. The M&NA owned half-interest in the station. The former depot foundation is to the west of the tracks near County Road 1062. A post office existed here 1913-1955.

52.0 **WAYNE HILL** – The railroad crests the grade at 1580 feet above sea level at Frisco Milepost 303.7. Heading south, there is a downward two-mile grade of more than 1%.

55.2 WASHBURN – The Frisco served this community with a small (42' x 20') three-room wooden depot ("WU"), built in 1904 and abandoned and ready to fall down by 1960. The depot was located on the east side of the Frisco mainline in line with South Street at Frisco Milepost 306.9, two blocks north of the Highway 90 grade crossing. To the west at this location, look for the large white building near the tracks. That is the old tomato canning factory and warehouse. A siding once existed alongside the building for railcar loading. In fact, a 1914 Sanborn map shows that there were three tracks passing through town; an industry track to the west, then a siding and then the mainline next to the depot. In 1914, the canning factory wasn't where the white building stands today, but instead the Washburn Canning Company was a block north of the northernmost grade crossing at Washburn, along with a set of cattle pens.

The first documented settler was Judge Cureton of Washington County, Arkansas, who moved to the area in 1840 and bought the area where Washburn is now located. When Cureton died in 1853, his property was sold to James T. Keet, who laid out Keetsville and then opened a store there. Keetsville was destroyed in February 1862 as troops fought in an early Civil War battle. After the war, Keetsville was resettled starting in 1867. The next year, a petition was passed to rename the town Washburn, and a post office opened. Washburn, and the surrounding Washburn Prairie, were named in honor of Samuel Washburn, an early settler who reportedly ran a post office in his store.

The railroad was built just west of Washburn in 1879-1880, and the railroad named its station

O'Day, after John O'Day, a Springfield-based attorney for the railroad. O'Day and Washburn became sister cities, with the two communities growing together and sharing businesses and citizens. The town of Washburn was officially incorporated on August 4, 1880, while O'Day remained unincorporated. The two communities were basically merged in 1892 when the post office at O'Day was closed and merged with the post office at Washburn. About the same time, a common public school was built to serve both communities. With the merger, many of the old Washburn businesses moved closer to the tracks. The population grew quickly and a number of industries located at Washburn. While the population peaked at about 1000, today's population is about 450.

The John G. Harbin home, one mile south of Washburn, was the last stage stop in Missouri before entering Arkansas for the Butterfield Stage Coach mail route. Washburn is also located on the historic Trail of Tears and on the Old Wire Road.

61.3 SELIGMAN – This area was first known as Herdsville. About 1838, Jacob Roller moved to this area from Scotts County, Virginia. Soon, the village was renamed Roller Ridge in honor of Roller (Roller Ridge Road still serves this purpose). In the winter of 1879 and 1880, the railroad from Monett arrived in the area and the St. Louis & San Francisco Railroad platted a new town here. On September 27, 1880, railroad president, E. F. Winslow donated 80 acres for the purpose of building the town. The town was renamed Seligman in honor of Joseph Seligman. Seligman was an investment banker and founder of J & W Seligman & Company, Inc., now

Seligman Investments. (According to the company: "Since 1864, generations of investors have used Seligman® investment solutions to build their wealth. From financing the railroads to developing some of the first mutual funds to pioneering technology investing, the Seligman brand has a reputation for insight, integrity and independent thinking.") The town was incorporated in March 8, 1881. In 1936, M. & A. freight trains #211 and #212 were scheduled to meet here at 1:20pm. Train #211 was scheduled to arrive at 12:50pm, providing time for it to interchange traffic with the Frisco.

While some of the original downtown buildings still stand in Seligman, only a few are still used. This former general store still stands near the tracks, but is empty. Photo by Barton Jennings.

Seligman, his brother, and a cousin had invested in the railroad industry. Establishing himself as the original "finance capitalist," he insisted on a place on the board of directors of the Atlantic & Pacific Railway (A&P at that time was a franchise of the St. Louis & San Francisco Railway) in order to protect his investment. Through financial manipulations, political payoffs, and synchronization with his European supporters, Joseph Seligman managed to retain control over the A&P for many years. According to *Goodspeed's 1888 History of Barry County*, Joseph Seligman passed away in April of 1881. When the town was named in his honor, his widow, Babette, was so pleased she donated one acre of land and $500 to erect a church house. The local Seligman residents raised another $300, and the Union Church, still standing, was constructed in 1884.

Seligman became the temporary terminal point of the Arkansas Division of the St. Louis & San Francisco Railway upon its arrival. Construction soon restarted and the line reached Fayetteville, Arkansas, in 1881. Meanwhile, on June 26, 1880, the Eureka Springs Railway Company was granted a charter to build from the Missouri state line to the resort community of Eureka Springs, Arkansas. On September 21, 1880, a charter was also granted for the Missouri & Arkansas Railroad Company of Missouri to cover the mileage in Missouri. On February 27, 1882, the charters were combined as the Eureka Springs Railway. With this, construction of the line between Seligman and Eureka Springs began later that year and the first train operated over the line on January 24, 1883. Eventually, the railroad was extended under the name of Missouri & North Arkansas all the way to the Mississippi River town of Helena, Arkansas. The M&NA was reorganized as the Missouri & Arkansas and eventually abandoned soon after World War II. The line from here to Harrison, Arkansas, was preserved as the Arkansas & Ozarks in 1950. However, even the A&O failed and was abandoned in 1961.

Wayne (MO) to Seligman (MO)

On September 28, 1909, the Frisco depot ("SI") was destroyed by fire and rebuilt in 1910 as a frame building measuring 24' x 145'. The exterior featured plaster walls and a tin shingle roof. From north to south, the building included a freight room (20' long), express room (15'), baggage room (17'), women's waiting room (18'), ticket office (12'), general waiting room (30'), and an open covered porch (30' x 19'-9"). There was also a conductor's lobby in the general waiting room next to the ticket office. The *Cassville Democrat* reported on March 9, 1966, that the Seligman Frisco Station would be destroyed for good. Look for its foundation to the east of the Arkansas & Missouri Railroad tracks just north of Eureka Avenue. The station was the subject of an article in the August 1981 issue of the *NMRA Bulletin*, and included a number of drawings of the structure.

The foundations, curbing, and a few steps are all that remain of the former train station at Seligman, as shown by this 2019 photo. Photo by Barton Jennings.

At one time, there were a number of tracks at Seligman, Frisco Milepost 312.8, including a siding to the east of the depot and several long sidings to the west of the Frisco mainline. The depot siding was used by the M&NA to reach the station and to interchange freight traffic with the Frisco. According to an early Frisco map, from east to west at North Street, now Jefferson Street, there were six tracks. These were an 860-foot team track, the siding used as the M&NA mainline, the 1274-foot Depot Track, the Frisco mainline, a 1722-foot passing track, and a 1497-foot Commercial Track. Along the Commercial Track was an auto unloading dock across from the depot. All of these tracks and buildings are now gone except for the west siding, which has now been cut back to just a short spur track at its south end.

Over the years, fewer and fewer railroad artifacts remain along the M&NA. In 1988, these homemade fuel tanks were still at a customer site in Seligman, Missouri. Photo by Barton Jennings.

Seligman (MO) to Harrison (AR)

Construction on the Eureka Springs Railway began at Seligman in 1882 by the Western Construction Company. The railroad was backed by Powell Clayton, a former Union Army brigadier general and later governor of Arkansas. Clayton was an important figure in the attempt to turn Eureka Springs into a national resort community. He attracted interest from St. Louis and other regional cities, and particularly from officials of the Frisco Railroad. In late 1882, the Eureka Springs Railway was built east from Seligman, using engineering and equipment essentially identical to those of the larger railroad. On January 24, 1883, the tracks reached Eureka Springs and regular passenger service soon began, often handling connecting coaches, lounge and sleeper cars from the Frisco.

Reports from the time clearly show the mountainous terrain that the railroad crossed. It stated that of the 18.5 miles between Seligman and Eureka Springs, only 1.1 miles was level and 7.9 miles of track was curved. In 1900, the railroad was extended east to Harrison as the St. Louis & North Arkansas, with the Eureka Springs Railway being sold to the new railroad on July 31, 1900. The Allegheny Improvement Company was the general contractor, and progress was generally good except for the tunnel under Charcoal Gap. Until the tunnel was completed, track materials were moved by wagon around the tunnel. On March 22, 1901, track construction entered Harrison, and regular service started on April 15, 1901, after another month of final track and bridge work.

61.3 SELIGMAN – In 1886, the Eureka Springs Railway operated a daily passenger train between Eureka Springs and Seligman, as well as a daily mixed train. By 1911, there were two passenger trains in each direction, plus two mixed trains daily. Later, the daily Joplin to Helena passenger train #201 arrived at Seligman at 9:05am, and then departed at 9:30am. Train #202 would arrive at Seligman at 6:55pm if it was on time, and then depart at 7:10pm.

Seligman is still marked by the Arkansas & Missouri Railroad station sign. Photo by Barton Jennings.

The population of Seligman in 1900 was about 300, and it has grown slowly ever since, to 851 at the 2010 census. Several sources say that the name Seligman is a form of Yiddish and means "a jolly, cheerful person." For the Missouri & North Arkansas Railroad, it was the first outside connection, and one of the last junctions used by the last remnants of the system.

Initially, Seligman was a terminal for the Eureka Springs Railway and the St. Louis & North Arkansas (StL&NA). It was also a significant interchange location. A map from 1909 showed that a siding wrapped around the east side of the joint Frisco-StL&NA depot, known as telegraph code "SI". This station burned in 1909 and a new one was almost immediately built. Initially, there was a 50-foot turntable and an engine shed here, with the turntable later replaced with a 75-foot turntable, located on a spur off the south end of the siding. There was also a water tank south of the station. There was a small yard east of the Frisco mainline north of the station for the StL&NA, while the Frisco had two tracks west of the mainline.

The foundation of the station can still be found on the east side of the Arkansas & Missouri (ex-Frisco) mainline between Eureka Avenue and North Street. Across the street are the last of a number of stone buildings that used to be part of the busy downtown business district. This area is on a ridge with the Butler Creek valley to the east. Because of this, locating the new Eureka Springs Railway was difficult. Unable to build the line so that it came into Seligman south of the Frisco station, the railroad was forced to connect to the Frisco north of downtown and then back to the station.

Heading east toward Eureka Springs and Harrison, the railroad dropped on grades of as much as 2.66% as it descended to Butler Creek. The M&NA grade started north of North Avenue. It then ran behind the row of buildings to the east of the station area. Leaving Seligman, the railroad passed under the Eureka Avenue bridge and crossed several small streams. Much of this area was filled in when the highway bypass was built around the east side of town.

The Eureka Avenue and Main street signs are a reminder of when the M&NA connected Eureka Springs to Seligman. Photo by Barton Jennings.

Heading east on Farm Road 2285, the grade is briefly on the hillside to the north. A map from the early 1900s shows that the railroad once bridged over the road and then back where the road briefly curved to the south. This part of the road is in a cut and it can be seen how the railroad can cross back and forth. About a mile later, the grade can be seen near several houses to the north and then the road and railroad grade merge off and on eastward, before again becoming two grades near the Missouri-Arkansas state line.

After about two miles, the grade reduced to 1.6% or less to the White River at Beaver, Arkansas. Overall, the elevation of the railroad dropped from 1540 feet at Seligman to 934 feet at Beaver, an average of more than 1% over these eleven miles. There were several studies on how to reduce these grades, but the expense was always too much for the railroad. The grade can be followed closely by taking Farm

Seligman (MO) to Harrison (AR)

Road (FR) 2285 east from Seligman, a route that also closely follows Butler Creek. Where the road enters Arkansas near Poddy Hollow, the road becomes Highway 232.

Much of the M&NA right-of-way can be driven, including in this area around Pender, Missouri. Photo by Barton Jennings.

63.5 PENDER – Pender, Pender Switch on many early maps, was an original station on the railroad with a water tank. Instructions in the November 1923 employee timetable stated that "trains doubling Seligman hill will make cut at Pender, place head end in the clear and move rear portion of train to Seligman first."

A siding was reportedly installed in 1926, and later reports show that it could hold a dozen cars and was on the north side of the mainline. At least one photo shows a station or section house on the south side of the tracks near the water tank. The 1926 annual report of the Missouri & North Arkansas stated that the section house at Pender was retired.

Heading south, over the next four miles, the railroad had nine timber trestles over small streams that flowed into Butler Creek.

During the 1920s, many of the small timber trestles along Butler Creek were replaced by steel deck plate girder spans to handle heavier steam locomotives. This one was still in place near Pender, Missouri, in 1988. Photo by Barton Jennings.

67.8 PENDERGRAST – This 5-car spur track was shown in the June 9, 1907, timetable. The names Pendergrast, Pendergrass, and Pendergraft were used by a number of early families who settled in this area.

69.5 ARKANSAS/MISSOURI STATE LINE – This is the boundary between **Barry County**, Missouri, and **Carroll County**, Arkansas. The state line is just north of where Poddy Hollow comes in from the west, and north of Sugarloaf Mountain (1690 feet of elevation).

Missouri borders eight different states. No state borders on more. Missouri became the 24th state on August 10, 1821. Today, Missouri is the 21st largest and the 18th most populated of the states. Known as the "Gateway to the West," Missouri was the starting point and the return destination of the Lewis and Clark Expedition, as well as the starting points of the Pony Express Trail and Oregon Trail.

The Territory of **Arkansas** was admitted to the Union as the 25th state on June 15, 1836. It is the 29th largest state, and the 32nd most populated. This part of the state is the Ozark Plateau/Mountains. This is part of the interior highlands region, the only major mountainous region between the Rocky Mountains and the Appalachian Mountains. Arkansas is also the only state where diamonds are mined, and you can go mine them yourself at the Crater of Diamonds State Park.

Carroll County was the 26th county created in Arkansas, established on November 1, 1833. The county was named for Charles Carroll of Carrollton, also known as Charles Carroll III, a wealthy Maryland planter. Carroll's fame came from being the last surviving signer of the United States Declaration of Independence. He died on November 14, 1832. Carroll County is unique in that it has two Districts, meaning two county seats. Berryville is the East District county seat and Eureka Springs is the county seat of the West District. This arrangement came about due to the Kings River and the mountainous terrain, which was difficult to cross when the county was created.

Heading east, the railroad continued to follow Butler Creek to near Beaver, Arkansas. There were a number of small bridges used to cross streams that flowed into Butler Creek. The stone headwalls of many of these bridges can still be seen in a number of places throughout the valley. Short 30-foot deck plate girder spans were used at Mileposts 68.3, 69.7, and 70.3, all installed new in 1928.

71.4 WALDEN – Also known as Walden Switch, this was once a 42-car-long siding to the east and a few buildings, but no station. The company reported that a new siding was installed here in 1926. Walden was at an elevation of 998 feet and was located near the junction between Arkansas Highway 187 and County Road 232. Heading east, Highway 187 follows the old grade to near Beaver, where the railroad once stayed close to Butler Creek and the road climbed to run along a ridge top.

Bridge stonework can still be found in many places along the railroad. The area around this bridge headwall had been cleared in 1988, making it easy to explore near Walden, Arkansas. Photo by Barton Jennings.

A post office was once planned for Walden, but it was opened in 1905 in the community of Busch to the south.

Seligman (MO) to Harrison (AR)

71.7 DEMOCRAT HOLLOW – Located here is the Railway Winery at Trestle 71-7. This is a small farm winery and vineyard with twelve varieties of grapes and several fruits. The stone headwalls of Trestle 71-7 are easy to locate along the highway where a new 30-foot deck plate girder span was installed in 1928 to increase the line's tonnage capacity.

This stonework was still visible at Democrat Hollow in 1988. It once supported a small steel deck plate trestle. Photo by Barton Jennings.

73.1 BUTLER CREEK BRIDGE – The railroad once crossed Butler Creek and then passed through a narrow ridge heading towards Eureka Springs. The bridge consisted of a seven panel frame timber trestle.

73.2 BUTLER CREEK BRIDGE – This was a long 11-panel frame timber trestle that once crossed a deep stream channel. After Table Rock Lake was created, the water level raised to the point that the Butler Creek channel could no longer be seen, and only the tops of the remaining timber bents were visible. Officially known as Bridge 73-2, this structure was damaged during the May 5, 1960, flood, causing the Arkansas & Ozarks to embargo their line.

Trestle 73-2 was the end of the Arkansas & Ozarks. It collapsed under a freight on May 16, 1955, and then was damaged by flooding on May 5, 1960. In 1988, some of the bents still stood where it crossed Butler Creek. Photo by Barton Jennings.

This timber trestle was tall, estimated at more than 40 feet above the stream level. This bridge was always a challenge for the railroad, and it collapsed under an Arkansas & Ozarks train on May 16, 1955. This train was a light move of one diesel locomotive and a carload of strawberries that was considered a rush shipment. The GE 70-ton locomotive (#900) involved was pulled out of the stream by a Frisco wrecker and repaired in the Harrison shops. The carload of strawberries in Railway Express Agency car #6210 was later moved using a shoo-fly around the bridge.

Just south of the bridge, the railroad was built on a narrow shelf blasted out along Poker Bluff. This grade was used by the Eureka Springs Railroad, an early 1980s project of the Younger brothers (Dreat and Reat). They operated their tourist railroad for a few years south of Butler Creek and across the White River bridge at Beaver, closing by 1987. When the tourist railroad closed, much of the display collection was used to form the Missouri & Arkansas Railroad Museum, now a part of the Boone County Historical & Railroad Society. The former railroad grade is now the Town of Beaver Trail.

Like in many places along the railroad, the grade was squeezed between a river and a bluff. This right-of-way is located just north of Beaver, Arkansas. Photo by Barton Jennings.

Missouri & North Arkansas Railroad: History Through the Miles

The M&NA right-of-way required a great deal of rock work. This cut through Poker Bluff is located not far north of Beaver, Arkansas, on the right-of-way once used by the Younger Brothers and their Eureka Springs Railroad. Photo by Barton Jennings.

73.7 **BEAVER** – Beaver is a small town with a population of approximately 100. The town of Beaver was incorporated on July 21, 1949, and then re-incorporated on November 28, 1980. According to a Eureka Springs newspaper dated October 21, 1901: "The Beaver homestead is on high and level ground overlooking and including a picturesque arc of White River, on the opposite banks of which, rising sheer from the water's edge, are the famous Cedar Cliffs. The dense green foliage of the graceful cedars appliqued upon the limestone bluffs of dazzling white, forms a picture of striking and perpetual beauty – the same in Winter and Summer."

Beaver was not named for a local mammal, but instead for Squire Wilson Ashbury Beaver. Beaver was born in North Carolina, moved to Tennessee, and then to this location. In 1857, Squire and his wife

Emeline purchased almost 350 acres from the original owners, John and Sarah Williams. Some reports state that Emeline was the half-sister of Judge L.B. Saunders, a major area developer who was instrumental in the development of Eureka Springs and Berryville. The Beaver family opened a ferry across the river, attracting many travelers to the community. The Beaver Inn was also built to house these travelers, and the building became known as the "Old Confederate House" for its use as a military hospital during the Civil War. The Inn was also the location of the Beaver Ferry Post Office (September 22, 1879) and served some government functions since Squire Beaver was also a Justice of the Peace.

The post office soon closed, but opened again as simply the Beaver Post Office on October 3, 1881. Meanwhile, Beaver had become an official stagecoach stop and was known as Beaver Station by the stage line. The development of nearby Eureka Springs also impacted Beaver. During the early 1880s, Powell Clayton and his Eureka Improvement Company were building hotels and other businesses, using stone from a quarry built near Beaver. The quarry once employed more than 400 laborers, making the community boom. Located near the Beaver end of the Beaver Bridge, known by many as the Little Golden Gate Bridge, is a stone spring house that protects Beaver Spring. This spring was the first water source for settlers, and had earlier been used by native tribes. The original spring was protected by a wooden cabin, and the stone structure was built as other buildings in the area began to use stone from the local quarry.

This stone house is used to protect Beaver Spring, once located alongside the railroad at Beaver. Photo by Barton Jennings.

During the early 1920s, several firms were regular shippers from Beaver. The Nebraska Bridge Supply & Lumber Company shipped cedar posts for fencing and other purposes, as did M. W. Swope. Swope also manufactured and shipped hubs and spokes for wheels.

There are several buildings of note in Beaver. One of these is the Beaver Town Inn and General Store. During the late 1800s, Cash Mark Swope almost became Beaver itself. Having bought the Beaver Inn, he also opened up stores, bath houses, a lumberyard, grocery store, and other businesses. Swope also worked as the railway and express agent. Later, he moved the Beaver Inn to near the station and renamed it the Riverside Inn, and later the Stagecoach Inn. In 1901, Swope built a stone two-story general store, now known as the Beaver Town Inn and General Store, or the Beaver Town Lodge. Next to the Beaver Town Lodge is the former railroad station. This one-story wooden station was built by the railroad and was located between the mainline and the 18-car siding that was located against the White River.

The general store in Beaver has long been a fixture along the railroad. Here is what it looked like in 1988. Photo by Barton Jennings.

The former Beaver depot has been moved a short distance away from the tracks, but still exists as a part of the railroad's history. Photo by Sarah Jennings.

The ferry operated at Beaver for many years. The first bridge, a toll bridge, was built in 1926, but it washed out during a 1943 flood. A new bridge was quickly built, but it was replaced in 1949 by the current swing bridge – the "Little Golden Gate Bridge." This one-lane suspension bridge carries Arkansas Highway 187 over the White River. The bridge was built as part of the creation of Table Rock Lake, requiring the bridge to be raised forty feet or more.

The one-lane "Little Golden Gate Bridge" is a landmark of today's Beaver, Arkansas. The former railroad grade is at the north end of the bridge. Photo by Sarah Jennings.

The Pioneer Construction Company of Malvern, Arkansas, received the bid for the bridge on December 19, 1947. With the changes required by the United States Army Corps of Engineers, the bridge didn't open until 1949. Reportedly, the bridge was built without the benefit of an industrial crane. It is the only in-service suspension bridge in Arkansas.

The Beaver Bridge was added to the National Register of Historic Places on April 9, 1990.

73.8 WHITE RIVER BRIDGE – Known officially as Bridge 73-8, the White River bridge initially consisted of two iron through truss spans, measuring 250 feet in total. The bridge was built by the Delaware Bridge Company and was set on piers made from stone from a nearby quarry. Stone from this quarry was used for a number of buildings in the Eureka Springs area. In 1907, the iron spans were replaced by a steel bridge built by the Wisconsin Bridge & Iron Company of Milwaukee, Wisconsin. From the west, the bridge consisted of a number of timber spans, and then a 103-foot Warren pony truss. The east span was a 155-foot Baltimore through truss. The bridge is easily seen from the river's west beach at Beaver Park.

While the timber trestle approach spans are gone, the steel spans still exist on the White River bridge at Beaver. This 2019 view is from the park at Beaver. Note the Cedar Cliffs and Narrows Cut on the far shore. Photo by Sarah Jennings.

This is the White River bridge at Beaver, photographed from the top of Cedar Cliffs in 1982. Photo by Barton Jennings.

The White River starts as several branches in the Ozark/Boston Mountains in northwest Arkansas. It flows north into Missouri, and then east and southeast back into Arkansas. It eventually flows into the Mississippi River across from Rosedale, Mississippi, and south of Helena. On July 17, 1909, a water level gauge was installed on this bridge to obtain data for use in studying water power, water supply, flood control storage and navigation problems.

The White River played a significant role in the abandonment of the Arkansas & Ozarks Railway. During the late 1950s, the U.S. Army Corps of Engineers built the Table Rock dam near Branson, Missouri. When closed, the dam backed water up past Beaver, requiring a few miles of the railroad to be raised to stay above flood waters. Instead of having the railroad raised, the railroad owners, the Salzberg family, applied to abandon the line, ending service out of Seligman.

Seligman (MO) to Harrison (AR)

At the south end of the White River bridge, the railroad had to blast a 60-foot deep cut through a limestone ridge, known as Narrows Ridge or the Cedar Cliffs, that separated the river from Leatherwood Creek. The cut became known as the Narrows Cut, or simply Narrows. The Narrows area became a popular picnic location, and many parties were held along the streams in the area. During the early years of the railroad, special trains were often run to here for these events.

In the Beaver area, the railroad is flat for several miles, but then begins to climb up Leatherwood Creek to reach Eureka Springs. The grades approached 1.25%.

For several decades after the railroad was abandoned, many trestles still stood. This one was photographed near the Narrows Cut at Beaver in 1982. Photo by Barton Jennings.

73.9 LEATHERWOOD CREEK BRIDGE – The railroad passed through the Narrows and almost immediately crossed Leatherwood Creek.

74.2 LEATHERWOOD – This station was listed in the November 30, 1902, Timetable No. 17 of the St. Louis & North Arkansas Railroad. This location is near the second bridge crossing of Leatherwood Creek, Bridge #74-2, an 11-panel frame timber trestle.

74.4 LEATHERWOOD CREEK BRIDGE – This is the third crossing of Leatherwood Creek. It was a 12-panel frame timber trestle.

74.7 SMITH HOLLOW – To the east up Smith Hollow is the Ozark Southern Stone quarry. The quarry opened in 1883 as the Eureka Stone Company. Hungarian Benjamin J. Rosewater, an early businessman, postmaster, and development advocate at Eureka Springs, opened and operated the quarry. Rosewater, like many early settlers, had first traveled to Eureka Springs to take a cure for his health. His quick recovery led him to stay in the area and partner with Powell Clayton to modernize the community. Rosewater was also involved in platting the town, getting funding for the Andrew Carnegie Library, and later helped found the Commercial Club, today's Chamber of Commerce.

Eureka Stone Company provided much of the stone for area construction. During the peak of construction, special stone cutters were brought in from Ireland. The White River Limestone that was cut at the quarry was praised by these workers as having the best density and quality they had ever worked with. The limestone has been used in buildings such as the Crescent Hotel, the Basin Park Hotel, and the downtown Bank of Eureka Springs, as well as many others across the region. The quarry stayed open until the Great Depression, and then changed hands several times. Lowell Johnson acquired it in 2006 and operates it as Ozark Southern Stone.

74.8 LEATHERWOOD CREEK BRIDGE – This was a 15-panel frame timber trestle.

75.1 ELK RANCH – This community, located at an elevation of 954 feet, was originally known as Skelton for the family that farmed in the area before the Civil War. Their farm was the location of a small Civil War battle between a band of Confederate raiders and a small force of the First Regiment Arkansas Cavalry (Union). Reportedly, during the winter of 1863, the Confederate raiders had attacked a number of Missouri farms. While moving back south, they took over the Skelton farm. First Lieutenant John Williams and several troopers of the First Regiment Arkansas Cavalry attacked the encampment. Despite being greatly outnumbered, Williams routed the larger force.

When the Eureka Springs Railway built through the area, it was still a collection of mountain farms. As an effort to attract business, the creation of an elk ranch was tried, giving the community its name. The Riverside Land & Livestock Company acquired one thousand acres in 1900, first with the intent of breeding horses. Soon the ranch was raising elk, and later even Angora goats. There must have been some success, as a post office opened on September 18, 1909. The breeding of elk didn't last long, but a small hotel did open up at Elk Ranch. For the railroad, there was only a four-car spur track that was gone by the early 1930s. There was no depot, but there was reportedly a 14' x 24' passenger shelter (shown as 10' x 15' on a M&NA valuation map) and a mail crane. Fourteen lots were laid out on the west side of the tracks for the town. The post office closed on June 30, 1955.

75.7 **LEATHERWOOD CREEK BRIDGE** – Known as Bridge 75-7 (75-8 on some documents), this small 10-panel frame trestle was located where Leatherwood Creek flows beside Arkansas Highway 187. The bridge was upgraded with a 30-foot deck plate girder span in 1928. It was one of a number of bridges that were never repaired after being washed out on May 5, 1960.

76.2 **GASKINS** – Gaskins, or Gaskins Switch, was a stop on the Eureka Springs Railway. The stop was named for John Gaskins, an early settler who is known as the greatest bear hunter in the history of Carroll County. He built a cabin in 1864 on the north side of Leatherwood Creek for himself, his wife, and their 11 children. The Gaskins cabin still stands and has been used as the home for several restaurants, with the Gaskins Cabin Steak House operating in 2018. The cabin is the oldest standing property in Carroll County.

Not long after the railroad was opened, a post office opened here in 1886, but it was named Whitcomb. It closed in 1888. Nearby is the Gaskins Switch Cemetery where several generations of the Gaskins family are buried. Gaskins lost its stop when the railroad was extended east to Harrison, with near-

Seligman (MO) to Harrison (AR)

by Junction serving that purpose. A railroad section house was also once located here.

77.0 **LEATHERWOOD CREEK BRIDGE** – This was known as Bridge 77-1, and was just north of the north switch of the Junction complex of tracks. The bridge consisted of seven spans of a wood frame trestle.

Just north of this bridge is the location of the Abundant Memories Heritage Village, which sits atop part of the old railroad grade. Abundant Memories is a project that has resulted in the construction of a small community that aims to present the history of the United States through stories and displays.

77.5 **JUNCTION** – The station of Junction replaced Gaskins when the St. Louis & North Arkansas Railway Company extended the railroad south to Harrison. Junction was built where the stream from Livingston Hollow flowed into Leatherwood Creek, meaning the wye had several bridges to cross all of the streams. Bridge 77-4 was located between the wye switches on the mainline, while Bridge 77-4A was on the east leg of the wye. Both bridged Leatherwood Creek. Bridge 77-4 was described as being an eight-panel frame trestle, while Bridge 77-4A was a seven-panel frame trestle.

Junction became an important station as it was the wye that connected the new mainline with the former mainline to Eureka Springs, now simply a short branchline. To support the trains that either passed through or stopped to run to Eureka Springs, a number of facilities were built at Junction. The facilities at Junction actually started to the west, railroad-north. There was a 10-car siding to the east, located north of the Leatherwood Creek Bridge 77-1. In 1936, M. & A. freight train #211 worked Junction, being scheduled to be here from 2:10pm until 2:35pm. Train #212 was shown as only a through train with a scheduled time of 12:01pm.

Just south of the 77-1 bridge was a 27-car siding to the east. There was a standard 16' x 24' wooden 50,000-gallon water tank just south of the north switch, located on the west side of the mainline. It was supplied by a pump house obtaining water from Leatherwood Creek. The south switch of the 27-car siding was just north of the north wye switch. There was also a 17-car siding to the west of the north leg of the wye, whose north switch was on the mainline.

The railroad grade can be driven for a short distance to the railroad-north here from Arkansas Highway 23. Along this road, the concrete foundations of the original coaling facility and water tank are still visible, although hidden in the woods to the west. During the railroad's operating days, this area was cleared and there were few trees, but today the foundations used as part of the raised coaling track and 80-ton wooden chute are in the woods to the south (railroad-west). Here, nine concrete foundations can be seen. Note that they are various heights with the first two (railroad-south) taller than the rest. Some documents state that the coal chute had a steep approach grade and that a cable hoist was used to pull loaded coal cars up onto the coaling trestle. Part of the grade is still used as a driveway.

Over the years, several different coaling systems were used here, some benefitting from the raised coaling track that is now partly used as a driveway. Documents listed an "80-ton wooden frame elevated coal chute" that was replaced in 1942 with a "Red

Devil" transfer conveyor. This simple conveyor system was apparently successful as one was installed at Harrison in 1943 and Heber Springs in 1944, likely as labor saving devices during the war. The coaling dock was apparently staffed at one time as in 1927, a house was built for the coal chute foreman at Junction.

The concrete footings of the coaling trestle can still be found in the woods to the north of Junction. Photo by Barton Jennings.

Today, the wye area has been rebuilt as the north destination of the Eureka Springs & North Arkansas Railway. The bridges have been rebuilt and the grade is clearly visible. The route of the tourist railroad generally uses the original grade to Eureka Springs with a few exceptions. **For information on the Eureka Springs Branch, please see page 179.**

To the north of Junction is Livingston Junction Cabooses, providing luxury lodging in several cabooses. The operation includes three cabooses as well as a building that resembles a railroad station. The oldest caboose was built in 1926 for the Frisco. Another was built in March 1930 at the Aurora, Illinois, shops for the Chicago, Burlington & Quincy. The newest caboose was built in September 1967. All eventually became part of Burlington Northern before coming to Eureka Springs.

This is the location of the coaling trestle switch. Looking railroad-north, the spur track went to the left (west), while the mainline was to the right (east). Photo by Barton Jennings.

78.0   TRACK REALIGNMENT – Just south of Milepost 78, the railroad realigned the track in 1938. Records show that the curve was moved inward. The work required that 299 feet of the original mainline be moved to the east, with 2330 feet of new track added. Then 2510 feet of track was retired.

78.7   BRIDGE 78-7 – Heading south from Junction, the railroad climbed up through Livingston Hollow. This route can be followed on County Road 266 for a short distance. The railroad generally stayed above the stream, with only one major bridge required, this one.

Only a few remnants of this former 238-foot long, 15-panel timber span bridge still exist. The bridge was one of many that mysteriously burned in January 1923 during the railroad strike. It had to be fully rebuilt before the line could reopen, and was a source of issues through the end of the operations of the Arkansas & Ozarks.

Construction on this bridge started in 1900 and ended in 1901, and many parts are almost 70 feet tall. Because it was almost impossible to drive piles into the rock, the original bridge was a frame trestle, but eventually the bents were rebuilt with piles. Some sources call this the largest wooden railroad trestle built on the railroad. On August 3, 2011, the remains of the bridge were listed in the Arkansas Register of Historic Places.

80.0 CHARCOAL GAP TUNNEL – This was the location of the only tunnel on the railroad, and the second railroad tunnel built in Arkansas. It is located at the upper end of Livingston Hollow at an elevation of 1270 feet, passing under Charcoal Gap. For years, this location had a short siding or spur track on the north side of the tunnel, located to the east of the mainline. Known as "Track No. 6" in some railroad documents, the track was often used by maintenance forces working on the tunnel. There was also a 20' x 24' section house here that was built in 1901. Earlier, there were short sidings on each end, both located to the west. Passenger schedules also showed the location to be a flag stop.

To build the tunnel, long cuts were required on either end, leaving approximately 700 feet of actual tunnel when completed. Railroad documents later indicated that the tunnel was 672 feet long, with 653 feet through solid rock with the rest supported by timber lining. An evaluation of the tunnel stated that the tunnel included "uniformly bedded limestone formation excepting about 18 feet at the south end which is timbered." The tunnel was holed through on January 7, 1901. The slow progress forced materials for railroad construction to the east to be moved by wagon. However, by early February, materials were moving through the tunnel toward Harrison.

While the core of the tunnel was through solid rock, the ends were through loose rock and soils. To protect the track at the north portal, retaining walls were used. The retaining walls were made of rough-faced ashlar stone, and stood ten feet high on the west side of the track and two feet high on the east side. There were no retaining walls at the south end of the tunnel.

With the railroad through the tunnel being abandoned in 1962, the right-of-way became private property, and the tunnel is still inaccessible without permission. Reports indicate that the center portion of the tunnel has caved in and that the approaches are heavily vegetated. The tunnel was listed in the Arkansas Register of Historic Places on April 4, 2007.

Heading south, the railroad curved numerous times, following Bee Creek out of the hills to the flatter farmland and pasture around Grandview.

81.8   BRIDGE 81-1 – This timber frame trestle consisted of nine panels. The railroad once crossed a small stream that flows south off of Boat Mountain.

82.7 BRIDGE 82-7 – This was a 12-panel frame wooden trestle. The small stream flows off of the west side of Brush Mountain, and flows south into Bee Creek just south of the old grade.

84.6 GRAND VIEW – Grand View, or today Grandview, is another community founded with the construction of the railroad. The area was already populated by several families, with the McElyea and Edmondson families well documented. The small community was named White Elm, but with the arrival of the railroad and a possible post office, a new name was wanted. Early histories of the area state that Brack Edmondson came up with the name, reportedly for the great views from the hilltops. A post office using the name Grandview opened on August 27, 1901. The post office was finally closed and moved to nearby Berryville in 1982 when Jack L. Ray, the postmaster, died.

Today, Grandview is a cluster of several dozen houses on Highway 143 north of U.S. Highway 62. The railroad grade can be seen in a few places as it comes in from the west, loops around the north side of the community, and then heads south to follow the Kings River to the Kings River bridge crossing. The railroad had a 37-car siding to the east, with a depot on the west side of the mainline. Kubat reported that the depot was a Standard #1 measuring 18' x 52' (some sources say 58'), and that there was no center waiting room, unique for the design. Grandview had the telegraph call of "RA" until at least 1933. Some sources state that the depot was gone by 1938 and replaced by a passenger shelter. The Grand View Canning Company operated here in the 1920s.

86.6 KINGS RIVER BRIDGE – The river was named for Henry King, a member of a prospecting expedition in 1827. He died during the expedition and was buried next to the river, which was given his name. The Kings River is a 90-mile tributary of the White River, flowing northward from the Boston Mountains to Table Rock Lake in Missouri. The river is somewhat unique in the region as it has never been dammed, and generally flows through woods and farmland. This makes it a popular floating and canoeing stream today, and is also known for sport fishing. The Kings River has been declared to be an "Extraordinary Resource Waterbody" by the State of Arkansas. This title limits development along the river and prevents human alterations to the streambed.

In this area, the river makes a number of tight bends and has carved a deep channel. The railroad crossed the river using three deck truss spans, each 100 feet long, on cut-stone piers, built by the Wisconsin Bridge & Iron Company. This arrangement required a nine-degree curve on the north end, one of the tightest on the entire railroad. On each end were timber trestles. Ten spans of the bridge were destroyed by fire on Friday, August 27, 1909. The bridge reopened two days later after new spans were installed. An investigation of the fire blamed it on burning coal falling from a passing locomotive.

As trains got heavier, the Kings River bridge was strengthened in 1929. Heading east (railroad-south) from the bridge, the railroad climbed out of the valley by following Clabber Creek to the wye at Freeman.

88.6 FREEMAN – This was the location of the wye for the branch line south to Berryville. The wye at Freeman, as well as the loop at Berryville, allowed trains to not have to back up while entering or departing Berryville. Coming from Seligman, trains heading to Berryville continued to the south, while Harrison-bound trains curved to the east. The mainline side of the wye had a 17-car siding to the railroad-west (compass-south), with the south leg of the wye coming into the siding before connecting back to the mainline. A standard 16' x 24' wooden 50,000-gallon water tank, supported by a railroad pump house using water from Clabber Creek, was located just south of this switch. The small frame depot was on the north side of the tracks near the south wye switch, but it was gone by the late 1910s. Freeman was named for J. W. Freeman of Berryville, a Director of the railroad. Freeman was also known for building miles of cement sidewalks and the first electric light plant in Berryville. The Freeman wye is located at the north end of today's Carroll County Road 4282 out of Berryville. **For information on the Berryville Branch, please see page 193.**

Train #211, heading toward Harrison and scheduled to pass here at 3:30pm, made a sharp curve to the east and continued to climb up Clabber Creek to Urbanette. Freight #212 was scheduled to pass westbound at 10:45am. The railroad crossed Clabber Creek on each side of Freeman (Mileposts 88.4 and 88.8) using 30-foot deck plate girder spans, installed about 1928. The route is to the south of today's County Road 434. Heading east, the grade crosses Highway 221 and then passes Blackjack Church before reaching Urbanette, Arkansas. Black Jack was once a construction camp for the railroad and featured a school, which moved to Urbanette in 1907.

91.7 URBANETTE – Urbanette, known across the region as Hump, was founded in 1902 about six miles north of Berryville when the railroad built through the area. The history of the community states that it was founded by a Mr. Urban and his father-in-law, a Mr. Bennett. Both were from Texas and they built much of Urbanette, including a store, hotel, livery stable, and restaurant. The two worked to attract area business, and other industries arrived such as a sawmill, flour mill, and a large set of stock pens. Urbanette was soon an important county shipping center for cattle.

On February 10, 1902, a post office opened at Urbanette, and later railroad section forces were moved from nearby Black Jack to the community. To attract the railroad, Urban and Bennett had built a number of frame houses. In 1907, the Black Jack school moved to Urbanette, and a new two-story concrete block school building opened in 1913. By 1922, the Farmers Canning Company, canning tomatoes and apples, was in business at Urbanette. Also in the community was the Berryville Canning Company, Haves Canning Company, and the Basore Brothers Milling Company. An early M&NA map shows that the siding was to the east, and it served, north to south, a canning factory, stock pens, a warehouse, and a mill. Despite all of this, the community never incorporated.

The school closed sometime during the late 1950s, and the post office in 1971 when the service moved to Berryville. Arkansas Highway 21 was built through town and it was paved during the early

1950s, connecting the town with Berryville. Today, Urbanette is several blocks of houses and foundations from when the town was a booming industrial community.

For several years after the railroad was built, towns along the route petitioned the Arkansas Railroad Commission for many services, including stations, side tracks, passenger service, and agents. Urbanette was one of these communities. After a series of complaints and hearings, on April 21, 1909, the Arkansas Railroad Commission ordered the construction of a depot at Urbanette, Arkansas. For many years, the railroad had a 26-car siding to the east (compass-north), with the depot and then a passenger shelter to the west near the north siding switch. When the Green Forest depot was destroyed in 1938, the Urbanette depot was moved there. The station reportedly measured 20' x 46'.

At Urbanette, County Road 459 to the west, and Urbanette Lane to the east, run along or on top of the old grade. The railroad continued eastward running along the base of Brothers Knob and Wilkins Mountain. In this area, the railroad passed Herd Springs. To the east of Berryville is a chain of hills that forced the railroad to loop around them to the north. These included Sisters Knobs, Brushy Knob, and Brothers Knob. Herd Springs is on the east slope of Brothers Knob. U.S. Highway 62 curves to the southeast to cut through Jennings Gap to get through Anderson Mountain and to Green Forest, and is not close to the old railroad grade.

93.2 INDIAN CREEK BRIDGE – The railroad crosses the south branch of Indian Creek to the northeast of Brothers Knob and north of Wilkins Mountain.

Indian Creek flows northward and eventually into the White River, today's Table Rock Lake, just across the border in Missouri. The 1933 masters thesis of Margaret E. Bell, "Place Names In The Southwest Border Counties Of Missouri," stated that the name Indian Creek came about because of a Delaware Indian settlement located in Stone County, Missouri, near where the creek flowed into the White River.

95.7 CISCO – This area was originally known as Braswell Springs, named for the springs once claimed by early settlers Samuel and Phoebe Braswell. When the railroad arrived in 1901, the station was known as Braswell Switch or Braswell Spring. The area soon developed into a logging and cordwood center and Isaac "Ike" S. Norton opened a general store, the first in town. The Cisco post office opened on July 7, 1903, with Ike Norton as the postmaster. The post office was named Cisco, reportedly after the Cisco (sometimes spelled Sisco) family, some of the first settlers in Carroll County.

Cisco grew with additional stores, several grist mills, a sawmill, and a blacksmith shop. According to the *1922 Canners Directory*, the Green Forest Canning Company was in business here, canning tomatoes, apples and sweet potatoes. Other documents show that the Crawford Canning Company had several buildings along the siding on the east side of the mainline. As area transportation improved, Cisco began to shrink and the businesses moved off. The last major industry, a canning company, eventually closed due to a tomato plant blight and pressure from stricter federal regulations. The post office closed at the end of the day on June 30, 1949.

Cisco is now a small cluster of rural homes along County Road 641 at an elevation of 1308 feet. Little of the town remains. During the last years of the Missouri & Arkansas Railway, there was a 43-car siding to the east that also served the canning factory. Earlier, a second siding off the main siding was used to serve the canning plant. Just west of the canning plant was a 10' x 12' passenger shelter on the east side of the siding. Other maps showed the shelter and a mail crane on the west side of the mainline, across from the canning plant. From Cisco, the railroad followed the Braswell Branch for a short distance before turning south toward Jennings Gap and then Green Forest.

In 1927, as part of the work improving the railroad, small bridges at Mileposts 95.4 and 95.6, both just north of Cisco, were retired and replaced by culverts and fill.

96.1 YOCUM CREEK BRIDGE – This is the west fork of Yocum Creek, and can clearly be seen on topographical maps. The railroad crossed the stream using a mix of fill and bridge, just northeast of where County Road 613 crosses the same stream north of US-62. The bridge was improved with a new 30-foot deck plate girder span in 1928. The railroad grade is now used as a farm road by a large turkey grower. Yocum Creek, sometimes spelled Yokum or Yoachum, forms in the Green Forest area and flows northward, entering the Long Creek branch of Table Rock Lake in the very northeast corner of Carroll County.

The name Yocum comes from John Yocum, a Missouri resident who moved south into Green Forest in 1831. He then moved into northern Carroll

County in 1836 and built a mill on what became Yocum Creek. A community soon developed, also using the name Yocum. John Yocum had reportedly earlier been a silver miner and he traded with local Delaware Indians, often using silver coins that he minted, known as Yocum Dollars. A post office opened at Yocum on June 8, 1882, but closed on October 31, 1907. The Yocum Roller Mills, also called the Yocum Milling Company, was formed in 1893 to enlarge the grist mill, and a cotton gin was later built. Most were destroyed by a series of fires in the 1920s.

98.0 YOCUM CREEK BRIDGE – This timber trestle was replaced with a new 50-foot deck plate girder span in 1928.

99.0 NORTON – Norton was a short 4-car spur track to the west to serve a canning company, installed in 1927. It was located immediately north of the grade crossing with U.S. Highway 62. The canning industry was always an important, but seasonal business, on the railroad. Reports indicate that there were as many as 75 canning plants, mostly canning tomatoes, along the line during the 1940s.

Seligman (MO) to Harrison (AR)

This grade and culvert are easily seen from U.S. Highway 62, and is where the short track of Norton once was. Photo by Barton Jennings.

100.5 GREEN FOREST – Welcome to the home of the creator of the modern *Cosmopolitan* magazine – yes, that *Cosmopolitan* magazine. The modern style of the magazine is due to the work of Helen Gurley Brown, the editor-in-chief of *Cosmopolitan* magazine for 32 years (1965-1997). Born Helen Marie Gurley in Green Forest on February 18, 1922, her father Ira was once Commissioner of the Arkansas Game and Fish Commission. Before she was ten, the family moved to Little Rock after her father won election to the Arkansas state legislature.

By 1948, Helen Gurley had moved to Los Angeles and gone to work with the advertising firm of Foote, Cone and Belding. There she worked for advertising executive Don Belding, eventually with the responsibility of writing copy. Her work earned her three Frances Holmes Advertising Copywriters awards, becoming one of the nation's highest-paid copywriters. In 1959, Helen Gurley became Helen Gurley Brown when she married movie producer David Brown, the producer of movies such as *The Sting, Jaws,* and *Driving Miss Daisy.*

Helen Gurley first became nationally famous as the author of the 1962 non-fiction book *Sex and the Single Girl.* The book stated many of Helen's beliefs, encouraging women to become financially independent and experience sexual relationships before or without marriage. The book made many bestseller lists and sold more than two million copies. This led her to the editor-in-chief position at *Cosmopolitan* magazine, even though she had no experience in book or magazine editing. However, her major move was to have the magazine written by women who matched the target market. The result was a magazine that grew to be one of the largest women's magazines in the world.

A second noted writer from Green Forest is David Crockett Graham (born March 21, 1884), an American Baptist minister and missionary who researched and wrote about a number of subjects. In particular, he was a noted archeologist, anthropologist, naturalist and field collector in Szechuan Province, West China, during the first half of the 1900s until Mao Zedong took over the country. During this time he collected and sent almost 400,000 zoological specimens to the Smithsonian Institution. Of these, more than 230 were new species and 9 were new genera, of which 29 were named after him. He later wrote three books published by the Smithsonian Institution, and has been called "One of a handful of Western missionaries whose scientific work was respected by other scientists – and of even fewer scientists whose religious work was respected by other missionaries" by Charles F. McKhann in his research on the minister.

City of Green Forest

Green Forest is located between Scott's Prairie to the west and the homestead of John J. Grim to the east. John Scott was one of the first settlers in the area and became a noted blacksmith and bellmaker. A post office opened in the area on November 16, 1855, but reportedly closed on August 8, 1856. As part of an attempt to create a town, John J. Grim opened a new post office with the name Green Forest on July 29, 1867. The name Green Forest reportedly comes from a stand of shade trees on the edge of Scott's Prairie. The trees were used as the location of the community's public square. Like many area communities, what buildings that stood when the Civil War began were gone by the war's end, and the town had to start growing again.

Several houses were built by the 1880s, and J. R. Hanby built a flour mill, saw mill, and cotton gin in 1887. These mills attracted other businesses and Green Forest was incorporated on February 22, 1895. Like Berryville, many of the early buildings were built of brick by Charles Pyron, Sr. Another area builder was James B. Reeves, who also was a farmer, lumberman, mayor, and the founder of the Green Forest Canning Factory. All his work earned him the title of "Father of the Tomato Industry."

A major attempt to move the county seat from Berryville to Green Forest was made in 1887. Residents of Green Forest went as far as creating the newspaper the *Arkansas Tomahawk* to promote their cause. However, a series of elections kept the courthouse where it was. By 1900, the area population was almost 1000 residents and the approach of the railroad was adding interest in the community.

The tracks arrived near Green Forest in early 1901 and the first passenger train stopped on April 15, 1901. A major issue with the railroad was that it followed Dry Creek about a mile south of the Green Forest Public Square. The depot (telegraph call "KN") was on land owned by Allman Wyatt who hoped to convince the businessmen of Green Forest to move to what he called New Town. Soon, his plan worked as almost 500 people had moved to near the depot and industry such as a canning factory, a cotton gin, several flour mills, a roller mill, a sawmill, and a number of businesses had made the move. Green Forest was a center of the canning industry according to the *1922 Canners Directory*. Among the firms listed included the Green Forest Canning Company, J. W. Bingham & Sons, Charles S. Hulsey Canning Company, and J. M. Wells. All reported that they canned tomatoes and apples, with sweet potatoes and peaches also listed by several of the canners.

This former cannery building still stands at Green Forest, and is located just a short distance from the restored M&NA depot. Photo by Barton Jennings.

Green Forest was nearly destroyed by a March 18, 1927, tornado. The storm killed several residents, destroyed the high school, and damaged many of the homes and businesses. It was again hit by a tornado on June 9, 1937, this time destroying the railroad depot and many buildings near it. However, the town slowly rebuilt and is today another base of the poultry business in North Arkansas. It is also the home of the North Arkansas Livestock Auction facility and its regionally famous Cattleman's Steakhouse. Located at an elevation of 1340 feet, the population in 2010 was 2761.

The Railroad

When the railroad arrived, it was forced to pass south of town as Green Forest sits on a notable hill. The original 18' x 72' depot was built in 1901 and destroyed by a tornado in 1937. The building was replaced with the 20' x 46' depot (built 1913) from Urbanette, Arkansas. At the time, the station agent was busy handling freight business from companies such as the Green Forest Cooperative Creamery, the Green Forest Mill and Elevator Company, and the ties being sold by W. P. Coxey. The daily freights, southbound #211 and northbound #212, were scheduled through Green Forest at 4:15pm and 9:45am respectively.

By the 1940s, the depot and 20-car siding were located just north of Bridge 100-7. The depot was located on the east side of the mainline and the siding was to the west. There were several long spur tracks just north of the depot. For years, there were also several small section and motorcar sheds not far south of the depot, and a water tank was also here.

There were also several industry tracks north of the station to serve a warehouse and the local cannery. After the Missouri & Arkansas closed, the depot was sold to Larro Feeds, who unloaded sacks of feed on the siding and used the building as a warehouse and feed store. The station has been preserved and restored and is used as a meeting facility and display building. It has been moved approximately one block north to where the cannery stands, but is still located on South Broadway Avenue. It should be noted that today's 9th Street was once named Depot Street.

This view of the Green Forest depot is from 1988, long before its restoration as a community meeting center. Photo by Barton Jennings.

The former railroad grade from U.S. Highway 62 to the southeast side of town is still an important feature as it is used as the city limits for Green Forest. Heading south, the railroad followed Dry Creek, turning to the northeast just north of the current Green Forest Waste Water Plant. It then turned to the east and crossed Dry Creek on a route used to-

Seligman (MO) to Harrison (AR)

day by Carroll County Road 902. The railroad again curved to the northeast just short of South Fork Dry Creek and crossed U.S. Highway 62. Passing Reves Spring, the railroad again crossed Dry Creek and headed on to Coin.

The depot at Green Forest has been moved a short distance, restored, and is used today for community meetings. Photo by Sarah Jennings.

102.5 DRY CREEK BRIDGE – The railroad crossed Dry Creek as it curved going from southeast to northeast. This kept the railroad north of Bradshaw Mountain, Round Mountain, Blacklick Mountain and Pine Mountain. Small streams flowed north off all of these mountains, eventually draining into Dry Creek. This bridge consisted of 11 panels, all of timber piles. The Green Forest Waste Water Plant is located in this area today.

During the 1950s, the Arkansas & Ozarks proposed to build a spur track south from here (Milepost 102 in the documents) to a new sand facility on Bradshaw Mountain. The 1½ mile line would serve the facility to move sand to Oklahoma, Texas, and other markets where oil drilling was taking place.

According to a report from the time, the project was promoted by a group of oilmen from Oklahoma and Texas who were drilling in older fields using newer techniques that required special sands and mud as part of the drilling process. Unfortunately for the railroad, no track was ever built and the business didn't materialize.

103.5 DRY CREEK BRIDGE – The railroad turned back to the southeast and crossed the creek using a 10-panel frame wooden trestle. The grade in this area is used by County Road 902.

104.9 DRY CREEK BRIDGE – This 12-panel timber pile trestle (122-feet long) crossed the area where South Fork meets the main channel of Dry Creek. This area has changed some over the years, but is the general location of Reves Spring.

106.2 DRY CREEK BRIDGE – The railroad used a short steel bridge to cross the creek, one of a few west of Harrison from the original construction. The bridge, from the north, consisted of three spans of wood frame trestle, 120 feet of steel deck plate girder (two 60-foot spans), and three more timber frame spans. The bridge was 217 feet long when it was built in 1901.

106.3 COIN – Today, Coin is an unincorporated community in Carroll County, consisting of a few houses and farms. During 2010, the Coin Township, one of twenty-one in the county, had a total population of 655. According to the Arkansas History Commission, on April 9, 1891, a post office opened at Coin. The post office was to be named Russelley Store, but

Seligman (MO) to Harrison (AR)

the name Coin was used instead. It closed temporarily in 1893 before reopening, and then closed again in 1907. A nearby post office with the name Markley opened in 1906, but was moved to Coin in 1911. The Coin post office closed on August 5, 1944, and mail service was moved to Green Forest.

The railroad was built through Coin in 1901, and a 21-car siding was built to the east in 1926. A small passenger shelter was also here for several decades. The Evans Canning Company had a canning plant at Coin that lasted at least until the 1940s, located on the siding. A railroad tool house was located north of the canning plant, and a mail crane was alongside the mainline west of the plant. The railroad grade departs to the southeast and follows Racetrack Hollow, curves east at Patty Spring to cross a low ridge, and then stays above Long Creek to reach Alpena. Parts of the route can be driven (CR-815 east of Patty Spring and CR-813 near Alpena).

The area to the south of Coin was once part of the fruit belt of Carroll and Boone Counties, Arkansas. The area along U.S. Highway 62 was once lined with fruit trees, primarily apple. For decades, this was the home of Banta's House of Apples and Orchard, a major attraction and the source of fresh apple pies and home cooked meals.

107.7 BRIDGE – This 14-panel pile timber trestle crossed a small stream that formed in the Patty Springs area, and then flowed to the north down Racetrack Hollow and entered Dry Creek near Coin.

110.0 MAPLES SUMMIT – This summit was shown on early M&NA track profiles and it was listed as being at an elevation of 1267 feet. The James Gunter Maples family moved from Tennessee to the area north of Carrollton during the early 1850s, and is often cited as one of the early settlers in the Alpena area. James Gunter Maples, who died in 1897, is buried in the Carrollton Cemetery. During the 1800s, a small community with the name Maple existed near his farm. Do not confuse this location with the community of Maple, or Maple Spring, located northeast of Urbanette on Arkansas Highway 21. County Road 813, a dirt road just west of Alpena, heads north from US-62, briefly using the retired railroad grade before the grade heads west toward Patty Spring through the summit area.

110.4 COUNTY LINE – The railroad is basically heading east-west as it exits **Carroll County** to the west and enters **Boone County** to the east, approximately at the junction between U.S. Highways 62 and 412 on the west side of Alpena. **Boone County** was originally part of Carroll County, but was separated on April 9, 1869, as the 62nd county in Arkansas. The county was named Boon, as was the first newspaper – the *Boon County Advocate*. The name Boon came from the economic boon that the new county was expected to create. However, the state bill was titled *An Act to Organize and Establish the County of Boone and for Other Purposes*. There was never an explanation for the change in spelling, although some claim that the county was named after Daniel Boone. Arkansas Governor Powell Clayton, later a major party involved with starting the railroad, signed the bill into law. The county seat is Harrison, the headquarters community of the Missouri & North Arkansas, and today the home of the general office of FedEx Freight and an important economic center in Northern Arkansas.

On June 2, 1953, the Arkansas & Ozarks proposed to realign this curve to eliminate a 12-panel frame timber trestle at this location. The change would have eliminated 180 feet of the line and moved the curve inward on higher ground to eliminate the need for the bridge.

111.0 ALPENA – Alpena was farmland until the railroad built through the area in 1900. The first settler was reportedly John Boyd, who received a land grant along Long Creek in 1849. By the Civil War, a few other settlers lived in the area, located just a few miles from Carrollton, then the county seat of Carroll County. The area was destroyed by armies and guerila forces during the war, and it took a decade for the region to recover.

During the late 1890s, plans were made to extend the Eureka Springs Railroad eastward, and the pass in the area seemed to be a logical route. As the line was under construction, the location became a construction camp, especially for forces building the bridge across Long Creek. A town grew up, and with Carrollton not being on the railroad, many of its buildings were moved to the new town, which was platted in November 1900. A post office opened in early 1901 with the name Estes, but it was changed to Alpena Pass before the end of the year.

The name Alpena doesn't come from a clear source, but the town's website states that it was the name of one of the railroad cooks when the town was founded. However, it is known that area farmers cut ties and sold them to the railroad at Alpena. Because of this, the town grew quickly, with several hotels, at least three general stores, a drugstore, two blacksmith shops, a doctor, several churches, and a school within a few years, all serving a population of 450. A report from 1908 stated that there were six general stores, a flour mill, a sawmill, a hub and spoke factory, and several woodworking mills, plus a bank that had opened the previous year. The Alpena Canning Company soon opened to can tomatoes and apples.

On May 31, 1913, Alpena was incorporated, shortening the town's name to what is used today. However, the population began to drop, especially as the railroad moved its facilities away – the section house was closed in 1926 – and the community suffered from flooding in 1927. The exodus of residents continued during the Depression and World War II, and the population was less than 300 by 1960, when the town began to grow again. The construction of U.S. Highway 62 through Alpena in 1933 and then its modernization and the construction of U.S. Highway 412 have led to recent growth, with the current population being about 400.

Many of the original buildings still stand at Alpena, but many of the storefronts are empty. These buildings once stood across the street from the M&NA depot. Photo by Barton Jennings.

The railroad passed through Alpena just north of U.S. Highway 62, and the 18' x 72' Standard #2 station was located approximately where the public pavilion now stands. The depot, which used telegraph call "PA", was on the south side of the mainline, with a 32-car siding to the north (railroad-east). Just north of the depot was a standard 16' x 24' wooden 50,000-gallon tank, with water obtained from Long Creek. There was also a short spur track further north, approximately where the Dollar General currently stands. Until the end of the railroad, crossties for Koppers was the primary business at Alpena. The depot was reportedly torn down about 1960.

111.4 LONG CREEK BRIDGE – Long Creek forms south of Carrollton and flows north to Alpena and then on north to enter Table Rock Lake just south of the Arkansas-Missouri state line. The stream was a major land feature in the area and was noted in many descriptions of the Carroll and Boone County areas. The waterway was so important that Long Creek Township was named for it. Long Creek has also been a problem for the area as it has had several historic floods, especially as part of the Great Flood of 1927.

The railroad track curved to the northeast leaving Alpena, crossed the Long Creek bridge, then curved along the side of the ridge to head east. The bridge was in the middle of a scenic S-curve. There was a curved timber trestle, then two deck truss spans (90-foot and 130-foot) set on cut stone piers. The bridge was strengthened in 1929 to increase its Cooper E-40 rating. The bridge piers still stand and can be reached from the Alpena Community Park walking trail.

There are several lessons that can be learned while exploring these piers. The first are the large number of concrete blocks that once each held five wooden piles in place. When originally built, the trestle on the north end of the bridge was built using frame bents sitting on concrete and stone pads. However, during flooding, Long Creek left its banks and cut through this area. To protect the trestle, about 18 inches of concrete was poured around the base of each bent. Many of these pours still exist and are used as a retaining wall in the area. Another lesson can be learned by examining the northernmost concrete pier. Several of the large blocks are now broken, and it can be seen that the blocks are poured concrete with large rocks used as filler material.

These stone piers of the Long Creek Bridge can be found in the Alpena Community Park. This part of the trestle stood over dry land except during high water, and can be explored closely by those who want to. Photo by Barton Jennings.

Seligman (MO) to Harrison (AR)

This stone pier of the Long Creek Bridge still stands in the stream near the south end of the bridge. Photo by Barton Jennings.

115.0 LITTLE ARKANSAS – This station, shown in the timetable during the 1940s, was a simple flag stop at U.S. Highway 62, and there were no side tracks. For years, the highway bridge had a small marker that stated that it was built to cross the railroad. The highway bridge was built in 1938 and was removed in 2001 when U.S. Highway 62 was improved to a four-lane highway.

Earlier during the 1920s, there was a short 7-car railroad siding here with the name Jennings. The name likely came from one of several families by that name who lived in the area. The Sunday, March 27, 1921, issue of the *Arkansas Gazette* reported that during the strike of the early 1920s, "spikes were pulled from ties at Jennings Spur, six miles north of Harrison." The Jennings spur track was retired in 1926.

Heading to Batavia, the railroad headed south, staying east of what is today Arkansas Highway 392.

117.4 BATAVIA – Batavia is located at an elevation of 1489 feet as the railroad used this pass to cross the ridge to reach Harrison, Arkansas. The town started in 1881 when Roswell Underwood settled in the area, and then opened a post office with the name Batavia in 1883, named after his former home in New York. The town grew slowly, even after the railroad built through the area in early 1901. However, the creation of the fruit business did positively impact the region. In 1905, Carroll County resident George W. O'Neal began planting apple and peach trees about a mile from Batavia. Within a few years, he had more than 10,000 trees planted on his Pilot Knob Fruit Farm.

Pilot Knob Fruit Farm was not the first business venture of O'Neal. He dealt in public land scrip, gaining a great deal of knowledge about homesteading, mining and timber claims, and other land laws. He also shipped out about 150 car loads of timber each year through his Ozark Post and Timber Company. He also owned land or options on land in Louisiana and Alabama. His business office was in Harrison.

The second fruit grower in the area was Frank Warning. Warning had originally arrived in the area to deal with his mining interests. He held options on a great deal of mining land and was the principal owner of several mines in the Boxley district, including the Bill Dugan Mine. Having worked on a number of land sales in the area, he soon became involved with the fruit industry. He became a vice president of the Ozark Fruit and Produce Company and a stockholder in the Batavia Fruit Company.

The Ozark Fruit Company had 50,000 fruit trees by 1905, while the Batavia Fruit Company had 135,000 fruit trees scattered over 1431 acres. Warning had 240 acres of fruit trees on his own farm.

By 1914, there were several canneries located in Batavia to handle the fruit being grown. One of the canneries was owned by Jeff Jagger. A second cannery, owned by A. R. Centers of Alpena, was managed by W. A. Markley. Markley also managed a nearby grist mill. In 1944, the Markley Canning Company was still in operation and was located north of the depot. Reportedly, the cannery building still stands. The railroad also received shipments of railroad ties from J. D. Mashburn. About the same time, houses were being built on Main Street (today's Arkansas Highway 392), and a hotel, several stores, stockyards, and a blacksmith shop also opened. The post office closed in 1955, and Batavia today is an unincorporated town, although it was once busy enough to be incorporated.

The former railroad grade through Batavia is now Old Rail Road Road on the east side of town. There was once a small frame depot at Batavia that measured 16' x 32', as well as a set of stock pens that were retired in 1927. However, by 1940, there was only a 4-car spur track to the east. Some reports state that the Batavia depot was moved and turned into a house. Just south of Batavia, the railroad grade is used briefly by Highway 392 as it passes just east of Kennedy Mountain. Where the highway crosses Denning Creek, the railroad turned east to avoid the low hill where Batavia Baptist Church now sits. The grade is used as a private drive into a home. Coming into Capps, the grade is used by Rail Road.

The former M&NA grade through Batavia is used today as a road, and the street signs clearly note its former use. Photo by Barton Jennings.

118.8 BEAR CREEK BRIDGE – Most maps show this to be Denning Creek. Denning Creek flows northward through Bear Creek Springs (once an Osage Indian village), where it becomes Bear Creek. Bear Creek then flows to the north and eventually flows into Bull Shoals Lake, another lake created from the White River.

    The name Denning comes from the Denning family who lived several miles south of Bear Creek Springs. A small community was once there, and the Denning Cemetery still exists.

120.0 CAPPS – At Capps, the railroad grade is Rail Road, and then turns north just east of Old Capps Road at the Capps Cemetery. It loops around a low wooded hill and then turns east to head to Harrison, generally following the north side of Dry Jordan Creek. The

Seligman (MO) to Harrison (AR)

railroad had a 27-car siding on the railroad-east side that also served a canning factory. The factory was the Capps Canning Company in 1944. Some documents show that there was also a glass factory here. The railroad never had a station or passenger shelter at Capps, but there was a small cinder platform.

While there is documentation that a number of families lived on farms in the area, the town of Capps didn't get a post office until 1901 when the railroad was built through the community. Records show that there were a number of other possible names for the post office, including Holt, Parker and Tims. However, it was named after G. W. Capps, who promoted and operated lead and zinc mines. The name Capps Hill has long been used for the ridge that the community sits on. Capps is today an unincorporated community located about five miles west of Harrison at an elevation of 1440 feet.

The M&NA grade is also used as a street at Capps, but is known simply as Rail Road. Photo by Barton Jennings.

124.8 GULF SPUR – Approaching this track, today's Industrial Park Road closely follows the grade of the Missouri & North Arkansas. The railroad then crossed U.S. Highway 65, a road from Albert Lea, Minnesota, to Clayton, Louisiana. Just south of the grade crossing was a track to the east to serve the Gulf Oil facility. This area is now a collection of fast food restaurants and stores.

This is the grade crossing where on August 23, 1946, motorcar #705, operating southbound, was hit by a milk truck. Both the driver of the truck and the motorcar were killed, and #705 was so badly damaged that it became a source of parts to keep car #726 operating.

Heading south to downtown Harrison, U.S. Highway 62/65/412, Arkmo Drive, curves alongside Dry Jordan Creek. The highway often uses the grade of the former Missouri & North Arkansas. This area is now a series of shopping centers and large stores, but it was once a mix of warehouses, small factories, and stockyards.

125.2 BOONE COUNTY LIVESTOCK AUCTION – There was a six-car track to the west to serve this facility, which once loaded and unloaded many carloads of cattle and other livestock. During the 1930s, the Agricultural Adjustment Administration (AAA) built a stockyard with 27 pens in Harrison to serve as a transfer point for cattle shipments. AAA was buying cattle to boost the local farm economy by lowering farm production and raising farm prices. Much of the cattle that were bought were simply destroyed and not even made available to locals who were on the border of starvation.

Later, this area became the location of the Harrison Sales Company, reportedly the first public stock auction sales barn in Harrison. The first public sale was during April 1935. Parts of the facility lasted

Seligman (MO) to Harrison (AR)

into the 1980s, but nothing remains of the complex today.

126.3 HARRISON – This area, often protected from strong winds and along a stream full of fish, was the location of an early Osage village. The Osage, a branch of the Sioux, controlled the area, although Shawnee, Quapaw, and Caddo also traveled and hunted here. After 1808 when the United States awarded the land to the Cherokee, the area became a war zone between the Cherokee and the Osage. The U.S. Government removed both tribes by the 1830s and white settlers began to move into the Crooked Creek area.

There have been many claims about who the first European was that actually saw the location of today's Harrison. Some claim that a scouting party of Hernando de Soto visited the location, while others credit various French hunters or trappers. It is known that by the 1830s, settlers from Missouri, Kentucky, Tennessee, and North Carolina were moving into the area and the Crooked Creek post office opened in 1836. A nearby community, Stiffler Spring, was located on the property of Albert Stiffler. By the 1850s, the area was populated enough that many people were moving on west. Probably the most famous of these was the Baker-Fancher wagon train of 1857. This group traveled west across Utah, where between 120 and 140 men, women and children were massacred by Mormons on September 11, 1857. Mormon sources stated that the men were executed by the Mormon militia, while Paiute Indians executed the women and children. The youngest children were given to Mormon families to raise. The Mormons also took the cattle, horses and other valuables of the group. Later reports recorded that some of the surviving children claimed to have seen Mormons wearing the clothes and jewelry of their parents.

Two years later, a military party investigated the report and found the body remains and buried them, built a cairn over the graves, and made a large cross from local cedar trees. Eventually the children were given back to their families, but many Mormons demanded payment for the expenses involved with caring for them. It wasn't until 1876 that a trial was held, even though several participants turned state's evidence against the church members. Finally, Major John D. Lee, Mormon constable, judge, and Indian Agent, was found guilty and executed by firing squad, the only participant punished. The massacre has long been a sore subject in the region, but a series of meetings over the past several decades have worked to reduce this animosity between Northern Arkansas and the Mormon Church.

This memorial to the victims of the Mountain Meadows Massacre is one of many monuments located on the city square in downtown Harrison. Photo by Barton Jennings.

Reports about the Mountain Meadows Massacre impacted many of the families in the Harrison area, but the Civil War destroyed the community and most residents moved away to avoid the repeated raids and shooting. After the war, it took several years for Crooked Creek to recover. Two things helped this cause. The first was the creation of Boone County in 1869 and the selection of the area as the new county seat. The second push was the interest of Marcus LaRue Harrison, a Union officer who developed the new town of Harrison. He surveyed and platted the town, leading to the post office changing its name to Harrison in 1870 and the town's incorporation on March 1, 1876.

The Arrival of the Railroad

By the late 1800s, Harrison was a regional trade center and the Jersey Roller Mill opened in 1884. As a part of the mill, a dam was built on Crooked Creek for power. However, the lack of rail service made it difficult and expensive to move products in and out of town. The arrival of the railroad in 1901 created a sudden boom, attracting more people than jobs. The sudden change led to many residents resisting the progress, leading to Harrison's reputation as a community that doesn't welcome outsiders. Several reported peaks in crime led citizens to drive out many new residents, including African-Americans and unemployed railroad workers, in 1904 and 1909. These would not be the last of such incidents, as described in the history of the Missouri & North Arkansas during the strike in 1923.

The Boone County Courthouse opened in 1909, and the Boone County Jail opened in 1914. Both were designed by Charles Louis Thompson, considered to be one of the most prolific and successful architects in Arkansas. During the late nineteenth and first half of the twentieth centuries, his firm designed more than two thousand buildings. Both of these buildings are on the National Register of Historic Places. The entire downtown area is also listed as part of the Harrison Courthouse Square Historic District. Included is the 1929 Hotel Seville, built in a Spanish Revival (Mission) style and still used as a downtown hotel. A walk through downtown Harrison will find a large number of historical markers that explain the area's history.

The Hotel Seville is a historic downtown hotel and doesn't seem to quite fit in due to its Spanish Revival design. However, it is one of those places that anyone who is someone in Harrison will eventually visit. Photo by Sarah Jennings.

In 1912, a large brick high school was built in the Prairie School and International Style. It was the area high school (the Golden Goblins) until 1952 when it became the junior high, being used for that through 1987. Listed on the National Register of Historic Places (2007), it is now the home of the Boone County Heritage Museum, operated by the **Boone County Historical and Railroad Society**. The museum houses one of the largest collections about the history of the Missouri & North Arkansas Railroad.

The Boone County Heritage Museum is now located in the 1912 Harrison High School building. For those interested in researching the railroad or the Boone County area, this is the perfect place to start. Photo by Sarah Jennings.

The Boone County Heritage Museum includes a large collection of items related to the M&NA, including this bridge plate for a roadway that once crossed the railroad. Photo by Barton Jennings.

During the 1920s, Harrison was also the home of a number of industries. These included the Harrison Canning Company (canned tomatoes, apples, peaches, and berries), S. T. Brown Cooperage, Harrison Stave & Tie, Harrison Milling, and Citizens Ice & Storage. Many of these were impacted by the 1927 flood. A second major flood on May 7, 1961, led to more improvements and the removal of many businesses along Crooked Creek.

The Harrison area has always been rough, and even notorious bank robbers haven't stood a chance. On February 18, 1921, Henry Starr, known as the Cherokee Badman, and his gang attempted to rob the People's State Bank in Harrison. After having robbed more banks than both the James-Younger Gang and the Doolin-Dalton Gang put together, Starr was shot and killed by the former president of the bank, William J. Myers. Henry Starr came from a long line of outlaws, including his grandfather Tom Starr, his brother Sam Starr, and his sister-in-law Belle Starr.

Harrison was also the birthplace of Faye Copeland. She and her husband Ray were the oldest people ever sentenced to death (at 75 and 69 respectively). Even after moving to Missouri, both did business in the area between killing drifters that they hired to help them with their farm and criminal schemes. Ray, described as a thief, swindler, forger, killer, and sometimes cattle farmer, died while awaiting execution. Faye had her sentence commuted to five consecutive terms of life without parole. After a stroke that left her paralyzed, she was paroled and soon died.

On a more positive note, Harrison has also been the home of Brandon Burlsworth, Ida Callery, and Vance Trimble. Brandon Burlsworth was a local football player who was killed in an auto accident soon after he was drafted in the third round by the Indianapolis Colts. Friends created the Brandon Burlsworth Foundation, a Christian organization that sponsors efforts to help children with limited opportunities, including scholarships for lower-income students. Ida Hayman Callery was a teacher, suffragist, and feminist leader during the early 1900s. She pushed for equal education for women, but her calls for socialism and her belief that African-Americans were inferior led to more failures than success. Vance Trimble was a reporter who was awarded the Pulitzer Prize for National Reporting in 1960 for his reporting of nepotism and payroll abuse in the U.S. Congress.

Angel Falls and Harrison

A surprise to many people is that Harrison, Arkansas, has a connection to Angel Falls, Venezuela. Angel Falls is the world's highest uninterrupted waterfall, and is named after Jimmie Angel, a one-time resident of the Harrison area. While James Crawford Angel was born near Cedar Valley, Missouri, in 1899, his family soon moved to near Harrison and Jimmie was a common sight in the area. He took up flying, serving in the Canadian Flying Corps during WWI after pneumonia kept him out of U.S. Army Air Force. He was credited with shooting down four observation balloons and one plane over France before being sent home as being underage. Jimmie developed the reputation of being a daredevil pilot and a "hell-raising soldier of fortune," even working as a stunt pilot in the movies *Wings* and *Hell's Angels* with Howard Hughes. In exploring South America, he was the first to fly over Angel Falls (November 16, 1933), which was named for him as "Salto del Ángel," or Angel Falls. He later crashed near the falls while hunting for a legendary vein of gold, and his ashes were scattered over them in 1960. The falls are today part of Canaima National Park.

Today's Harrison

The modern Harrison began after World War II. For years, Harrison was the center of the parking meter industry. The Duncan Parking Meter Company came to Harrison in 1947 and manufactured and sold them from here for decades. The Duncan Parking Meter was developed by Donald Duncan, who also invented the "Duncan Yo-Yo." Walmart store #2 opened in Harrison in 1965. Another area company, Arkansas Freightways, later renamed American Freightways, became a major Less-Than-Load (LTL) freight carrier. It was so successful that in February 2001 it was combined with Viking Freight to become FedEx Freight, still based in Harrison. Harrison was also impacted by the creation of the Buffalo National River on March 1, 1972, 100 years after the establishment of the first National Park at Yellowstone National Park. John Paul Hammerschmidt, a native of Harrison and a member of the U.S. House of Representatives, was the primary author of the legislation.

Harrison has been the home of Cavender's Greek Seasoning since 1969. The firm started in 1948 in the Ozark Mountains when Spike and Katherine Cavender moved to the area. They went through a number of businesses before selling a family Greek seasoning spice mix that Spike had been using for years, and sharing with his friends. Tours are available of their facility (306 N. Industrial Park Road), and they operate a store downtown in the former Well-Worth Dime Store, once operated by the Cavender family.

Some have dubbed Harrison as "the most racist city in America" due to parts of its history and the presence of several groups in the area described as being white supremacists. The history of the 1904 and 1909 riots, and the 1923 move against the striking railroad union workers, haven't helped the town's reputation. However, Harrison is mostly a modern community whose population continues to grow, up from 12,943 in 2010 to an estimated 13,170 in 2016.

The Railroad Facilities

From 1913 until the Arkansas & Ozarks closed in 1961, Harrison was the operating and equipment maintenance headquarters for the railroad. Once the St. Louis & North Arkansas Railway Company decided to build east, Harrison became the first goal of construction. The Saturday, August 25, 1900, issue of *The Harrison Times* had a report about a meeting between railroad officials (O. W. Watkins – President, John Scullin – President of the Allegheny Improvement Company, and Samuel W. Lee – Chief Engineer) and leaders of the Harrison community. Harrison guaranteed $35,000 and 20 acres for depot and terminal grounds, plus "additional right-of-way to the Frazier Hollow east, or the forks, of the creek south" if the railroad arrived by April 15, 1901.

The land chosen for the railroad terminal was to the east of town and was owned by C. C. Murray. Initially, the facilities at Harrison were minor as a shop already existed at Eureka Springs. This included a 24' x 72' frame station that later became the operations building. However, a decision in 1912-1913 led to the plan to build a system shop and yard complex at Harrison. Ground was broken on March 15, 1913, for the expansion, which included five miles of yard and shop tracks, a 70' x 238' machine shop attached to the 6-stall roundhouse equipped with an 80-foot turntable, a stores building, a coach shop, several support buildings, and a new powerhouse for steam and electricity. There were also plans for a 118,000-gallon concrete reservoir watered from Mitchell Springs and a crane at the coal dock.

The railroad also wanted to build a new brick office downtown with a fireproof vault. However, in

Seligman (MO) to Harrison (AR)

1913, the railroad's general offices were moved to the second story of Dr. Leonidas Kirby's new building. The building still stands at 123-125 North Main Street on the northeast corner of Harrison's downtown square. A historical sign marks the building. In addition to the general offices, a new 24' x 76' depot was built to replace the original building. The new depot stood on the west side of the mainline between Prospect and Ridge Avenues, about where the Bank of the Ozarks building now stands. Harrison used several different telegraph calls over the years, including "H", "GM", "GO" and finally "DS".

The 1914 Sanborn Insurance Map showed the general arrangement of the new shops complex in Harrison, Arkansas. Note the many buildings involved, such as the roundhouse, machine shop, store house, and coach shop. In 1936, these facilities served daily freight trains #211 and #212. #211 was scheduled to arrive at 6:05pm and depart southbound at 7:00pm, while #212 arrived at 4:10am and departed toward Joplin at 8:00am.

The Kirby Building is still busy and houses a pharmacy on the downtown square in Harrison. Photo by Barton Jennings.

Missouri & North Arkansas Railroad: History Through the Miles

The Kirby Building is marked by this cornerstone, located on the top of the front of the building. Photo by Barton Jennings.

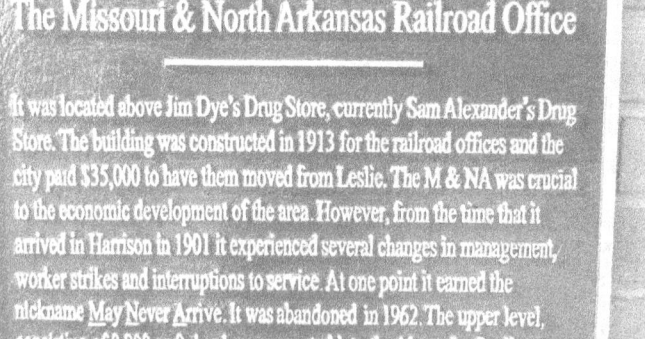

While some of the details aren't accurate, this marker notes the location of the M&NA general offices in downtown Harrison. Photo by Barton Jennings.

Seligman (MO) to Harrison (AR)

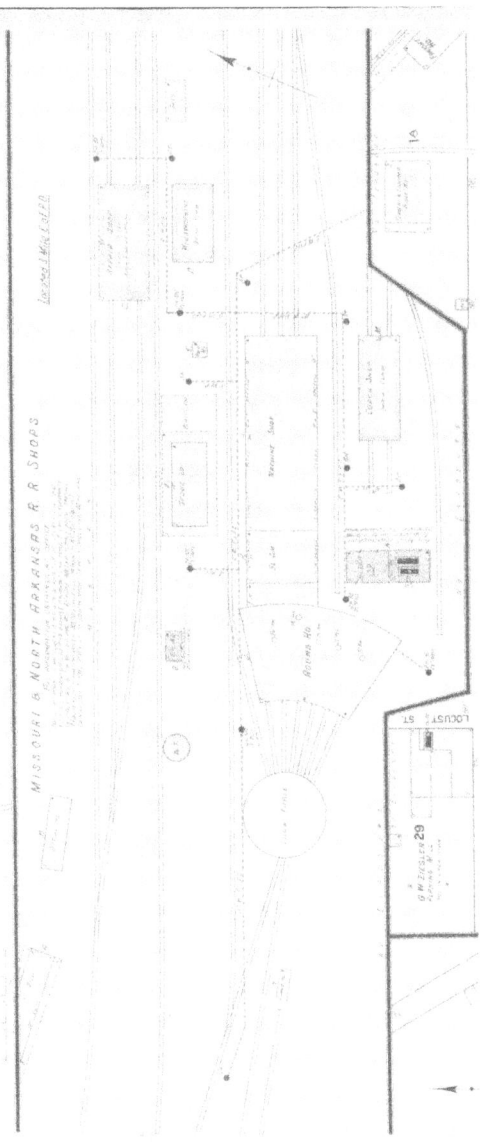

Sanborn Fire Insurance Map from Harrison, Boone County, Arkansas. Sanborn Map Company, June, 1914. Library of Congress, Geography and Map Division. https://www.loc.gov/item/sanborn00260_004/.

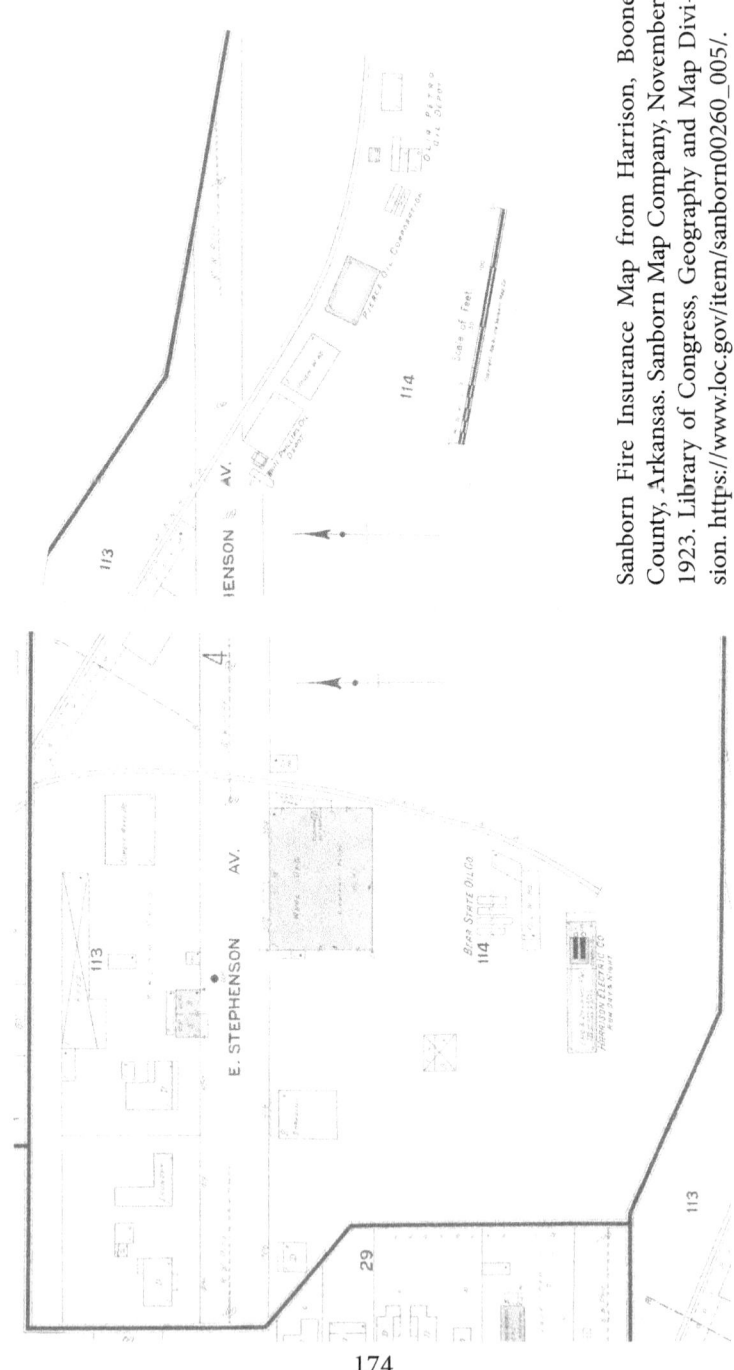

Sanborn Fire Insurance Map from Harrison, Boone County, Arkansas. Sanborn Map Company, November, 1923. Library of Congress, Geography and Map Division. https://www.loc.gov/item/sanborn00260_005/.

A map from the year 1923 showed that from north to south, there was a short siding and a spur west to Myers Mill. There were two tracks at the depot with the Standard Oil facility across the tracks to the east. Just south of Ridge Avenue was the Harrison Grocery Company spur, and a spur south to the Ice Plant and Carnation Plant. There was also a spur track to the freight depot, located just north of Stephenson Avenue. On the same lead and on past the freight depot was a set of stock pens and an ore dock.

The M&NA freight house was located on a spur track just west of the railroad's shop complex. The switch for this track was once at the intersection of Rush Avenue and Chestnut Street, where U.S. Highway 65 and Chestnut have an intersection today. Several rail users were on the same track beyond the freight house, and the area still consists of light industry. A spur track also headed south to the Harrison Electric Company, with the switch just north of the railroad's freight house.

On the west side of the yard complex was a turntable and roundhouse with a large backshop attached, then a large car shop and other shops. To the east was a 4-track yard with the railroad-south switch just before the Crooked Creek Bridge. The former depot and now operations building was located at the compass-west end of the yard. All of these facilities were located in the bend of Crooked Creek between downtown Harrison and the Crooked Creek Bridge at Milepost 127.1. There were also a number of shippers in the area, creating 679 carloads of traffic in 1945, the third most on the railroad that year. This volume was the reason that the Arkansas & Ozarks was created.

After the closure of the Missouri & Arkansas, many of the tracks were removed and the Arkansas & Ozarks based its operations out of the original wooden station at Harrison. During the 1950s, there were still a large number of rail shippers at Harrison. These included the Harrison Lumber Company, Hammerschmidt Lumber Company, Harrison Grocery Company, Rhodes Chevrolet, the Arkansas State Highway Department, Gulf Refining, and others. Outbound shipments generally included lumber, cedar fence posts, hardwood flooring, and crossties.

With the closure of the A&O, the tracks were removed, as well as most of the buildings. Today, some of the shop complex still stands and is used by several different businesses. Remaining buildings include the machine shop, the woodmill, the storeroom, and the car shop. All are easily visible just south of U.S. Highway 65 as part of Miller's True Value Hardware.

Also still standing is the diesel shop built by the Arkansas & Ozarks to replace the old shops which were much too large for the small railroad. The cinder block building is next to U.S. Highway 65 at the intersection with North First Street, just north of the old shops complex. Nearby is the Harrison Regional Chamber of Commerce building, built in 1985 to resemble a railroad station. Next to it is former Missouri Pacific caboose #13496. The caboose was built in 1950 as a steel model with a streamlined cupola. It was initially Chicago & Eastern Illinois #9. By 1970, Missouri Pacific owned a majority of the C&EI and took control of the railroad, modernizing the car and installing a standard cupola.

The large backshop building of the M&NA still stands in Harrison, used for other purposes today. Photo by Barton Jennings.

Across the highway from the original M&NA shops is the newer Arkansas & Ozarks engine house. Photo by Barton Jennings.

The M&NA never had a station this fancy, but the Harrison Chamber of Commerce built their building in a railroad style, and it is located near where the M&NA had their shops and station. Photo by Barton Jennings.

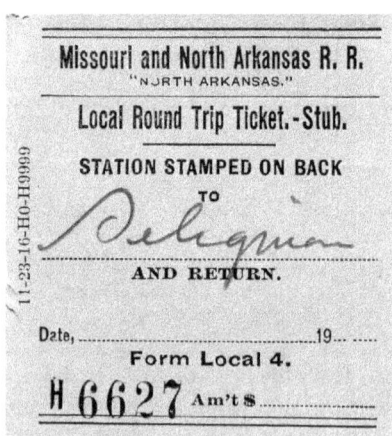

Missouri and North Arkansas R. R. Local Round Trip Ticket. From the collection of Barton Jennings.

Eureka Springs Branch

The railroad followed Leatherwood Creek from Junction to Eureka Springs for a total of 1.8 miles. This route was the original mainline until the railroad expanded east. The railroad climbed from 1026 feet at Junction to 1128 feet at the railroad depot in Eureka Springs. This was a steady one percent grade, surrounded by hills on all sides. The challenge for all train operations was that there was no way to turn a train at Eureka Springs. Therefore, the general operating rule was to back from Junction to Eureka Springs.

The general grade of this route is today used by the tourist railroad Eureka Springs & North Arkansas Railway. This is the longest piece of track built by the railroad to still exist in use.

Steam still ran on the right-of-way of the M&NA in 1986, as shown by this photo of Eureka Springs & North Arkansas #201 on November 9th during a photographer's event. Photo by Barton Jennings.

77.5 JUNCTION – The station of Junction was the wye that connected the Eureka Springs Branch to the mainline. For information about Junction, see information on the First District.

79.3 EUREKA SPRINGS – Welcome to "The City that Water Built." The healing abilities of the springs in the Eureka Springs area was known to generations of tribal members from across the region. Indian hieroglyphs from the area indicate that at least 14 different tribes visited the springs, and stories about the springs were told as far east as the Cherokee and as far north and west as the Sioux. These stories led to several efforts by European settlers to locate the waters. In 1832, Dr. Alvah Jackson, a graduate of Oxford and a surgeon from New Orleans, moved to the area and first heard about the legendary Indian Healing Spring. By 1856, Dr. Jackson had identified what he thought was the curing spring and used it to treat his son's eye infection. The cure worked and Dr. Jackson began bottling and selling his "Jackson's Eye-Water."

The Civil War prevented development of the springs, but they were used by troops of both sides to heal wounds and illnesses. Dr. Jackson established a hospital in a local cave during the Civil War and used the waters from Basin Spring to treat his patients. Many of these soldiers returned home and spread the legend about the cures. The fame of these cures started attracting visitors to the area, and during the late 1870s, Judge L. B. Saunders visited the spring with Dr. Jackson. He claimed that his crippling disease was cured by the spring waters and soon built a home nearby. His son, Burton "Buck" Saunders, built his own home, generally recognized as the first permanent settlement in Eureka Springs. Buck Sanders also began naming springs, and after several attempts, came up with the name Eureka Springs. The primary spring that Dr. Jackson used eventually became Basin Spring, still a core of the community.

The *Eureka Springs Herald* newspaper started printing in 1875 to promote the area. 1879 saw the construction of the first store and a number of houses, and the population reached 180. On August 8, 1879, the first Eureka Springs town committee was elected. Later, on October 21, 1879, the Eureka Springs post office opened. The town of Eureka Springs was officially incorporated on February 14, 1880. Within a few months, more than 15,000 people were at Eureka Springs looking for a medical cure, with most living in tents and caves. By 1881, Eureka was the fourth largest city in Arkansas, and in 1889 it was the second largest city, behind Little Rock. There were many arguments about land ownership as squatters claimed their spots and built basic buildings. To solve the problem, I. N. Armstrong was hired as town surveyor and told to survey and plat a town so ownership could be determined. An issue quickly arose after Armstrong finished his survey as it was determined that he had been selling lots, often the same lot to multiple people. It didn't take long for Armstrong to flee the town.

Improving Eureka Springs

It took until 1885 for mayor John Carroll to settle things, including settling several mineral rights claims on the springs, attempts to mine the springs, and even ownership claims of the many springs.

These claims had failed to be solved by county courts, federal courts, and even the U.S. Secretary of the Interior. The solution was that the springs belonged to the city, churches received free land, and that squatters could claim their land. The compromise was also helped by the fact that the timber companies had cut the trees and moved on and the mining companies found no valuable minerals.

Another factor that helped the situation was the creation of the Eureka Improvement Company. Former Arkansas Governor Powell Clayton organized the company in 1882 to build hotels and other city facilities. Powell Clayton can best be described as the father of Eureka Springs. While Dr. Alvah Jackson as grandfather of the city found the springs and started the promotion, Clayton developed the city as many know it today. Powell Clayton was from Pennsylvania, and moved to Kansas as a surveyor. He joined the Union army during the Civil War as a captain of Company E, First Kansas Infantry. By 1862, he was in Helena, Arkansas, and later commanded the military post at Pine Bluff, Arkansas. By the end of the war, he commanded the cavalry division of the Seventh Army Corps as a general. He bought several plantations around Pine Bluff and helped found the Republican Party in Arkansas. He became governor on July 2, 1868. As governor, he led Arkansas' efforts to fund the construction of railroads, the creation of public schools, and the start of the state's university system. Clayton also served in the United States Senate (1871-1877). He then continued his law practice, moved to Eureka Springs in 1882, and began his investments to develop the city.

In 1885, the Eureka Improvement Company was given all unclaimed land and a 50-year franchise to build and operate street cars, gas and water utility lines. The Improvement Company immediately went to work marketing Eureka Springs as a luxury resort. The company built gazebos at the various springs, created organized boardwalks and stair-step trails, retaining walls to add lots, and a bandshell at Basin Park. The group also raised Main Street, ending its nickname of Mud Street. Even today, Leatherwood Creek flows below the many buildings that line Main Street and some still use the basements that were once the ground floor.

The first proposal for a railroad to Eureka Springs was in 1881 when Richard C. Kerens arrived to explore the option. It was felt that visitors to a luxury resort should not have to endure several hours on a stagecoach covering rough mountain roads. The new railroad began service on February 1, 1883, making the town even more popular. To help justify the railroad, the Crescent Hotel was built in 1886. Kerens also built the Kerens Memorial Chapel in honor of his mother, a building known today as St. Elizabeth's Catholic Church. Kerens also donated the land for the Eureka Springs Carnegie Public Library, built in 1912. The town did attract its share of famous people such as Carrie Nation, who moved here towards the end of her life and founded Hatchet Hall on Steele Street.

It wasn't long, however, until the tourist business began to fade. Modern medicine disputed the curing power of such springs, and other similar resorts across the country also began to compete for guests. On November 25, 1919, the Ozarks Playground Association was formed to market the community as an attempt to end the slide in visitors. During the 1920s, Eureka Springs was still a town of some industry, many who were rail shippers. These companies included the Eureka Springs Canning Company (tomatoes, apples, pumpkins, squash, sweet potatoes and berries), the Ozarka Water Company, the Eureka Springs Electric & Ice Company, and the Eureka Springs Monumental Works. There were a number of timber-based companies such as John I. Bradley (hardwood) and the lumber mills of C. D. Bradley Lumber Company, R. B. Kelly Lumber Company and C. W. Phillips. There were even several ore companies such as Lewis Webber (onyx) and the Ore Rock & Ore Products Company (zinc).

Today's Eureka Springs

The Great Depression and World War II further impacted the community with the population down to 1770 residents, most serving local farms and operating local businesses. With land cheap and plenty of empty building available, some new residents were attracted, leading to some interesting changes. Gerald K. Smith and his wife Elna arrived in the 1960s and had the "Christ of the Ozarks" statue built on Magnetic Mountain. Other attractions such as the Great Passion Play and several country music shows soon followed, kicking off a new tourism boom in Eureka Springs. With the mix of tourists, Eureka Springs picked up the nickname of "The Town Where Misfits Fit." Today it is a town based again on tourism and local trade.

Eureka Springs is one of two county seats for Carroll County, split by the waters of the Kings River. Eureka Springs is a unique Victorian resort village, and a popular shopping and walking town. The entire city is on the National Register of Historic

Places as the Eureka Springs Historic District. Eureka Springs has been selected as one of America's Distinctive Destinations by the National Trust for Historic Preservation. Eureka Springs has historically been called "The Little Switzerland of America" and "The Stairstep Town" because of its mountainous terrain and the winding, up-and-down paths of its streets and walkways. The streets wind around the town, no two intersect at a 90 degree angle, and there are no traffic lights. As of the 2010 census, the city population was 2073.

For many years, Eureka Springs was a popular subject of *Ripley's Believe it or Not*. Besides the layout of the streets, Ripley featured such items as the church that is entered through its bell tower, the hotel with seven street level floors, and many other characteristics of this Victorian town. For fans of architecture, the old commercial section of the city has an alpine character, with a large number of Victorian homes covering the hillsides. Building surveys indicate that about 20% of the city's buildings were built in the 1890s, and they have a significant element of either Queen Anne or Second Empire styling. A number of commercial buildings are built of local stone. Many buildings have street-level entrances on more than one floor, with a number actually having entrances below street level.

Ozarka Water

A famous feature of the area around the Eureka Springs railroad station was the Ozarka Water Company. The company used water from the Ozarka Spring, located just above the station area. The water was stored here and then piped into glass lined rail cars designed to move the water. There were also special boxcars designed with racks to hold large bottles of water. There were distributors across the country who would bottle the water at the market. For years, the water was also served on Frisco passenger trains. Today, the brand is part of the Nestlé Waters group.

The Brownstone Inn was built in 1895 and served as headquarters for the Ozarka Water Bottling Company that drew its water from the nearby Ozarka Spring. The adjacent round house did not start as a tank for the water, but was instead used to hold coal gas (methane) for use in the street lights before electricity was available. At first there was just a large tank here, but by 1904 a stone building was built. The building was owned by Powell Clayton's Eureka Springs Gas Light Company. It was later used as a warehouse by the water company.

The first railroad cars used were the typical wooden refrigerator cars with large advertising on the side promoting Ozarka Water by the Eureka Springs Water Company. Later, the company used more traditional tank cars to move their product. The water shipments were important to the railroad, and Eureka Springs produced 463 freight car loads in 1945. After the railroad shut down, the water was trucked to Garfield and loaded into rail cars on the Frisco until the operation was moved from Eureka Springs.

The Eureka Springs Streetcar System

From 1891 until 1923, Eureka Springs had its own streetcar system. The operation started using mule-drawn cars in 1891, but the system was electrified by 1898. The original company was the Eureka

Springs Electric Light and Street Railway Company, chartered May 1, 1891. The initial route was from Basin Park along Spring Street to Harmon Park and then on its own right-of-way through Crescent Park to the Crescent Hotel, for a total of 2.5 miles. The initial power was mule, two for each of the five cars due to the steep grades, and a storage barn was built at Harmon Park.

The line was electrified in 1898, with a powerhouse and ice plant built just south of the railroad depot. To connect the system to the railroad, a line was built down Hillside Avenue. In 1900, the trolley system became the property of the Citizens Electric Railway Company. This company expanded its offerings by providing electric light and power, cold storage and ice facilities, and a recreational attraction at Harmon Park. The park facility included an auditorium and opera house where the Eureka Springs Parks and Recreation Department is now based. In 1900, the system had three motorized cars and four trailers, but a report from 1902 showed the line with twelve passenger cars and two pieces of non-revenue equipment. Ridership peaked about 1903 and the company added bottled water to their business using the name Eureka Springs Water.

About this time, the Ozark Traction Company was organized to build interurban lines to a number of nearby towns, but nothing was ever accomplished. The trolley line soon failed to pay many of its bills and was sold on February 26, 1910, to the Eureka Traction Company. In 1912, the system was expanded with a line from the railroad depot up Main Street and directly to Basin Park. According to the *McGraw Electric Railway Manual* of 1914, the system consisted of four miles of track, nine motor cars, and one other car. It also stated that the repair shop was near Auditorium Park. Revenues failed to cover the cost of the system and in late 1918, the Home Electric Company acquired the street railway, the electric company and the ice plant. As the equipment and track failed, and visitors started arriving by car and trains stopped running due to the strike, the system gave up and abandoned the operation by 1923.

The Railroad

For years, the railroad was the entrance to Eureka Springs. Pullman cars on regular trains arrived from St. Louis and other Midwest cities. An 1897 Sanborn Map for Eureka Springs showed what it was like during the early years before the railroad was extended east to Harrison and then on south to Helena. At this time, Eureka Springs was the base of the railroad and it hosted many of the facilities required by the railroad.

At the time, the depot was a 30' x 56' wood-frame structure with waiting rooms at each end with the ticket office in the middle. This center section also had several rooms on the second floor under the high roof. There was a separate "Colored Waiting Room" building south of the station at the end of the platform. To the north of the depot was a baggage room. Both of these smaller buildings were connected to the main station by a covered platform.

This Sanborn map from 1897 shows the location of the locomotive shops, freight house, station, and other structures as they existed in Eureka Springs before the extension to Harrison, Arkansas, was completed.

Eureka Springs Branch

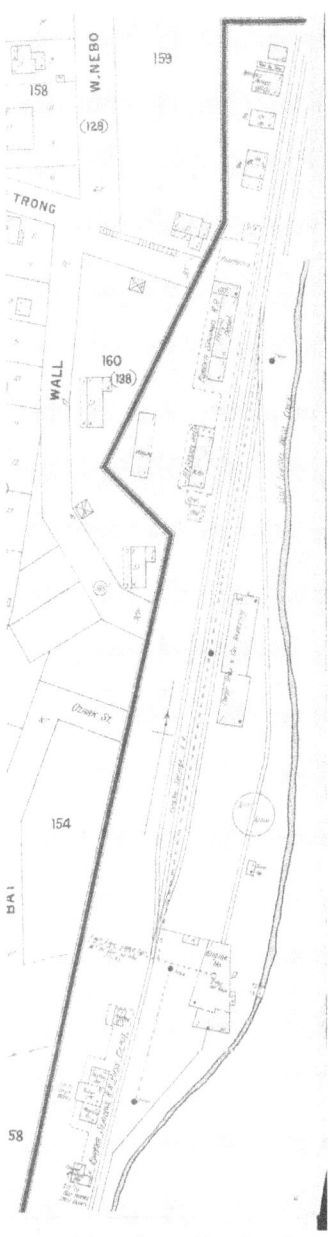

Sanborn Fire Insurance Map from Eureka Springs, Carroll County, Arkansas. Sanborn Map Company, May, 1897. Library of Congress, Geography and Map Division. https://www.loc.gov/item/sanborn00242_003/.

Further north were two sidings, one each side of the mainline. Along the siding to the west were a number of buildings, including a coal shed, the H. I. Seidel and Company warehouse, the Eureka Springs Freight Depot, several ice houses, and the buildings of the Waters Pierce Oil Company. East of the tracks was a lead onto a turntable, past a sand house, and then into a one-stall engine house. Between the track and the east siding was a "Carp'r Shop & Car Repairing" building. There was also a source of water for the steam locomotives. Located 300 feet south of the depot was an ice factory and electric light plant, marked as being in the hands of a receiver.

In 1913, a new 30' x 86' stone station was opened as part of the decision to move the shops and headquarters from Eureka Springs to Harrison. Many of the facilities were also closed. By 1940, the facilities at Eureka Springs were down to the depot (telegraph call "AW"), some stock pens, and a number of tracks. From the north, there was a two-car spur to the east to serve stock pens. Next was a 20-car spur track to the west that ended just north of the depot. To the east of the depot was a 19-car spur track that was often used for tie loading. South of the depot, the mainline ended at the Arkansas Power & Light Company facility. Just to the west was another 10-car spur track to where the water plant was located.

The Eureka Springs & North Arkansas Railway rebuilt the line and added a few new tracks as well as the former Frisco turntable, moved from its original Fort Smith location. The stone depot still exists and is used as the railroad's ticket office, souvenir store, and office. A number of passenger cars and machinery displays are also found in the area.

Eureka Springs Branch

The Eureka Springs depot was freshly restored in this December 1982 photo. The unique stone structure is used as the base of operations for the Eureka Springs & North Arkansas tourist railroad. Photo by Barton Jennings.

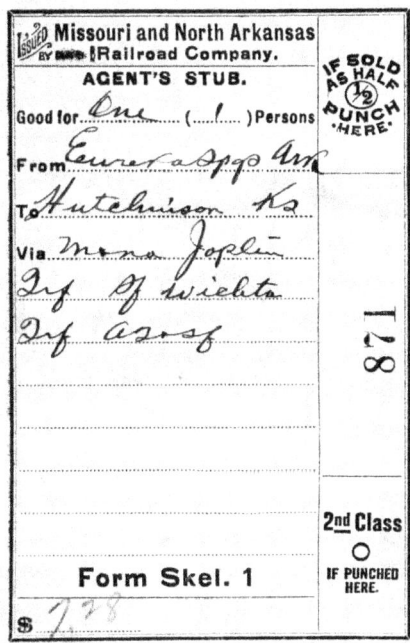

Missouri and North Arkansas Railroad Company Agent's Stub. Good for passage of one person from Eureka Springs, Arkansas, to Hutchinson, Kansas, via Joplin. Stamp on reverse side dated Jan 15, 1913. From the collection of Barton Jennings.

A photography event on the Eureka Springs & North Arkansas in November 1986 provided this image of steam on the former M&NA Eureka Branch, almost making the railroad come back alive. Photo by Barton Jennings.

Berryville Branch

The line from Freeman to Berryville followed a small stream that flowed into Clabber Creek near the wye. The elevation at Freeman was 1051 feet while Berryville is about 1200 feet, requiring a steady climb south. However, the wye at Freeman and the loop at Berryville prevented any need for a train to back up. The length of the branch was 2.6 miles.

Reports from the time of the building of the railroad indicate that Berryville obtained the right-of-way for the branch, and built the route. According to *The Green Forest Tribune*, the community was also responsible for the depot facilities. Berryville resident J. W. Freeman led the effort to obtain the land and build the route, using much of his own personal wealth.

J. W. Freeman was one of those responsible for bringing the railroad to Berryville, and he is buried there today along with much of his family. Photo by Barton Jennings.

88.6 FREEMAN – This was the location of the wye for the branch line south to Berryville. For information about Freeman, see information on the First District.

91.2 BERRYVILLE – When the railroad was built, Berryville was important enough to be served by a branch line, even though the mainline passed north of town. Berryville was served by a large loop track, allowing trains to reverse direction easily. On the loop, the railroad had a 32-car siding with the depot (telegraph call "B") between the two tracks. A 15-car spur track was located just west of the siding, and a short spur track once existed across the main track from the depot. The route of the loop track at Berryville was located north of downtown; signs of the loop can still be found. Railroad Circle Drive marks the southeast side of the loop, and the large Tyson Food plant basically uses the space the loop once encircled. On the northeast corner of the loop, several buildings still stand that were built to match the curve of the railroad.

The original depot at Berryville was built by H. B. Littleton, who had the contract to build the 15 depot buildings along the extension of the St. Louis & North Arkansas in 1900-1901. The Berryville depot was a common design also used at Freeman, Green Forest, Alpena, Harrison, Everton, St. Joe, Marshall, and Leslie. The building measured 18' x 72' and featured a waiting room, an agent's office, a "colored" waiting room, and a baggage room. The original depot was replaced in 1904 when the depot from Freeman was reportedly moved here. The story behind the need for the move is reported in the November 24, 1903, issue of the *Arkansas Gazette*. The article stated that in early November, some whiskey was stolen from the depot. At 1:00am on November 23rd, a fire destroyed the depot at a reported loss of $5,000. The newspaper stated that the "fire may have been set to cover up a repeat robbery."

The author once lived in Berryville, Arkansas, and walked by the former M&NA depot often going to and from school. He found the depot still standing and showing its use as a farm supply store during his honeymoon on the last day of 1982. Unfortunately, the building didn't stand much longer. Photo by Barton Jennings.

There is some confusion about this as the second depot reportedly measured 18' x 90', much too large for the depot that was once at Freeman. Some suspect that the depot used the shell of the former Freeman depot, but was greatly expanded. Kubat called the Berryville depot a "Standard #2" structure but also noted some questions about its size. After the railroad shut down, the depot was converted to a feed store and mill. It is now gone.

A number of older buildings that stood alongside the railroad still stand today, including this stone warehouse at Berryville. Photo by Barton Jennings.

History of the City of Berryville

The history of Berryville is similar to many small North Arkansas towns. It started as a central location for farmers to meet and trade for goods, often with a spring as a water source. In this case, the first known settlers were William and Joel Plumlee, Sr., Tennesseans who arrived in 1836. They obtained land in the area as squatters, with Joel obtaining 160 acres which now includes the location of Berryville's Public Square. A town began to grow as Joel built and operated a roller mill. For those who don't know, a roller mill uses cylindrical rollers to crush or grind grain, an alternative to traditional millstone gristmills.

About 1846, Blackburn Henderson Berry and his wife Eliza, also Tennesseans, arrived in Carroll County and soon bought the property of Joel Plumlee. The local spring became known as Berry Spring, and talk began about creating a town. By 1850,

Berry and Arthur A. Baker created a design for the community based upon three main streets and 24 lots. Baker was another settler of the area, arriving at today's Berryville about 1840 as a blacksmith. Baker later changed careers and became a doctor and opened his own apothecary in town.

Another Tennessean, local schoolteacher Arnold Champlin, actually surveyed the plat. Blackburn Berry opened a store, bought more land, and then donated property for the Public Square, another city park, a school, and then the Cumberland Presbyterian Church. Baker also donated land for the church. On July 13, 1852, the Berryville post office opened with Isaac Plumlee as the postmaster. Berry also helped create the Old Berryville Cemetery when his wife Eliza died of typhoid fever in 1854. Her large stone marker is still a historic landmark, although her grave and marker have been moved to the newer Berryville Memorial Cemetery.

Berryville was basically destroyed during the Civil War, with only three buildings still standing by the war's end. The founder of the post-war Berryville was Judge L. B. Saunders, who moved to Berryville in 1867 to open a store and to enroll his children in Clarke's Academy. Clarke's Academy was founded on January 14, 1867, by Professor Isaac Ashbury Clarke. Clarke moved to Berryville from Tennessee, and after the Civil War started a school to replace the one that had been burned. Saunders built a home where the Berryville City Hall now stands, and his store has been replaced by the St. George (aka Grandview) Hotel. Saunders and his son C. B. Saunders were involved with a great deal of area development. C. B. Saunders named nearby Eureka Springs, and donated much of his gun collection to

Berryville that is now displayed as the Saunders Museum. Saunders Heights, located just north of town, was also donated to Berryville to be used as a park.

Boone County was created from the eastern part of Carroll County, so the county seat of Carrollton was no longer centrally located. After several votes, the county seat was moved to Berryville in 1875. This choice led the town to be incorporated on March 23, 1876. The courthouse was built of local brick and opened in late 1880. A third floor was added in 1904. The building is now the home of the Heritage Center Museum. 1880 saw the first public school after the Civil War open, on land donated by former blacksmith and now Dr. Arthur A. Baker. Another leader in developing Berryville was Charles Pyron, Sr., another Tennessean. Pyron manufactured brick and built many of the buildings in town. Among these was the St. George Hotel, later called the Grandview Hotel and advertised as the "only hotel with pure spring water, free bath room, and pure mountain air."

By 1889, the town of Berryville had a population of about 400 people and several employers such as a canning factory and the second largest flour mill in the state. Over the next decade, Berryville was overshadowed by the nearby health resort town of Eureka Springs. The county seat duties had already been divided and Berryville was now responsible for the Eastern Judicial District. As the St. Louis & North Arkansas Railroad built eastward, a branch was built to reach the industry at Berryville. On June 15, 1901, a major parade and celebration was held for more than 2000 spectators to welcome the railroad.

During the 1920s, Berryville was the home of a number of small industries that used the railroad.

Berryville Branch

These included the Berryville Canning Company (tomatoes, apples, and berries), the Berryville Milling Company, Everett & Son Milling Company, and the A. L. Hanby lumber mill. Many of these companies were gone by the 1950s, but the railroad continued to serve shippers like the Lion Oil bulk plant, Hanby Lumber, Berryville Supply, Ocoma Foods, and the Carroll County Farm Bureau. Since the 1960s, Berryville has been the home of a major poultry processing facility, eventually earning the town the title of "Turkey Capital of Arkansas." The town has also been the home of plants owned by companies like Kraft Foods, Tyson Foods, LaBarge Electronics, William Kaye Manufacturing, and Kerusso, the leading producer of Christian clothing. The downtown area has also been recognized as the Berryville Commercial Historic District, added to the National Register of Historic Places in 2016. Berryville had a population of 5356 in 2010, making it the largest city in Carroll County.

Missouri and North Arkansas ticket from Green Forest, Arkansas, to Berryville, Arkansas. From the collection of Barton Jennings.

Missouri & North Arkansas Railroad: History Through the Miles

Missouri & North Arkansas Route Guide
Second District –
Harrison (AR) to Heber Springs (AR)

The Second District of the Missouri & North Arkansas/ Missouri & Arkansas, defined as being from the company's headquarters at Harrison south to Heber Springs, included the track built by the St. Louis & North Arkansas to Leslie by 1903, and then extended by the Missouri & North Arkansas to Heber Springs in 1908. This part of the railroad was unique in that it had no connections with other common carrier railroads, just a logging railroad at Leslie. This part of the railroad included a number of grades, and featured some of the most curvy and scenic parts of the entire railroad.

The mileposts presented are from *Missouri & Arkansas Railway Company Time Table No. 7*, dated Sunday, February 25, 1945, and a June 28, 1925, timetable of the Missouri & North Arkansas. However, it should be noted that mileposts for many of the station locations have changed slightly over the years.

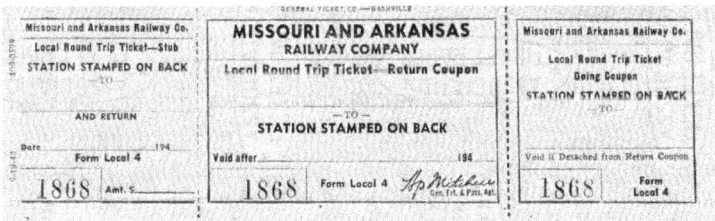

Missouri and Arkansas Railway Company Local Round Trip Ticket. From the collection of Barton Jennings.

SECOND DISTRICT

SOUTHWARD

THIRD CLASS 325 Local Freight Mon. Wed. Fri.	SECOND CLASS 11 Manifest Freight Daily	FIRST CLASS 1 Passenger Daily	Siding Capacity		Distance from Joplin	Maximum Grade	TIME TABLE No. 7 Effective 12.01 A. M. SUNDAY February 25, 1945 STATIONS
			Pass.	Other			
Lv 6.00AM	Lv 7.00PM	Lv 11.59AM	Yd.		126.33	1.75	DN........HARRISON.....CTWX
							4.69
6.20	7.20	f 12.11PM	27B		131.02	1.75	........BELLEFONTE........*
							5.59
6.30	7.44	f 12.24	28B		136.61	1.75	..........OLVEY...........*
							4.75
6.45	8.05	s 12.36	32B	18	141.36	1.60	D........EVERTON..........W
							6.92
7.10	8.30	s 12.51	36B		148.28	1.75	,..........PINDALL..........
		M2 M326					7.06
7.40	9.00	s 1.03	39B		155.34	1.60	,..........ST. JOE.........
							6.38
8.10	9.30	s 1.23	25B		161.72	1.30	,..........GILBERT........W
							5.49
8.35	9.55	f 1.40	13B		167.21	1.30	..........ZACK.............*
							3.67
8.55	10.15	1.49	41B		170.88	1.75	........JAMESON...........
							1.89
9.02	10.22	s 1.53	16B	4	172.77	1.75	D........MARSHALL..........
							2.12
9.10	10.30	f 1.59	9B		174.80	0.44	..........BAKER............*
							6.86
10.08	11.15	s 2.14 / 2.34	44B	53	181.75	0.30	DN........LESLIE.........WY
							4.79
10.23		f 2.46	7N		186.54	0.00	..........RUMLEY...........*
							5.27
10.43 M2	11.50PM M12	s 2.59	21B		191.81	0.00	..........ELBA............
							9.19
11.17	12.25AM	s 3.19	38B		201.00	0.50	..........ARLBERG........W
							4.90
11.32		f 3.30	7N		205.90		..........LYDALISK..........
							4.38
11.52AM	1.00	f 3.39	34B		210.28	0.15	..........OAKVALE..........
							4.75
12.22PM	1.30	s 3.50	34B	79	215.03	0.00	D........SHIRLEY..........W
							8.26
12.52	2.00	f 4.12	20B		223.29	0.50	..........PARTAIN..........
							4.10
1.07	2.15	s 4.21		258	227.39	0.30	..........EDGEMONT..........
							2.23
1.15	2.23	s 4.27	28B	22	229.62	0.50	..........HIGDEN...........
							7.23
1.42	2.50	s 4.42	33B		236.85	0.60	..........MILLER...........*
							6.47
Ar 2.05PM	Ar 3.15AM	Ar 4.57PM	Yd.		243.32	0.45	DN....HEBER SPRINGS....CWY
Mon. Mon. Fri.	Daily	Daily	End Connected B—Both N—North S—South				116.99
325	11	1					

Missouri & North Arkansas Railway Company Time Table No. 7, Sunday, February 25, 1945. Second District, southward. Courtesy Boone County Historical & Railroad Society.

Second District – Harrison (AR) to Heber Springs (AR)

COND DISTRICT

TIME TABLE No. 7 Effective 12.01 A. M. SUNDAY February 25, 1945 STATIONS	Maximum Grade	Station Numbers	Telegraph Call	NORTHWARD		
				FIRST CLASS **2** Passenger Daily	SECOND CLASS **12** Freight Daily	THIRD CLASS **326** Local Freight Tues. Thurs. Sat.
DN.........HARRISON.....CTWX — 4.69	....	126	DS	Ar 1.41 PM	Ar 5.00 AM	Ar 2.05 PM
.........BELLEFONTE.........* — 5.59	1.75	131	......	f 1.30	4.35	1.50
............OLVEY............* — 4.75	1.75	137	......	f 1.17	4.13	1.31
D........EVERTON........W — 6.92	1.75	141	RN	s 1.06	3.50	1.15
,........PINDALL............ — 7.06	0.64	148	......	s 12.51 M1-P326	3.20	12.51 M1 2-P
,........ST. JOE............ — 6.38	1.75	155	......	s 12.34	2.45	12.16 PM
.........GILBERT........W — 5.49	1.67	162	......	s 12.19	2.15	11.55 AM
.............ZACK............* — 3.67	1.37	167	......	f 12.02 PM	1.45	11.30
.........JAMESON............ — 1.89	0.00	171	......	11.53 AM	1.32	11.17
D.......MARSHALL........... — 2.12	0.75	173	MR	s 11.49	1.25	11.10
............BAKER............* — 6.86	1.28	175	......	s 11.43	1.10	10.55
DN........LESLIE.........WY — 4.79	....	182	K	11.28 11.08	12.45 AM	10.30
............RUMLEY..........* — 5.27	0.60	187	......	f 10.56	....	9.42
............ELBA............ — 9.19	0.60	192	......	s 10.43 M325	11.50 PM M11	9.22
.........ARLBERG........W — 4.90	0.60	201	......	s 10.23	11.17	8.48
.........LYDALISK............ — 4.38	....	205	......	f 10.12	....	8.33
.........OAKVALE........... — 4.75	0.50	210	......	f 10.03	10.43	8.13
D........SHIRLEY........W — 8.26	0.45	215	SN	s 9.53	10.25	7.43
..........PARTAIN............ — 4.10	0.60	223	......	f 9.31	9.45	7.13
.........EDGEMONT........... — 2.23	0.50	227	......	s 9.22	9.29	6.58
.........HIGDEN............ — 7.23	0.60	230	......	s 9.16	9.20	6.50
..........MILLER...........* — 6.47	0.50	237	......	s 9.01	8.55	6.23
DN.....HEBER SPRINGS....CWY	0.60	243	HB	Lv 8.46 AM	Lv 8.30 PM	Lv 6.00 AM
116.99				Daily	Daily	Tues. Thur. Sat.
				2	**12**	**326**

Missouri & North Arkansas Railway Company Time Table No. 7, Sunday, February 25, 1945. Second District, northward. Courtesy Boone County Historical & Railroad Society.

𝕸𝖎𝖘𝖘𝖔𝖚𝖗𝖎 𝖆𝖓𝖉 𝕬𝖗𝖐𝖆𝖓𝖘𝖆𝖘 𝕽𝖆𝖎𝖑𝖜𝖆𝖞 𝕮𝖔𝖒𝖕𝖆𝖓𝖞

1936
Pass
-Mrs.W.G.Degelow & dtr. **No. 1338**
Nancy, wife & dept.dtr., AGFA
StLSW Ry Lines

GOOD BETWEEN ALL STATIONS UNTIL JANUARY 31, 1937, UNLESS OTHERWISE SPECIFIED HEREON, AND SUBJECT TO CONDITIONS ON BACK

VALID WHEN COUNTERSIGNED BY MYSELF OR D. C. KUDER
COUNTERSIGNED BY

VICE-PRES. & GEN'L. MGR.

Missouri and Arkansas Railway Company 1936 pass for the wife and daughter of an Assistant General Freight Agent. From the collection of Barton Jennings.

United States Railroad Administration
Missouri and North Arkansas R. R.
HEBER SPRINGS, Ark.,
TO
HARRISON, Ark.
Good for One Continuous Passage, commencing not later than one day after date of sale. Subject to tariff regulations.   Gen'l Pass'r Agent.

4366

United States Railroad Administration / Missouri and North Arkansas R. R. ticket for passage from Heber Springs, Arkansas, to Harrison, Arkansas, a trip spanning the Second District. From the collection of Barton Jennings.

Harrison (AR) to Heber Springs (AR)

126.3 HARRISON – For information about Harrison, see the First District section.

127.2 CROOKED CREEK BRIDGE – Crooked Creek starts just east of Mystic Caverns near Marble Falls in Newton County. It then flows north to Harrison where it turns east and flows through Yellville before entering the White River. Crooked Creek has a national reputation for its smallmouth bass fishing, and many people float the stream while fishing. According to the State of Arkansas, Crooked Creek is "the blue-ribbon smallmouth stream of the state" and features deep pools, fast chutes and clear water. While the stream passes through Harrison and Yellville, most of its route is through rolling hills, mountainside bluffs, bottomland thickets, and lush pasturelands. Around Harrison, Crooked Creek has been channelized and a levee has been built to protect the city from flooding.

This two-span deck plate girder (DPG) bridge was built by the Wisconsin Bridge & Iron Company and was completed in early March 1902. From the north, the bridge consisted of eleven frame bent timber panels, two 60-foot DPG spans, and seven frame bent timber panels. Construction on the bridge delayed track laying on the extension to Leslie. For years after the railroad was abandoned, the stone piers and at least one span remained. These were removed by 1970 when a new highway was built through the area. This bridge was the one that union activist Ed C. Gregor was hanged from in 1923 during the violent strike against the Missouri & North Arkansas. The Brotherhood of Locomotive Engineers and several other railroad unions offered a $5000 reward for information that would lead to the arrest and conviction of those that hung Gregor. Reportedly the reward was never made, but neither was the one for $2000 for the arrest and conviction of railroad union members who burned or bombed several M&NA bridges.

This area was once the edge of town and the Erwin sawmill was located just south of the north end of the bridge. Leaving Harrison, trains faced a steep and curving route as they headed south. Having a local yard locomotive push the train over the Crooked Creek bridge and up the hill was not uncommon. The route is now covered by U.S. Highway 65/412 to near the junction with South Main Street/Business Route 65. Here the railroad turned east toward Bellefonte, staying north of the highway and a few housing subdivisions.

128.5 SCHNEITTER SPUR – Documents from the early 1940s show that there was a 3-car spur to the west here, which was built in 1930 according to the railroad's annual report. The customer located here was large enough that the Arkansas & Ozarks preserved the line this far south. This location would have been just east of the manufacturing complex at the junction between the U.S. Highways and the business route. The name Schneitter is found in Harrison records as the Schneitter Lumber Mills Company. The company advertised that it had a sawmill 1½ miles southeast of Harrison and bought pine, oak, gum, cottonwood, ash, cedar and walnut.

The October 6, 1930, issue of the *Fayetteville Daily Democrat* had an article that read "H. E. Schneiter combines his Plainview, Ark., and Kennett, Mo., sawmills and moves them to Harrison."

One of the current manufacturing plants here is Claridge Products and Equipment, Inc., one of the largest Visual Display Board manufacturers in the world. It has been in business for more than sixty years and is a NWBOC (National Women Business Owners Corporation) certified women-owned company. The plant creates a steady flow of trucks in and out of Harrison.

129.0 OZIER SUMMIT – Identified as being at an elevation of 1182 feet, this grade top was shown in early railroad documents. This was the top of the two miles of 1.75% grade up from Harrison Yard. The Ozier family moved to this area from Tennessee during the mid-1800s. The Ozier family had a farm on Old Bellefonte Road during the early 1900s.

129.8 CHAPMAN – Chapman was approximately where the grade crossed Old Bellefonte Road, and was likely named after the Chapman family who lived in the area and conducted some mining. A benchmark shows the elevation at this location to be 1170 feet above sea level. This nine-car spur track was retired in 1926.

131.0 BELLEFONTE – Coming into the Bellefonte area, the railroad followed Brush Creek and then Huzzah Creek just north of today's town on U.S. Highway 65. The railroad then looped to the northeast along Huzzah Creek to go around a low ridge. At the north end of the ridge, the railroad turned to the southeast, following a branch of Huzzah Creek. At Bellefonte, the railroad had a 27-car siding on the east side of the tracks, with the depot to the west. The Standard #1 frame depot at Bellefonte, measuring 18' x 58', still stands at the intersection of Center Avenue and Cash Street, used as a home. The depot was built in 1901 without a center waiting room, a somewhat unique design. Over the years, its exterior was covered with local field stones. Some modifications have been made, including several additions. The building was listed on the National Register of Historic Places in 1992.

The Bellefonte depot was easy to photograph in 1988, with only this small addition altering its look. Photo by Barton Jennings.

The other side of the stone-covered Bellefonte depot was little-altered in 1988. Photo by Barton Jennings.

The first purchase of land in this area was by John Simms, who bought land from the U.S. government in 1854. His purchase included a large freshwater spring that later became an important source of water for the community. Multiple names were used for the community as it began to grow. In 1848, a post office opened using the name Hussaw. Meanwhile several settlers were trying to name the town after the spring, coming up with "belle fonte" which one of them thought was Latin for "beautiful spring." In 1852, the post office changed its name to Mount Pleasant. Just before the Civil War, Bellefonte was the largest community in the region and reportedly featured eight blacksmiths, eight merchants, a tanner, a wagon maker, two masons, two carpenters, and was the regional market center for cattle.

The Civil War saw both Northern and Southern forces take and camp at Bellefonte, but much of the town seemed to have survived. After the war, Bellefonte began to grow again, but suffered a major defeat when Harrison was chosen as the county seat of the new Boone County in 1869, even though Bellefonte was a much larger town. In 1871, the post office finally changed its name to Bellefonte and the town was incorporated on July 17, 1872. About the same time, North Arkansas College, a private high school, opened at Bellefonte and attracted many students to the community.

In 1882, much of Bellefonte burned and the town's incorporation was lost. The town slowly rebuilt, but unlike many other area communities, the arrival of the railroad did not have a large impact. Instead, with Harrison being the county seat and only a few miles away, most business development skipped Bellefonte. However, some businesses such as a leather factory, cotton gin and a flour mill did open here. The railroad also built several facilities, such as a cotton platform and a coal house, both of which were retired in 1929.

In 1963, Bellefonte again incorporated and today features several stores that cater to the highway traffic. Its population was 530 in the 2010 census. In 2013, Bellefonte gained national attention when Mayor James Wiggins, age 90, was recognized as the oldest active mayor in the United States.

Rusty Wheels Old Engine Club

South of Bellefonte at 5722 U.S. Highway 65 South is the Rusty Wheels Old Engine Club with their collection of farm equipment, machinery and tools, and even a railroad steam locomotive. The club hosts at least two operating shows each year, although the railroad steam locomotive is generally not operated.

The railroad steam locomotive displayed was built by Baldwin in 1919 as Portland Cement Company (Petoskey, Michigan) #10. The 0-6-0T was sold to Kenneth Stanaback in 1965, and he rebuilt the locomotive to an almost new condition, even turning it into a 2-6-0. Without ever operating the locomotive at his home near Grand Rapids, Michigan, he transferred the ownership to Reat and Dreat Younger and their tourist operation at Beaver, Arkansas. Locomotive #4, as it was renumbered, changed hands after the railroad closed during the mid-1980s. It was first leased to the non-operating Krazy Horse Ranch and Railroad Park near Branson, Missouri, and then eventually wound up here.

132.2 HUZZAH CREEK BRIDGE – Follow Cash Street, the former railroad grade, to reach Huzzah Creek. The concrete piers for this bridge's 60-foot deck plate girder span still stand, and are located where the railroad changes direction from heading to the northeast and starts heading to the southeast. Huzzah Creek forms not far south of the junction of U.S. Highways 62 and 65 southeast of Harrison. It flows to the northeast and into Crooked Creek. The area where the creek forms is known as Huzzah Prairie, or Hooza Prairie. This area was a natural prairie that was used for grazing by early settlers.

South of here, the railroad grade is briefly used by Huzzah Road and then passes under U.S. Highway 62 alongside a branch of Huzzah Creek. A highway bridge was built here in 1940 that stated the bridge was built for the Arkansas State Highway Commission and the United States Bureau of Public Roads. It was replaced by this new bridge in 2006.

134.5 CECIL SUMMIT – Early Missouri & North Arkansas documents show this top of the grade location, listed as being at 1156 feet. This is the second summit that southbound trains faced out of Harrison, all with grades of 1.75%. The Cecil family lived in this general area, and several members also lived in nearby Harrison. The most noted member of the Cecil family was probably W. H. Cecil, who was on the Harrison committee to attract the railroad shops to Harrison. He was also a 1912 delegate to the national Progressive Republican convention from the 3rd congressional district.

The summit grade is today Mikes Road, located just north of Old Olvey Road. Mikes Road uses the old railroad grade from Old Olvey Road to the point where Mikes Road turns due north. Look for the gated grade to the east. Heading south from here to Olvey, the railroad followed Meeks Creek.

136.6 OLVEY – The post office at Olvey opened in 1884 with the name Enon. In 1887, it was changed to Pedlo, and then to Olvey in 1904. It closed in 1955 as mail service was moved to Harrison. Multiple names seem to be common for the area, with the nearby Enon Cemetery also once known as the Gosset Cemetery. The name Olvey is also used for Olvey Township, one of twenty current townships in Boone County. The township is rural in nature with a population of 440 in 2010, at an elevation of 1013 feet.

The railroad arrived at Olvey by June 1902. During the 1920s, Olvey was the location of the Seymour Canning Company, a canner of tomatoes. The name Olvey Canning Company is also found in the *Arkansas Marketing and Industrial Guide* of 1921. The plant was sold in 1925 to Arvil Chester Williams and renamed the Williams Canning Factory. The plant survived the Depression and had a contract to provide canned tomatoes to the military, packaged under the name *Royal Red Tomatoes* and advertised as being "Packed in the Heart of the Ozarks." The factory burned in late 1942 and was rebuilt as the Crawford Canning Company. The canning plant changed ownership in 1967, and didn't close until 1977. The building was later turned into a home, but burned down on April 5, 2004.

The railroad arrived from the northwest by following Meeks Creek. Just west of the north switch was Bridge 136-5. The siding was shown as being 28 cars long and was to the southwest, with the wooden depot between the siding and the mainline. Kubat stated that the depot was a Standard #1 building measuring 18' x 58'. The building was sold on November 15, 1945, and replaced by a small shelter. Olvey was a telegraph station until the early 1920s using "VR" as its telegraph call.

Exiting Olvey, the tracks continued to follow Meeks Creek and Old Olvey Road. The railroad continued straight where Old Olvey Road turned east, eventually becoming the grade for Meeks Creek Road. Where Meeks Creek Road turns sharply to head directly south, the railroad grade curves off to the southeast and climbs several low ridges over Shirley Summit to reach Hog Creek, which it follows to Everton. Parts of this route can still be followed on maps and in the field, thanks to the tree lines the grade created.

138.0 SHIRLEY SUMMIT – The top of the summit and the railroad grade can be found on many topographical maps as a benchmark at an elevation of 1062 feet, northwest of the Newton Cemetery. This was the third southbound summit from Harrison, identified by the Missouri & North Arkansas. It was shown to be at an elevation of 1063 feet and again at the top of grades as stiff as 1.75%. It was a short climb of less than a mile for southbound trains, but about three miles long for northbound trains.

139.5 BRIDGE 139-5 – This bridge was described as being 131 feet long and 33 feet high. Located just west of the intersection between Jones Road and Rally Hill Road, it bridged across the road and the creek to the south. This was one of several bridges that were burned on January 10, 1923, during the strike of the 1920s.

141.3 EVERTON – The railroad opened to here on July 15, 1902. Even as the railroad was building toward the site, James Logan Rush of Jasper, Arkansas, was platting a town on seventy-five acres of land in a valley at 856 feet of elevation. With the railroad's arrival, a post office opened later in the year. The town quickly attracted residents and a school opened in 1903. Within a few more years, the town featured a sawmill, cotton gin, and a number of businesses typical for a growing mountain community. Fruit was also a growing business, several flour mills opened, and the Everton Mining and Development Company operated several area lead and zinc mines. Everton was incorporated during 1913 and the town was rebuilt several years later after a major fire. The Seymour Canning Company opened to produce canned tomatoes and other vegetables and fruits that were grown locally. The Bell Brothers Lumber Company also operated at Everton. At one time there was an ore dock at Everton, but it was retired in 1926, the same year that a new cotton platform was built.

Possibly the most famous industry to ever operate at Everton was the Uncle Sam Cob Pipe Works, a manufacturing plant that made corn cob pipes. Opened in 1923 by Joseph Migliore, the firm manufactured thousands of pipes a day that were sold across the country. The initial company was known as the Arkansas Cob Pipe Works and was located in the former general store and office of the Everton Mining and Development Company, about four miles east of Everton at Emide. The pipes were made from a special corn that was bought at prices above the regular price of corn, buying the firm the loyalty of area farmers. About 1929, the name Uncle Sam Cob Pipe Works was also being used, using a Pyatt, Arkansas, address (a station on the nearby Missouri Pacific). This gave the firm two options for shipping. In 1937, a new factory was built two blocks north of the M&NA depot, and the old factory turned into a house. Even though the firm had its ups and downs due to labor and supply costs, competition, and government wage policies, the firm continued to survive until it closed in 1942 due to a lack of labor at the beginning of World War II. During the company's operation, it supplied pipes to such people as General Douglas McArthur and New York City Mayor LaGuardia. Many of the pipes where shipped over the railroad using the mail or the Railway Express Agency.

Everton was also the location of what is probably the most successful of the efforts of the Manda Corporation. In 1936, the Everton Silica Sand Company opened to mine a rich seam of sand, founded by former railroad employee H. C. "Hallie" Ormond. The sand was shipped by rail to a glass factory in Tulsa, Oklahoma, with more cars going to the Lava Soap plant in Kansas City, Missouri. The railroad provided more than investment money to the Manda Corporation; the plant used the boiler from M&NA steam engine #16, a Baldwin 4-4-0 (construction number 32856) that was built in 1908 and retired in 1935. Employing 20 to 25 workers, the plant featured crushing and washing units, a drying facility, sand storage, a pump house for wash water, and several bins for loading railcars. In 1939, the plant was sold to the Silica Products Company, which shipped about 100 carloads per month. Because of the sand plant, Everton was one of the four largest sources of traffic for the railroad, creating 627 car loads in 1945. The sand company operated until the railroad closed in 1946.

With the closure of the cob plant and the sand plant in the 1940s, Everton began to shrink back to a small mountain town. The school was closed and sold to the local Methodist congregation and students went to nearby Valley Springs for their education. This building was placed on the National Register of Historic Places on September 10, 1992. The Everton Baptist Church, located on Rally Hill Road, is located in the former corn cob plant. The post office is still open, but there are currently no businesses at Everton. The population in 2010 was only 170.

Harrison (AR) to Heber Springs (AR)

The Everton Methodist Church is just a few blocks from the railroad and is located in the Everton school building. Photo by Barton Jennings.

Just north of the Everton Community Center is the former corn cob pipe factory, now used as part of the Everton Baptist Church. The railroad once operated where the road now exists. Photo by Barton Jennings.

Everton had a 32-car siding to the north (railroad-east), with an 18-car spur track off of the south end to the sand plant alongside Clear Creek. The 18' x 72' Everton frame depot (Standard #2) was located between the mainline and siding. While the station is gone, the community has built a community center that is a replica of the original depot, and located it near the original site of the M&NA depot. For years, the depot used the telegraph call of "RN". There was also a standard 16' x 24' wooden 50,000-gallon water tank, and the concrete footings still remain. A private contractor pumped water to the tower from Hog Creek.

One of the first buildings that you see when you enter Everton is the new Community Center, built to resemble a railroad station to honor the community's history. Photo by Barton Jennings.

141.6 CLEAR CREEK BRIDGE – Heading south out of Everton, Clear Creek Road follows the railroad grade for several miles. The grade almost immediately crossed the Marshall Branch and then the main channel of Clear Creek. Clear Creek Road uses a low-water bridge across both streams.

Clear Creek forms on the hillsides to the north of Pindall, flows north to Everton, and then to the northeast before it enters Crooked Creek near Pyatt, Arkansas. Clear Creek was the reason James Rush located Everton where he did. Clear Creek provided water power as well as irrigation for local farmers. Later, the Everton Silica Sand Company mined the sand and stone that the creek had deposited in the area.

144.4 COUNTY LINE – **Boone County** is to the north while **Searcy County** is to the south. There have actually been two Searcy Counties in Arkansas. The first was established on November 5, 1835, created from western Izard County to represent the growing mountain population in the area. This Searcy County included land that later became Marion and parts of Boone, Baxter, and Stone counties, as well as today's Searcy County. During September 1836, the county was renamed Marion County to honor Revolutionary War hero Francis Marion. As the population increased, a new **Searcy County** was created on December 13, 1838, using the southern part of the original Searcy County.

The name Searcy comes from Richard Searcy, a prominent civil servant, major landowner, and circuit court judge during the early 1800s. Searcy was the first clerk and judge in the Arkansas Territory. The county is still mostly rural with a population of 8195 in the 2010 census. Marshall is the county seat.

For the food buff, Searcy County can be an interesting attraction. The Greater Searcy County Chamber of Commerce declared Searcy County the "Chocolate Roll Capital of the World™" and has trademarked the term and a local treat known as the Chocolate Roll™. The dessert consists of pie dough spread with a mixture of cocoa powder, shortening, and sugar. The mix is then rolled up and baked. The Marshall High School also hosts a Chocolate Roll™ Festival where various versions compete against each other for the annual championship.

148.2 PINDALL – From Everton to Pindall, the railroad generally followed Clear Creek. Clear Creek Road uses the grade leaving Everton, and for some distance beyond. Before the road leaves the grade, it is known as Side Track Lane. Past the end of the road, the grade continues to the south, weaving between several hills. The line passed Dugger Spring and the Glencoe Cemetery before coming beside U.S. Highway 65 and arriving at Pindall. Pindall had a depot on the east side of the mainline with a 36-car siding to the west. The 20' x 36' wooden depot is currently next to the Pindall post office, near several closed gas stations. The building appears to be used for storage by the owners of a nearby house. Records show that the station was sold in late 1945 and replaced by a small shelter.

The Pindall area first received a post office in 1904, known originally as Big Hurricane Switch. It was almost immediately renamed Kilburn Switch, or simply Kilburn, for a local businessman named Kilburne, the owner of the land where the railroad was built. In 1908, the name Pindall was assigned to the post office. The name Pindall comes from Xenophon Overton Pindall, a member of the Arkansas House of Representatives, Arkansas State Senate and Acting Governor of the State of Arkansas. Pindall became governor when Arkansas Governor John Sebastian Little resigned due to mental and physical illness on February 11, 1907. This made the president of the State Senate, John Isaac Moore, governor. When the legislative session ended in May, 1907, Pindall was selected as the next president of the State Senate, making him governor. He held that title until January 11, 1909. Pindall was later a noted criminal attorney.

While thousands of people drive by this small structure daily, few probably recognize that it is the former M&NA depot at Pindall, Arkansas. Photo by Barton Jennings.

Pindall was part of the lead and zinc boom in the area. About two miles west of Pindall was the Big Hurricane Mine, opened in 1903 as a source of zinc. The railroad built a track to serve it and named it Hurricane Switch. The mine closed in 1905, then reopened during World War I (1915-1918). The mine reopened a final time during World War II due to the demand for zinc.

Besides mining, for many years Pindall was a regional business center and the home of two timber manufacturing companies, as well as a railroad tie loading point for several others. There was also a canning factory that processed beans and tomatoes, and the Pindall Strawberry Association. A stock pen was used for many years to load sheep (retired in 1929), and there was a cotton platform here for several decades. With all of the industry, Pindall was incorporated as a town in 1912. The town has never been very large, and its population was 112 during the 2010 census. The railroad has climbed 200 feet in the seven miles since Everton, with the elevation being 1060 feet.

The street (Searcy County Highway 15) one block south of U.S. Highway 65 closely follows the old railroad grade leaving town to the south. The grade turns south and then makes a horseshoe curve to turn east to follow Mill Creek to St. Joe, Arkansas.

149.5 RAINBOLT SUMMIT – Heading south from Pindall, the railroad climbs almost 100 feet to climb over Rainbolt Summit at 1150 feet. This is the fourth summit that southbound trains out of Harrison had to face. The southbound grade was almost nine miles long while the northbound grade was essentially a dozen miles long, both with grades as much as 1.75%.

Emanuel Bellefiel Rainbolt was born in Tennessee and moved to this area before the Civil War, and died here on January 18, 1861. The Rainbolt family continued to live in the area, giving the summit their name.

150.4 CLUTES – For a number of years after the railroad's construction, Clutes was a 15-car spur track that served a sawmill. The track was retired in 1927. Clutes, or simply Clute, was located where the railroad turned east to follow Mill Creek toward St. Joe. The railroad crossed Mill Creek more than a half-dozen times heading towards St. Joe.

153.6 MILL CREEK BRIDGE – The bridge, from north to south, included two panel trestle spans, two 30-foot deck plate girder spans, and three wooden frame approach spans on the south end.

153.8 MILL CREEK BRIDGE – The bridge used two 30-foot deck plate girder spans, with one wooden frame span on the north end and two wooden approach spans on the south end. Mill Creek forms on the north side of Chinquapin Spring Ridge near the Kilburn Cemetery at Chinquapin Spring. Mill Creek flows east to near St. Joe, and then to the southeast before flowing into the Buffalo River south of Duff. The M&NA used the creek's route west of St. Joe.

The Chinquapin, also known as the Ozark Chestnut, once filled the woods from Arkansas and Missouri east to the Carolinas. The tree has been described as being a "heat-tolerant hard-wood specimen perfect for southern forests due to its fondness for the acidic, dry and rocky soils." This very much matched the conditions in the Ozark, Ouachita, Appalachian and Allegheny mountain ranges. The Chinquapin nut was popular with wildlife like bears, squirrels and deer. Early settlers also harvested the nuts. The wood was also rot-resistant, and was popular for railroad ties and fence posts. This led to heavy logging of the trees. This, combined with the chestnut blight, almost wiped out the tree. There are efforts today to introduce a version that is resistant to the chestnut blight.

154.0 MERCER – Mercer was a 7-car track that served a tipple on the east side of the mainline. It was located just south of the bridge over Mill Creek. The area around St. Joe was known for its lead and zinc mines, as well as marble, lime and limestone. Mercer was a lead mining community with its own ore loading facility. There was also the W. A. Bonner Marble and Limestone Company quarry. Most of the area mines closed around the time of World War I and the early 1920s. However, the Moark Stone Company still operated here in 1944 at what was called Mercer Spur. Records show that there was never a station or passenger shelter here.

154.1 MILL CREEK BRIDGE – The bridge used two 30-foot deck plate girder spans, with two wooden approach spans on each end.

154.2 MILL CREEK BRIDGE – This bridge used a single 60-foot deck plate girder span to cross the creek, with four timber frame panel spans on the north end and three on the south end. This steel bridge was one of many acquired in 1901 from the Wisconsin Bridge & Iron Company.

155.0 MILL CREEK BRIDGE – This crossing of Mill Creek used a single 30-foot deck plate girder span.

155.3 ST. JOE – The railroad reached St. Joe on September 15, 1902. St. Joe had its Standard #2 depot located between the mainline and a 39-car siding (2065 feet) to the west, and U.S. Highway 65 crossed the south end of the siding. The 18' x 72' depot, built in 1902 with a long cinder platform, still stands today after being used as a church, a school, and a feed store. It was then abandoned and sat unused for more than a decade, still sitting on its original site next to U.S. Highway 65.

Before being restored, the St. Joe depot served many uses. The author remembers the building as being across the highway from what was the bus station, and saw it often during the 1960s. Here the building sits abandoned in December 1982. Photo by Barton Jennings.

The building was placed on the National Register of Historic Places on August 11, 1993, and then bought by the City of St. Joe in 2009. After several years of work, the wooden depot was restored to a like-new look. The south end of the depot included the freight house while the north end included the ticket office and waiting room. For years, the depot used "J" as its telegraph call.

The St. Joe depot has been restored on its original location, and features the colorful paint scheme of a typical station along the line. Photo by Barton Jennings.

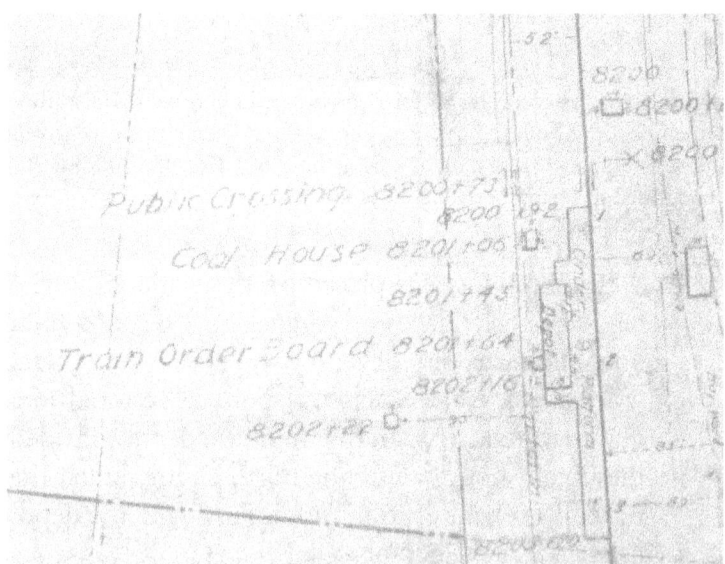

This part of the St. Joe Valuation Map shows the depot area. Note the coal house and the long cinder platform that was once here. Courtesy Boone County Historical & Railroad Society.

Because of the mining in the area, the railroad had several ore docks at St. Joe, with at least one retired in 1926. There was a 50-foot freight house just north of U.S. 65, and a 112-foot-long freight dock to the south, both on the west side of the siding. Further south was once an oil tank and ore bins. At one time there was a sawmill just west of these buildings, supported by a spur track.

There are several conflicting stories about the history and naming of St. Joe. The stories generally agree that the first settlers arrived about 1860, living on several area farms. Apparently, some mining was going on by the late 1800s. One story from this era says that the name St. Joe came about because a number of miners from St. Joseph, Missouri, were working the area in 1900. However, the post office opened in 1877, claiming a similar reason for the name. There are also reports that an early name for the area was Monkey Run.

The arrival of the railroad in 1902 helped the mining in the area prosper, and the town to grow. Almost immediately, St. Joe was incorporated. The railroad allowed the lead and zinc mines to ship out their ore, and the population boomed to almost 1000 miners. Mines such as *Davy Crockett*, *Excelsior*, *Lucky Dog*, and *Mercer* operated in the area. The newspaper *Mountain Wave* reported on the activity, stating in 1904: "There is a great deal of mining talk going on here. St. Joe is situated in the heart of some of the best mineral land to be found in the North Arkansas zinc fields....and it will not be long until her fame as a great mining center will be known throughout the world."

Besides the lead and zinc, limestone was also a major source of business in the area. Located not far west of St. Joe was the St. Joe Lime and Crushed Rock Company. The company produced both crushed limestone and fine lime, again shipped by rail. The company was later shown to be the Moss DeVoy Lime & Stone Company.

During the late 1910s, St. Joe was the location of at least four stores, a grist mill, several hotels, a blacksmith, several cafes, a bank, and a number of other typical businesses. The population peaked at a reported 2300 residents during this time. World War I greatly increased the price of lead and zinc and the mines boomed, even with a shortage of labor. However, the prices dropped greatly after the war and the mines closed, no longer able to turn a profit due to the unique way the ore was concentrated in deposits and not in ore veins.

After World War I, business changed from mining to timber, and in 1921 there were lumber mills being operated by W. E. Brown, F. E. Crank, J. J. Miller, J. A. Rogers, L. H. Wall, and Calvin Williams. The town and the railroad also handled cattle, cotton, and other farm produce. Eventually, the town let its incorporation drop and most of the original buildings were torn down or allowed to fall down. During the late 1990s, St. Joe attempted to re-incorporate but its population was too small to legally do so. Therefore, the community simply reactivated the original charter for the first St. Joe, which was located a short distance away from the railroad station and later downtown area.

Today, there is little business at St. Joe besides a gas station and convenience store, a post office, and the St. Joe Public Schools complex. Ozark Timber and a few small hotels are located nearby. Tourism from the nearby Buffalo River has also helped the area. In 2010, the population was 132, but the community is slowly growing. Today, St. Joe is one of thirteen communities that are part of the Ozark Byways, a program that promotes small towns in the north central Arkansas region.

160.0 DUFF – Duff was located where the railroad grade that follows Dry Creek junctions with Arkansas Highway 333 near Zion's Light Baptist Church, several miles north of Gilbert. However, it was never an official station on the railroad. The county history states that the first flour mill in Searcy County was established by Billie Mays and Reden Baker on Dry Creek at Duff in 1887. The mill processed both wheat (19,960 bushels) and corn (5227 bushels) according to an 1898 report. A post office opened at Duff in 1890, but it closed in 1905 when William Mays moved his store and the post office to the nearby railroad town of Gilbert. While the railroad passed close to Duff, there is little evidence to show that any tracks were built to serve local shippers.

In the 1922 report of the Arkansas Commission of Mines, Manufactures and Agriculture entitled *Minerals in Arkansas*, several reports were made about Duff. One covered the Cason shale outcrops at Duff, which also contained manganese and iron minerals. The second material reported on was Brassfield limestone. This limestone was noted for its fossils as well as its gluconite (an iron potassium phyllosilicate) content.

160.6 DRY CREEK BRIDGE – Immediately to the north of Arkansas Highway 333 are two 40-foot through plate girder spans that the railroad once used to cross Dry Creek. The spans still sit on their original concrete piers, and were acquired in 1901. The plate girder spans were noted in Missouri & North Arkansas records as being "half through girder spans," meaning that the track was about the middle of the span as opposed to either riding on its top or bottom cross members. Bridge records show that the bridge also had a two-panel pile timber trestle on the north approach and a three-panel pile timber trestle on its south approach.

The Dry Creek Bridge is easily seen from Arkansas Highway 333, and has long been an attraction for those who follow the railroad. Photo by Barton Jennings.

Dry Creek drains the hillsides to the north. It gets its name because the stream often goes underground for long distances. Much of this underground water surfaces again as Gilbert Springs, once the water source for the M&NA water tank at Gilbert.

161.7 GILBERT – Welcome to the "coolest town in Arkansas" as recognized by the National Weather Service. The town is known for often having the coolest temperatures in Arkansas, summer and winter. This area was homesteaded soon after the Civil War by William S. and Agnes Jane Moore. In 1885, the homestead was sold to Thomas and Alpha G. Vinson. Gilbert came about when the railroad built through the area and the land was sold to W. S. Mays about 1900. With the survey completed, the town of Gilbert was announced and businesses began moving to the area. One of the first was the Mays General Store, built by Billy Mays in 1901, with a second building added in 1906. The store was sold to Buck Mays and Tom Mite during the 1920s, but became the Baker's Country Store in 1926 when W. Riley Baker bought it. By 1950, it was the only business in the community, and it also began to house the post office. In 1979, the store was sold to Mike Mills who renamed it the Gilbert General Store. With the creation of the Buffalo National River, Gilbert became a tourism center and the general store still sells groceries and other supplies, and is also the home of Buffalo Camping and Canoeing. The building was added to the National Register of Historic Places in 1983.

The Gilbert General Store is still a major attraction and is a regular stop for many who are floating the nearby Buffalo River. Photo by Barton Jennings.

A series of historical markers stand next to the Gilbert General Store, many of which focus on the railroad, such as this one. Photo by Barton Jennings.

The town of Gilbert, shown as Buffalo in some early documents, was founded in 1902 as a railroad construction camp, and there was once a wye track here to turn trains. The name honored Charles W. Gilbert, secretary-treasurer of Allegheny Improvement Company, which was building the railroad for the Missouri & North Arkansas. Over the years, Gilbert also held a number of positions with the railroad. Crews stayed here for many months as the construction of the nearby Buffalo River bridge was a bigger project than was planned for. The railroad was completed to Gilbert on December 1, 1902, and an 18' x 52' depot with no center waiting room, and a 24' x 40' section house, were quickly built. There was a standard 16' x 24' wooden 50,000-gallon water tank, supported by a pump house acquiring water from Gilbert Spring, on the river side of the mainline, with a 25-car siding to the east. There were also several section tool houses at Gilbert, and an ore dock that lasted until 1926. A post office opened in 1903. Records show that a new 24' x 40' frame depot was built in 1917.

The footings of the M&NA water tower still stand near Gilbert. They can be found by walking a short distance along the Old Railroad Trail at Gilbert. Photo by Barton Jennings.

Gilbert became a trade center, with timber and ore major sources of area revenues. Business reports for Arkansas stated that Gilbert was a shipping point for lead, zinc, cotton and timber. Area history states that there was a cedar slat mill, a stave mill, several storage yards for stave bolts and railroad ties, cattle pens, a cotton gin, a grist mill and a flour mill, two hotels, several general stores, a grocery store, and a saloon.

Starting in 1920, Gilbert was the destination for a colony of the Christian Church (Disciples of Christ) from Illinois. Preacher John A. Battenfield had claimed that he had discovered secrets within the Hebrew text of the Old Testament that told him that soon a great war would be fought between Catholics and Protestants and that the world would end about 1923. Soon, World War I began and he obtained a number of followers who went with him to prepare for the great event. A small religious school was started, preaching the utopian visions of Battenfield. However, his belief that all possessions belonged to his church, and the failure of the world to end, cost Battenfield much of his credibility. To save things, he announced that he could return life to a dead person. A 1925 attempt failed and then he suffered a reported nervous breakdown and moved away. Soon most of his followers did the same thing.

The population of Gilbert peaked about 1930 with 116 residents. With the closing of area mines, the end of most of the timber business, and finally the railroad, most of the other residents also left Gilbert by the late 1940s. The railroad sold its depot in 1945 and replaced it with a simple shelter made from timbers from the fire-damaged backshop at Harrison. By 1950, the population was down to 51. Although the welcome sign says the population is 33, the 2010 census found a population of 28. With the creation of the Buffalo National River, Gilbert became the only private property on the river. Today it is a popular tourist destination with guest houses and cabins for rent, and camping facilities. It is also a popular float origin or destination, and a fishing center.

The creation of the Buffalo National River suddenly put Gilbert back in the spotlight, making it a busy place much of the year. Photo by Barton Jennings.

Gilbert Old Railroad Trail

The railroad grade from Gilbert to the remains of the Missouri & North Arkansas bridge over the Buffalo River is now the Old Railroad Trail. The trail begins between the historic Gilbert General Store and the river, and heads 1.7 miles to the northeast using the former grade of the railroad. Much of this route is on a narrow grade cut into the bluffs along the river. A few of the highlights of the trail are the former water tower footings less than 100 yards onto the trail, a series of cliffs above the grade, the remains of a large timber trestle and several stone culverts near Stilltown, terrific views of the Buffalo River, and the Buffalo River Bridge piers.

The Gilbert Old Railroad Trail is often on a cut ledge above the Buffalo River, and often features bluffs such as these. Photo by Barton Jennings.

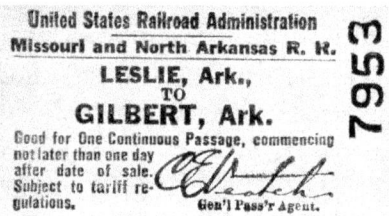

United States Railroad Administration / Missouri and North Arkansas R. R. ticket for passage from Leslie, Arkansas, to Gilbert, Arkansas. From the collection of Barton Jennings.

162.8 STILLTOWN – During the 1920s, there was a 7-car spur track here to serve a sawmill known as Stilltown, or Still. There were also a few company houses and a store for the workers. The railroad's 1928 annual report stated that the spur track was retired that year. The location can be found as a rare open and flat location between Gilbert and the Buffalo River.

Harrison (AR) to Heber Springs (AR)

The Stilltown area features some of the most beautiful stonework along the railroad. This stone culvert is hard to find, but it is a part of an extensive drainage system that also includes a cave under the railroad grade. Watch your step exploring in this area as a single slip can result in a long fall. Photo by Barton Jennings.

This culvert can be found where the Old Railroad Trail crosses a small stream. Nearby are the remains of a timber trestle, along with the stone-lined earthen approaches. Photo by Barton Jennings.

163.5 BUFFALO RIVER BRIDGE – All that remains today are several tall concrete piers that once held the three 150-foot through truss spans built by the Wisconsin Bridge & Iron Company. The bridge also included one 90-foot deck plate girder span and curved timber approaches on each end. In particular, the northern end featured a tight loop as it approached the bridge. The bridge was listed as an overhead obstruction that would not clear a man riding on the top or side of a car, especially as freight cars got larger. It was also the southern-most bridge on the railroad built to the E-40 bridge rating; those further south were rated as E-50.

On July 16, 1909, a water level station was installed on the bridge to obtain data for use in studying water power and storage problems for the Buffalo River. The installation report stated that "Bear Creek is tributary to Buffalo River from the right bank about one-fourth mile above the station."

After the railroad was abandoned, the bridge was quickly removed. However, parts of it were not the original structure. About 11pm on February 19, 1929, the center span of the bridge collapsed under train #211 as it headed south from Harrison. The span took nine freight cars with it. To get the railroad back in service, a temporary timber trestle span was built, but it washed out five days later in a flood. Five days after that, work started on the new steel span. Today, all that remains are the tall concrete piers, piers that were completely covered by December 1982 flood waters.

Once the railroad crossed the Buffalo River, it began to climb up the Brush Creek watershed. There were several bridges built in this area, but 1927 records show that short steel bridges at Mileposts

165.6 and 165.9 were retired that year. The southern half of this climb can be driven into Zack.

A highlight of the Gilbert Old Railroad Trail is finding the former M&NA bridge piers where the railroad crossed the Buffalo River. Several piers stand in the open in the river, while others are buried in vegetation on the hillsides along the river. Photo by Barton Jennings.

167.2 ZACK – Zack was an old mountain community that grew when the railroad built through it in 1903. With the railroad, Zack became a shipping point for wood products such as cross ties, bolts, staves, and lumber. It also became a fruit and vegetable center, especially for apples and strawberries. For a number of years, the Flintrock Strawberry Association was based here. Blowing Cave, located across Brush Creek from the Zack passenger shelter, was turned into a storage facility to hold the fruit. To move the fruit to the railroad, a tramway was built from the cave to the railway siding.

Zack was also a shipping point for lead and zinc ore, with some early newspaper articles stating that as many as 100 ore wagons a day were unloaded at the depot. There was also a canning factory, a grist mill, and several stores. With all of the activity, a post office opened in 1907. Reportedly the original name was to be Zif. The name Hensley Switch was also used locally for the community, a name also used for nearby Hensley Hollow, both named for the local Hensley family. The railroad also showed the station as Hensley in 1907. The post office closed in 1955. A few houses still exist at Zack, located at the junction of Zack Road and County Road 416.

The railroad had a 13-car siding to the east at Zack, with the 12' x 38' passenger shelter on the west side of the mainline. A mail crane was also located here, to the west about 100 feet north of the shelter. For a number of years, there was a railroad dam on the creek to be used by a watering station. The railroad also had a gravel pit in this area.

The bridge at Milepost 167.4 was one of several destroyed during the strike of 1922-1923. It was burned on January 10, 1923.

168.8 GRAVEL PIT – This gravel pit was used for track ballast and other projects. The railroad often assigned their steam shovel (X3) to this pit to mine the gravel and load railroad cars.

170.9 JAMESON – Jameson was short spur track in the 1920s, located to the west of the mainline, that was later extended as a 41-car siding in 1929. John Jamison and his family settled in the area during the

1830s, building a home at the mouth of the Jamison branch of the Buffalo River. During the late 1800s, the Jameson family located in the St. Joe area and was involved with mining. Some records show that the two families were related, but spelling their names differently.

172.7 MARSHALL – Marshall, station "MR", dates back to the need for a county seat for the new Searcy County. The Arkansas State Legislature approved the location of the new town on December 31, 1856, located about five miles east of the old county seat of Lebanon. The town was named Burrowsville after Napoleon Bonaparte Burrow, a planter and politician from near Van Buren in Crawford County. Eleven acres was bought from George and Rachel Norman for five dollars to obtain the land, and a community immediately began. On July 21, 1857, the nearby post office of Lebanon (opened in 1840) was moved to Burrowsville.

The Civil War essentially destroyed Burrowsville, especially since the Confederate Nitre & Mining Bureau produced niter for gunpowder in the area. Both Confederate and Union forces destroyed the town, built their own structures, and then destroyed them again. After the war, Union supporters wanted to celebrate the victory by changing the town's name to Marshall, named for U.S. Chief Justice John Marshall, a change approved on March 18, 1867. The post office changed its name at the same time.

Marshall began to rebuild over the next several decades, and the City of Marshall was incorporated in 1884. A new Searcy County courthouse was built in 1889, making it today one of the oldest active courthouses in Arkansas. The courthouse was placed on the National Register of Historic Places in 1976. Marshall was on the edge of the mining boom, but survived primarily on the timber industry and by being a supply town for area farmers. Things improved when the St. Louis & North Arkansas Railway Company built through town, and some industry was able to locate here to serve markets across the country.

In 1909, the Cincinnati Cooperage Company established Marshall's first stave mill. According to the *Arkansas Marketing and Industrial Guide* of 1921, there were a number of small firms here. Lumber led the list with hardwood firms operated by Charles T. Anderson, E. E. Bookmiller, L. W. Fields & Son, J. T. Karnes, Frank Regmier, and D. W. Salyer. There was also the H. C. Fields Lumber Company, the A. L. Hayes Company (tight barrel staves), and A. Peltz (brooms). Additionally, Charles H. Anderson manufactured brick, and there was the Duff Milling Company and the Marshall Roller Mill. By 1944, there were Cities Service Oil Company, J. A. Karnes Stave Mill, Marshall Canning, Midland Tie and Timber, Moss Tie and Timber, and Standard Oil. Today, the primary industries at Marshall are timber processing, cattle and tourism. Marshall also attracts crowds on weekends due to the Kenda Drive-In theater, which opened in 1966. Marshall is not large, and its population was 1355 in the 2010 census.

As was done in many communities, the residents of Marshall campaigned to have the railroad pass through their town. To help with this, $2000 was raised to help pay for a railroad station. Construction to Marshall was delayed by work on the Buffalo River bridge, but the railroad reached Marshall on August 3, 1903, and there was a large celebration held at the depot location when the first train arrived. In 1936, Marshall was served by daily #211 and #212 in the middle of the night. Freight #211 was scheduled to depart at 10:22pm while #212 departed at 1245am. By the 1940s, Marshall had a 16-car siding to the west of the mainline, with the depot on the east side near the siding's north switch. West of the siding was a spur track that served the Standard Oil terminal.

The depot was originally located just north of the intersection of Arkansas Highway 27 and East Main Street. The railroad crossed Highway 27 here and then turned to the northeast, closely followed by today's highway. After the railroad was shut down, the building was remodeled as a house. In 1982, the depot was moved closer to the highway and used as a store. By 2002, the depot was moved further to the northeast along the highway and was restored. Unfortunately, the former M&NA depot burned down August 6, 2005, reportedly from a lightning strike. The station was described as a Standard #2 building that measured 18' x 72'.

Many of the M&NA stations were sold over the years for other uses. The Marshall station, shown here in 1987, was used as a home and later as a business before it burned in 2005. Photo by Barton Jennings.

The Railroad Grade to and from Marshall

From the Buffalo River, the railroad used a grade up Brush Creek, some of which is now Zack Road, County Road 46. The railroad was heading south as it arrived at Marshall. The old grade passes just west of the Searcy County Civic Center and curves east near the north end of the Marshall High School football field. The grade is north of U.S. Highway 65, with parts used by Duvall Street, Ruff Street, and Fair Street.

To head south from Marshall, railroad surveyors found a series of hills. This required the railroad to loop to the northeast around Devil's Backbone Mountain through what was known as Gap of the Mountain. For the railroad, this summit was at 1199 feet, with grades up to 1.75% in each direction. From the north, the grade started at the Buffalo River near Gilbert. From the south, the climb essentially began at Helena, with the steep grades starting near Heber Springs.

The grade from Marshall to Baker and on to Leslie can essentially be driven. Take Arkansas Highway 27 north and then turn east to Baker on Arkansas Highway 74. At Baker, turn south on Rail Road, Searcy County Road 54, and follow it toward Leslie. Rail Road basically uses the former railroad grade until Rail Road curves sharply to the east to meet County Road 74. Here, the railroad grade curves across the field and stays just to the west of Main Street into Leslie.

Harrison (AR) to Heber Springs (AR)

Most of the old grade between Baker and Leslie can be driven as it serves as Rail Road. The road is gravel and passes through a number of small farms. Photo by Barton Jennings.

174.9 BAKER – While the grade through Baker was a regular travel route through the area known as the Gap of the Mountain, the town wasn't founded until the St. Louis & North Arkansas Railway Company built through the gap in 1902. The June 9, 1907, railroad timetable showed a station with the name Williams near here, which included a 13-car track. In 1907, an application for a post office with the name Saratoga was rejected by the United States Postal Service, which substituted the name of Baker. The name Low Gap was also suggested. The name Baker was very common in Searcy County. Littleton Baker was one of the three commissioners appointed in 1856 to select the new county seat for Searcy County. Some of the Baker family were part of an 1857 wagon trail heading to California that was massacred by Mormons at Mountain Meadow, Utah. Seventeen children survived, including Twittie Baker who moved back to Searcy County and lived in Leslie. John Baker built a store in the county in 1878 that was operated by his brother Asa, one of a chain of Baker Brothers Stores in northern Arkansas. Finally, Reden Baker built the first flour mill in Searcy County.

At its peak, Baker included eight stores, a grist mill, and a blacksmith shop. Baker was reportedly the largest timber shipping point in the county next to Leslie. The railroad had a short 9-car siding to the east and passenger trains stopped when flagged. The Baker passenger shelter was also to the east, and just north of the siding. The original shelter was retired and replaced in 1926. A mail crane existed for the life of the railroad on the west side of the tracks across from the station platform. The post office closed in 1955 and mail service was moved to Marshall.

175.7 **WILLIAMS SIDING** – This was a short 13-car siding located near the top of the grade, and used to hold cars when trains doubled the hill.

177.7 **COVE** – The location of this M&NA station was believed to be just south of the intersection with today's Grape Vine Road. Cove was likely named for Wiley's Cove, the valley that was the home of Chief Wiley. In 1907, there was a 5-car track in this area named Bryant. The railroad reportedly had few facilities here, but the location is shown on early railroad documents. There are some reports that the railroad once had a small building here that housed a telegraph key. The key was used by crews to alert the dispatcher that they had reached the top of the grade, and to receive permission for helpers that needed to drop back down the grade. It was also a flag stop during the 1920s.

Harrison (AR) to Heber Springs (AR)

Heading south, the railroad angled to the southeast, but looped around Brushy Mountain before again heading southeast to Leslie. The railroad crossed a number of small streams that flowed off the hills to the east and into Trace Creek, located just to the west. One of these bridges, located at Milepost 178.0, was burned on January 10, 1923, during the infamous M&NA railroad strike.

181.3 LESLIE SHOPS – Grading of the St. Louis & North Arkansas Railway Company reached Leslie during early 1903, and the line was completed and regular service begun on September 11, 1903. Leslie was the end of track for several years, making it an important location. Until the new Leslie station was built in 1913, this location was the base of operations at Leslie. It was also the area where the cooperage firms built their mills. The railroad ended here for several years, and a three-stall engine shed, shop building, yard tracks, stock pens and a wye were built. There was also a standard 16' x 24' wooden 50,000-gallon water tank with the water coming from nearby Cove Creek.

The intersection of Ice Plant Road and Rail Road marks the location where the railroad approached the original cooperage area of Leslie from the north. Heading south, the road soon leaves the grade of the railroad as it once cut across what is today pasture. Photo by Barton Jennings.

Over the years, the Missouri & North Arkansas actually had two groups of tracks at Leslie. To the north of Begley Creek were the original tracks, with a wye to the east, along with several sidings and spur tracks that served the cooperage plants. In the yard area, there were three yard tracks to the east of the mainline, plus two locomotive service tracks that featured a coal dock and cinder pit. Further to the east was the wye track. To the west of the mainline was a short scale track plus a long spur track that served the stock pens. There was also a spur track that served the Lenker Hub Mill and an ice plant near Begley Creek.

A wooden depot was initially built near the other facilities at the wye. For awhile, the railroad also used two passenger cars as offices at Leslie. Photos from September 1913 show the two cars with roofs added being used as the "Superintendents Office" as well as the "Western Union Telegraph and Cable Office." It is believed that these cars were retired when the new stone depot opened in 1913 to the south. The shops also closed about this time when the new shops at Harrison opened.

Maps from 1910 show that the cooperage plant was east of the railroad at the end of the wye track. To the west of the mainline was "Dink Town" and the mill's housing. Some maps show the community as the "Chandler-Griffin Addition." The "H. D. Williams Tram Line" is shown as crossing the M&NA cooperage track just east of the wye, then looping along the south leg of the wye before turning to the west. It then crossed the M&NA mainline about 500 feet north of the Begley Creek bridge, passed through Dink Town and bridged over Cove Creek, before climbing into the hills to the west.

H. D. Williams Cooperage Company

Heading from Joplin to Helena, H. D. Williams Cooperage was the first of three major lumber companies that operated on and along the Missouri & North Arkansas. Along with the Doniphan Lumber Company and the Chicago Mill & Lumber Company, these companies provided a great deal of business and revenue for the first several decades of the railroad.

The H. D. Williams Cooperage Company operated first in Poplar Bluff, Missouri, but moved to Leslie in 1906 after acquiring large tracts of timber and the plant of the Leslie Stave Company. Timber was an issue for the company as after 21 years in southeast Missouri, the company was out of wood that could be used in their products. At Leslie, the company located a stave and barrel plant, plus a large outdoor timber storage yard, on sixty-eight acres. The new plant was quickly proclaimed the largest of its kind in the world.

The primary product of the H. D. Williams Cooperage operation was white oak whiskey barrels. At its peak, the company produced 3000 to 5000 barrels daily, shipping them across the country, with many even going to Europe for the storage and aging of wine. Many of the barrels were manufactured to order, with sizes ranging from 160 gallons to as little as one gallon. Many of these were built for specific products such as whiskey, wine, brandy and other alcoholic beverages, while others were used for products like crude oil, cotton seed oil, lard, and other similar products. Many of the smaller kegs were used for fruit and vegetable packing.

Many of the staves (individual barrel boards) were shipped unassembled to their buyers to save on shipping charges. However, the Missouri & North Arkansas still moved many carloads of assembled barrels. Timber that was not suitable for the production of staves was still used by the company. Other products such as telephone or telegraph pins and brackets, table stock for furniture, wagon hubs, and many other smaller products were made from these timbers. Scraps were even used for dunnage, bracing, and even to fire boilers at the mill. Little was allowed to go to waste.

Williams Cooperage Logging Railroad

To provide the timber, the company bought from timber companies all along the railroad. Many early railroad stations were created based upon this business. The company also controlled 130,000 acres of trees to the south and west of Leslie. To reach the timber, the cooperage company built a standard-gauge logging railroad, known by some as the Leslie, Mountaintop & Southwestern. The line headed west from the cooperage, crossed the M&NA and Cove Creek, and followed the watershed up Nubbin Hill Mountain. Once across the ridge, the line dropped down to the Middle Fork Little Red River and followed it upstream for many miles. A logging community was built at the end of the railroad at a place that became known as "End of the Line." There, a company store, a boarding house and other facilities existed until the 1920s when the timber was gone and the mills closed.

A number of logging camps and "green mills" were spread throughout the hills, and a reported

1200 men and more than 300 teams of mules and horses were kept busy handling the timber. At its peak, almost 20 miles of logging railroad was being operated, many with steep grades through the mountains. To operate the railroad, the company had several Shay locomotives as well as a traditional locomotive to switch the yard. Records indicate that the Missouri & North Arkansas rented locomotives to the cooperage company to handle this switching and to move cars along the valley routes.

The first Shay locomotive arrived on a Missouri & North Arkansas flatcar on November 4, 1906. Reportedly, a second locomotive arrived just before Thanksgiving. The first locomotive was a 2-truck, 20-ton Shay built in October 1906 under construction number 1791. It was named "H. D. Williams" and assigned #1. It was built to burn wood but was later rebuilt to burn coal. The Shay was sold to the Export Cooperage Company as their #1 in 1915. It then went to the Southern Iron & Equipment Company as their #1559, which almost immediately sold it to the Scotland Lumber Company in Ravenswood, Louisiana, as their #1. It then went to R. J. Hackney Lumber Company at Ravenswood before being scrapped in late 1926.

Another Shay locomotive built for the company was construction number 2319, built in May 1910. This was a larger locomotive, rated at 32 tons but still with two trucks. Like #1, the locomotive was sold to the Export Cooperage Company. It was shown to be for sale by the mid-1920s and was eventually scrapped.

For those who don't know, a Shay locomotive is a slow speed geared locomotive, the most widely used geared steam locomotive. Logger Ephraim Shay designed the locomotive in the late 1870s and then Lima Locomotive Works of Lima, Ohio, built the locomotives. An estimated 2770 Shay locomotives were built by Lima between 1878 and 1945, weighing as little as 6 tons and as much as 160 tons. Those of Williams Cooperage were on the small size, but were very typical for the era.

A third Williams Cooperage locomotive was an old 4-4-0 that had started as a 6-foot-gauge locomotive on the New York, Pennsylvania & Ohio, a part of the Erie Railroad. It was reportedly built in March 1882 and rebuilt in September 1896. The locomotive was sold to the Cotton Belt as their #153. H. D. Williams acquired it as their #2 during April 1909. This small locomotive was used around the yard where timber was seasoned and stored until needed.

Dink Town and the Cooperage Industry

The cooperage plant was on the north side of Leslie. Besides the plant and storage yard, the company also had about 60 homes for its employees and their families. A unique part of what became known as "Dink Town" was its large black population, which had followed the stave mill from Poplar Bluff. At the time, there were as many as four stave mills, plus a number of sawmills, at Leslie. These began to consolidate by 1909. In the July 1, 1909, issue of *The Lumber Trade Journal*, an article covered the closure of one of these. "The Rice-Brown Lumber Company is dismantling its sawmill at Leslie and will ship the machinery to Higdon, where it will extend the manufacturing of yellow leaf pine. The company will quit the manufacture of hardwood lumber at Leslie and has sold to the Williams Cooperage Company

100,000 feet of white oak logs in its yards there. The company will maintain its wholesale and retail yards at Leslie. O. D. Curie will continue as local manager."

The H. D. Williams Cooperage Company mill only operated six years before a fire on November 26, 1912, burned most of the complex, leaving only the company office building and boiler house. A much smaller plant was built in 1913, but the company declared bankruptcy in 1915. The company was sold at auction by court order on March 9, 1916, with the Mississippi Valley Trust Company of St. Louis buying it for a reported $243,000. The Mississippi Valley Trust Company was the firm that forced the cooperage company into bankruptcy on October 1, 1915. On April 6, 1916, the Export Cooperage Company of Leslie was incorporated to acquire and operate the assets. With this, operations continued, despite the 18th Amendment to the U.S. Constitution (1919) which started Prohibition. The Export Cooperage Company closed in 1923, as did many of the other Leslie firms, and almost 1000 workers lost their jobs. The situation became so bad that the Red Cross was called in to help feed the children of the former workers. Various reports state that the logging line was gone by 1926.

181.5 BEGLEY CREEK BRIDGE – This stream was the dividing line between the cooperage industry to the north and the town of Leslie to the south. The stream was originally known as Begley's Creek and was named for early settlers Henry and John Begley. The railroad bridge consisted of two 30-foot deck plate girder spans mounted on concrete piers. The north approach included three timber spans and the south approach had seven timber spans.

181.7 LESLIE – Even as white settlers arrived in the area, this valley was still the home of a number of Indian families. This area was the home of Chief Wiley, and the area became known as Wiley's Cove. Samuel Leslie settled in the area in 1838, bringing with him his family and several slaves to operate a farm. He also opened a store and trading post. The small isolated community served the region and received a post office in 1842. Settlers cleared the land in the valley and operated farms, but the rough surrounding hills remained mostly untouched. On November 9, 1887, the post office changed its name to Leslie at the request of Andrew Jackson Leslie, the son of Samuel Leslie.

As the St. Louis & North Arkansas Railway was building south, Leslie was still a village of only several houses and a single store. However, when construction stopped here in 1903, the town began to boom, especially as timber companies discovered the white oak and other timber in the surrounding hills. The first stave mill opened at Leslie in 1903, and soon what was billed as the largest stave mill in the world was located here. A. L. Barnett, the Leslie Stave & Heading Company, J. C. Myers Lumber, and Peken Cooperage also soon had facilities. About 1910, Ed Mays established the Mays Manufacturing Company in Leslie and began producing barrel staves. Mays also supported the construction of the first electric light plant and ice plant in Leslie.

Another major industry in the area was fruit, led by the Elberta Fruit Farm. By the early 1900s, the farm had more than 11,000 fruit trees with an announced plan to plant 6000 more in 1905. Elberta Fruit produced many of their own trees, having created a hardy stock that reportedly grew straight and could handle the winds and weather conditions of the area. This and other area farms supported several canning plants, including the Derickson Canning, Creamery & Cold Storage Company at Leslie.

As the land was cleared, farming became a larger source of income for locals. Cotton, corn and even wheat was grown locally. This led to the construction of the Leslie Roller Mill, a 3-story, wood-frame roller mill built in 1910. The mill specialized in processing locally-grown wheat. The building survived until 2004 when it was destroyed by a severe storm. Farming and grazing is still popular in the area. During the 1950s, Leslie was recognized as the "Whittling Capital of the World" and today it is known for its weekend country music shows. In 2010, the population was 441, and in 2017, much of the downtown area was designated as the Leslie Commercial District and listed on the National Register of Historic Places.

The Missouri & North Arkansas Railroad

A wooden depot was initially built near the other facilities north of Begley Creek, but it was replaced with a nicer 22' x 100' cut-stone station downtown in 1913 as a gift to the community after the shops were closed and moved to Harrison. The stone reportedly came from the quarry near Smith Hollow, west of Eureka Springs. At the depot was a 16-car siding that wrapped around the building on the east side of the mainline. Further south was a 40-car siding to the east, as well as several spur tracks. The railroad also had a "Roadmaster's House" and a tool shed in this area. Leslie was served in the middle of the night by freights #211 and #212. #211 was scheduled to pass

Leslie at 11:15pm, and #212 had a schedule of being at Leslie at 12:01am.

The stone station still stands just south of Oak Street, also known as Arkansas Highway 66, as a part of the Derickson Lumber Company complex. The structure was listed on the National Register of Historic Places in 1992, which states that the station "is the only tangible evidence of the railroad remaining in Leslie." For many years, the tracks ran just to the west of the depot and passenger trains stopped so passengers could eat in the café that was located in the north end of the building. The telegraph call for Leslie was "K" and an agent lasted here until the end of the railroad, using the square bay window on the track side. Since the closure of the railroad, the station has been used as storage for the lumber yard, but some original windows and doors, as well as some of the interior details reportedly remain. Across the tracks to the west of the Leslie station was the Derickson Canning, Creamery & Cold Storage Company. Today, Derickson Lumber owns the stone station and the land around it.

Heading south from Leslie, the railroad stayed to the east of Cove Creek to near where it flows into the Middle Fork Little Red River, squeezing between Chicken Wilson Knob to the west and a series of ridges to the east. The railroad then followed the east bank before crossing the Middle Fork and swinging east.

The Leslie depot is often surrounded by building materials, but is clear for a photo in December 1982. This station was built of stone as a consolation gift to the community after the railroad shops were closed and moved to Harrison. Photo by Barton Jennings.

184.4 NOAHS – Also known as Noah or Noah's, there was a 9-car siding here. The location apparently was never a stop for passenger trains, but was used by local timber cutters to move their cuttings to area mills.

185.3 COUNTY LINE – Heading south, the railroad crossed from **Searcy County** into **Van Buren County**. **Van Buren County** was created on November 11, 1833, from parts of Conway, Independence and Izard counties. It was named for Martin Van Buren, who was Vice President at the time of the county's formation, and later President of the United States. Parts of Van Buren County were later used to create Stone County (1873) and Cleburne County (1883). The county seat is Clinton, southwest of Shirley, and the county has a population of approximately 17,000.

185.4 MIDDLE FORK LITTLE RED RIVER BRIDGE – Just south of the county line the railroad curved east, crossed the Middle Fork Little Red River, and then curved back to the northeast to follow a bend in the river. In doing so, it crossed back in to Searcy County. The river starts just north of Una, Arkansas, in very northwest Van Buren County. It flows north and then east, collecting a large number of small streams as it winds between hilltops. The Middle Fork is seldom straight as it heads east along the county line between Searcy and Van Buren Counties, and then Stone and Van Buren Counties. The river eventually flows into Greers Ferry Lake in Cleburne County.

The Middle Fork is one of three forks that eventually join to create the Little Red River. The South Fork actually starts just on the other side of a ridge from where the Middle Fork begins. The South Fork flows into Greers Ferry Lake near Clinton. The third fork is known as Devils Fork. The Devils Fork starts in northeastern Cleburne County and flows to the southwest to Ida where it enters Greers Ferry Lake.

The railroad bridge is gone, but the four piers still stand. This bridge consisted of 190 feet of deck plate girder (DPG) spans built by the Wisconsin Bridge & Iron Company. Specifically, the bridge included a 50-foot DPG, a 90-foot DPG, a 50-foot DPG, and then a number of timber spans on the south end. It can be glimpsed from Rumley Road, especially in winter.

185.5 COUNTY LINE – The railroad has crossed the Middle Fork (MP 185.4) and curved back to the northeast, passing back into **Searcy County**. Much of the railroad grade in this area is used as Rumley Road, known as Van Buren County Road 86, and Searcy County Road 187. It connects with U.S. Highway 65 just south of the highway bridge over Peyton Creek.

186.4 COUNTY LINE – The Middle Fork curves back east and the railroad re-enters **Van Buren County**.

186.5 RUMLEY – Rumley is an unincorporated community that sits on the Searcy-Van Buren County Line. Some sources say that Rumley was founded in 1866 by Henry Rumley, and within a few years the town consisted of several houses and a small community store. By late 1906, the Allegheny Improvement Company was building the Missouri & North Arkansas line through the area. This gave a small boost to the community and a post office opened in 1907. For a while the post office was considered to be in Van Buren County, and then when the county line was adjusted in 1910, it was declared to be in Searcy County. The railroad had a mail crane to drop off and pick up mail. Before 1918, the mail crane was on the east side of the tracks about 160 feet north of the passenger shelter. Later it was moved to the west side of the tracks and about 150 feet south of the shelter.

Rumley had a passenger shelter on the west side of the mainline with a short 7-car spur track to the north. Apparently, business picked up at Rumley about 1931 as the passenger shelter had a freight room added that year. The employee timetable in 1936 showed that there was a 13-car siding at Rumley, and that freight trains #211 and #212 were scheduled to meet here at 11:32pm. For a number of years, the Bentley Brothers Lumber Mill operated here. Today, Rumley is simply a cluster of several country homes.

187.2 COUNTY LINE – The river and the railroad curve back north just past Rumley Hollow and pass back into **Searcy County**.

187.8 COUNTY LINE – The railroad continues to follow the Middle Fork Little Red River and turns back to the south to cross back into **Van Buren County**.

189.0 SHAIN – In *Missouri & Arkansas Railway Company Time Table No. 7*, dated February 25, 1945, Shain is listed as an additional flag stop for passenger trains. It is also stated that there were no side tracks at Shain, although in 1923 there was a six-car spur track here. The community of Shain dates to 1899 when William F. Shain moved to near Leslie and built a home. Shain also built a sawmill, which attracted the interest of the railroad. During construction of the Missouri & North Arkansas, William Shain rented space in his house to railroad workers. He had so much business that he soon built the Shain Hotel. The sawmill reportedly burned down about 1915, ending many of the local jobs. Most of the Shain family eventually moved away, and the hotel business went away. What remains at Shain is now private property.

Some speculate that Paul Henning, creator of television shows such as *Petticoat Junction*, *The Beverly Hillbillies*, and *Green Acres*, may have been influenced by the town of Shain and its hotel. Henning had traveled in the area when he was young, and there are some similarities between the Shady Rest Hotel from *Petticoat Junction* and the Shain Hotel.

However, no comments or records from Henning support this theory. Instead, it is probable that the hotel is based upon one at Eldon, Missouri, where his wife used to visit her grandparents and her female cousins. Paul Henning did credit the many visits to the mountains around Branson for many of his stories.

191.8 ELBA – Elba was located where Linn Creek and Half Moon Creek flow into the Middle Fork Little Red River. Today it is simply a few houses and farm buildings, plus the old hotel, but in 1920 it was the location of a number of lumber companies. The lumber mills included G. W. Bradley, J. N. Keeling, and J. W. Whillock. To the west is Styles Mountain and to the east is Half Moon Mountain.

A post office opened here in 1907 with the name Scullin, but it was changed to Elba in 1908. The post office closed in 1954. Daily passenger service using a mixed train reportedly began in February 1908, operated by the construction company. When the railroad officially opened, the 20' x 34' Elba depot was on the east side of the mainline near the north switch of a 21-car siding that was to the west of the mainline. There was a mail crane here during the late 1930s and early 1940s.

In the 1945 employee timetable, Elba was an important railroad station and siding. Trains were scheduled to meet here. In that timetable, northbound passenger train #2 was scheduled to meet local southbound freight #325 at 10:43am, while northbound freight #12 was scheduled to meet southbound freight #11 at 11:50pm. It is interesting that in the same timetable, Elba was not listed as a telegraph station, although it was shown as "BX" in the late 1920s. The station was retired and sold in 1945.

194.0 COUNTY LINE – Heading south, the railroad makes a loop to the north as the Middle Fork swings around Half Moon Mountain. There was essentially no straight track through this area and the grade dropped steadily, creating a challenge for northbound trains. At the end of Half Moon Mountain, the railroad passed from **Van Buren County** into **Stone County** as it headed east (railroad-south) at an elevation of 800 feet. The railroad continued to follow the Middle Fork through Arlberg and Lydalisk in Stone County.

Stone County was created from parts of Independence, Izard, Searcy, and Van Buren Counties on April 21, 1873. The county name comes from the many natural stone formations in the area. The county seat is Mountain View, the home of the Ozark Folk Center and Blanchard Springs Caverns, managed by the United States Forest Service. The county has seen a steady population growth thanks to a number of retirement and lake communities, and its population was 12,394 in the 2010 census.

196.5 BARNETT – Barnett was a timber town that began when the railroad built their line through the area. Reports indicate that timber was loaded here and shipped to the lumber mills and cooperage plant at Leslie, and elsewhere along the railroad. Barnett was located on the Middle Fork Little Red River near Cane Hollow at an elevation of 755 feet, giving the timber companies access to the dense forests on Half Moon Mountain. Later, coal was discovered and mined, although the mines soon flooded and coal never became a major business.

Barnett was never a large community with no mills and only a small general store. By 1945, Barnett was simply a flag stop with no side tracks and just a passenger platform. However, in 2006, a local resident built a new railroad depot based upon the railroad's "Standard #3" plans. The depot is known by some as Devil's Bend.

197.0 ORMOND – A 15-car track was built here in 1932. During the early 1930s, Ormond was a needed source of revenue for the railroad as the Ormond brothers operated a rock quarry that was selling stone to the federal government for bank stabilization on the Mississippi River. Some of the stone was also used for the new levees being built in response to the 1927 floods. The track was retired by late 1939.

In this area, the railroad again turned north to go south, looping around a corner of Half Moon Mountain. As the tracks turned back south, Sawmill Hollow was across the river to the north. Heading south, the river and the railroad passed between Half Moon Mountain to the west and Angora Mountain to the east.

201.0 ARLBERG – Coming in to Arlberg, the Missouri & North Arkansas passed through some of the most scenic territory in Arkansas. Winding along the Middle Fork Little Red River, the railroad was surrounded by tall mountains in what was called the "Colonnades of the Little Red River." Arlberg grew quickly with the arrival of the railroad as it became a loading point for railroad ties and other timbers. Much of this timber was shipped to the cooperage plant at Leslie, but Ham & Perkins was manufacturing chair stock here in 1921.

Arlberg predated the arrival of the railroad, and was actually one of the first towns settled in the region. Arlberg was located in a wide spot along the river where streams from Miller Hollow and Bane Hollow flow into the Middle Fork, with Angora Mountain to the north. Arlberg was initially a typical mountain town that supported the many mountain farms in the area. During the 1860s, the Arlberg area was the home of Bill Dark, reportedly a Confederate deserter and murderous felon. Dark routinely robbed locals until a home guard was formed to protect the local citizens. The legend states that Dark was eventually killed by fifteen-year-old Jim Berry, who Dark tried to rob at his home between Arlberg and Lydalisk. The story was covered in the 1953 article "Voice of the Hills" in the *Mountain View Herald*. Jimmy Driftwood (James Corbitt Morris) wrote the article and later recorded the song *The Ballad of Jim Berry* in 1972.

Jimmy Driftwood was an American folk music songwriter and musician from Arkansas who wrote more than 6000 folk songs, including *The Battle of New Orleans* and *Tennessee Stud*. In 1959, Driftwood had six songs on the popular and country music charts, and his song *The Battle of New Orleans* won the 1960 Grammy Award for Song of the Year. Driftwood, who regularly visited friends at Arlberg, also became involved in many Arkansas preservation issues. He campaigned to stop a proposed dam on the Buffalo River and helped with the effort to establish the Buffalo National River. He also helped to establish the Ozark Folk Center, preserve Blanchard Springs Caverns, and founded what became the

Arkansas Folk Festival, which attracts more than 100,000 people each year.

Things began to change at Arlberg in 1906 when the railroad arrived. Suddenly the timber business boomed and a canning factory opened. A post office opened in 1908, a school soon opened, and Arlberg became the largest town in Stone County. A number of farmers sold timber to agents operating out of Arlberg, and the railroad had several spur tracks where cars would be spotted for loading. The railroad agency closed in 1930.

During the 1930s, Arlberg was the home of the Arkansas Academy, an orphanage founded by James "Uncle Mac" MacKrell. MacKrell was a radio personality who was heavily involved in state politics, even running for governor twice. MacKrell first became famous for reading the Sunday morning comics on central Arkansas radio. He later created the evangelical radio program *Bible Lover's Revival* which was broadcast starting in 1938 and lasting for ten years. The orphanage moved from Arlberg to Mabelvale (near Little Rock) after flooding damaged the facility in the late 1930s.

The Great Depression and the cutting of most of the area timber hurt the community, but the floods of the late 1930s ended the future of Arlberg. The final blow was the abandonment of the railroad in the late 1940s. With most businesses and residents gone, the post office closed in 1955. The downtown area is now simply a square of dirt streets, a few houses, and a low-water bridge across the river on Angora Mountain Road. A few remains of the canning factory and the orphanage can still be found in the brush, and the footings of the old railroad water tower still stand.

At its peak, the railroad had a 38-car siding to the west with a Standard #3 22' x 40' depot on the east side of the mainline, next to the river. Until the late 1920s, Arlberg used the telegraph call of "RG". There were once several spur tracks for loading timber products and for delivering goods for the local stores. To water the steam locomotives pulling the trains, there was a standard 16' x 24' wooden 50,000-gallon tank. Water was pumped 1000 feet from the Little Red River. The railroad also had a track maintenance section based here and track inspectors to check for landslides were also commonly based here. Because of the long siding, trains often met here.

Heading south toward Helena, the railroad again turned north as it left Arlberg as the river looped around the north edge of Sally Flats Mountain, passing Moon Bluffs, a scenic highlight. Across the river from the point of the mountain is Meadow Creek, where there is now a small vineyard. This is the area where Jim Berry reportedly killed Bill Dark. This area was once full of small farms owned by families such as the Kenners, Godseys, Harpers, Smiths, and Bloodworms. Most of these valley farms raised corn and hogs. Parts of the railroad grade are still used as farm access roads.

202.6 BETTS – The spur track at Betts once held six cars, but it was retired in 1929. The Betts family has long lived in the Stone County area, and Grant Betts and his wife operated the Mountain Home Hotel in Arlberg for many years. Betts was not an official flag stop for passenger trains.

205.6 LOST CREEK BRIDGE – Lost Creek starts to the south in Van Buren County near Arkansas Highway 110. It flows north along the west side of Lute Mountain and east of the large plateau of Sally Flats, before entering the Middle Fork Little Red River here. The bridge included a 60-foot deck plate girder span which remains today.

205.9 LYDALISK – Located at the north end of Lute Mountain, Lydalisk was another mountain town created because of the timber industry. A post office opened on September 18, 1915, with the name Lydalisk, although the original name was to be Arnold, and the railroad actually used that name until the late 1910s. After the timber boom ended, the post office closed on May 29, 1937, with mail delivery moved to Arlberg. The railroad had a short 7-car spur track to the west with the switch on the north end. A mail crane was used until the post office closed.

The name Lydalisk reportedly comes from the name of the first postmaster, a Mr. Lisk, and the daughter of the first railroad agent, Lyda Thomas. Lydalisk is today a ghost town. Lute Mountain Road passes through the old town site and uses a low-water bridge to cross the Middle Fork. Parts of the old grade, now known as River Road, can be driven using four wheelers, a popular recreational activity in the area.

Heading south, Lute Mountain is to the west of the old railroad grade, while Harper Bluffs and Nubbin Ridge are to the east.

208.0 COUNTY LINE – The railroad grade is running north-south here, and trains heading towards Helena crossed back into **Van Buren County** where there is a large island in the river. Not far south of here is Kinder Slough, a flat area across the river to the east. Kinder Slough is an alluvial fan created by deposits from Tick Creek, Pour Off Hollow and Still Hollow, which drain the hills to the east.

210.3 OAKVALE – Oakvale was a 34-car siding to the west with a mail crane and passenger shelter until the late 1920s. The community was located where Bear Branch exits the mountains to the west and flows into the Middle Fork Little Red River. Across the river is Simkins Point which forces the river to make a tight bend. Post office records show that a post office was here 1916-1923. It was originally to be called Oak Vales; it was actually named Friehl. However, maps show it as Oakvale. Today the community is another railroad ghost town.

This part of the river is a popular floating destination because of the number of rapids. Just south of Oakvale is the Walter Diggs Rapid, a serious Class III hazard between high bluffs and a willow jungle. There is also a boulder garden in the river to make navigating difficult.

The north end of River Road from Shirley reaches just south of here. North of here, the road is gated. However, bicyclists and hikers are currently allowed, although there are clear warnings that this can end if any vandalism takes place. Heading south, the grade is often squeezed between the river to the east and the mountain to the west. Approaching Shirley, the rail grade crosses open pasture on a high fill once designed to keep the railroad above the flood waters of the Middle Fork Little Red River.

Harrison (AR) to Heber Springs (AR)

River Road ends at the former station of Oakvale, a former small community and railroad siding. Today this area is mostly trees with limited river access. Photo by Barton Jennings.

214.6 MIDDLE FORK LITTLE RED RIVER BRIDGE – This bridge is unique in that it still stands and is used as a highway bridge. It is now owned by Van Buren County and used by River Road, County Road 125, to cross the river and follow the old grade of the railroad north to Oakvale. The main span of the bridge is a Baltimore through truss set on large concrete piers, a modification of the Pratt truss development by the Pennsylvania Railroad in 1871. The 154-foot main span was built in 1908 by the Wisconsin Bridge & Iron Company. There were once two deck plate girder spans, each 55 feet long. The Interstate Commerce Commission showed that there were two girder spans south of the through truss span. Later, the bridge was rebuilt with a single deck plate girder span on each end. The total length of the bridge was 340 feet.

Missouri & North Arkansas Railroad: History Through the Miles

The remaining through truss span of the Little Red River Bridge near Shirley still stands and is used by River Road. Here is a view of the bridge in 1988. Photo by Barton Jennings.

The bridge was rebuilt in 1978 for road use, and now includes a 56-foot steel stringer span (north span), the 154-foot truss span, and a 136-foot concrete T-beam span on the south end. The bridge was part of the Arkansas Historic Bridges Recording Project. It has also been listed by the Historic American Engineering Record and was placed on the National Register of Historic Places on January 21, 2010.

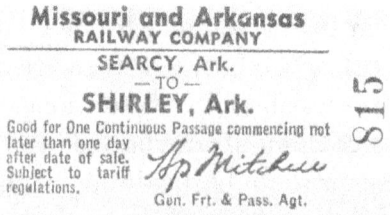

Missouri and Arkansas Railway Company ticket for passage from Searcy, Arkansas, to Shirley, Arkansas. From the collection of Barton Jennings.

Harrison (AR) to Heber Springs (AR)

For a great adventure, drive across the Little Red River Bridge and north along the river on the former railroad grade, now River Road. Photo by Barton Jennings.

215.0 SHIRLEY – Shirley was a town that was created by the fact that the Missouri & North Arkansas could not build on its desired route. The original plan was to build through Settlement, an existing town in the area. However, sheer bluffs kept a reasonable route from being built so a new route was chosen through the site of today's Shirley. The first settlement was in 1859 when John G. Nixon and Elijah M. Sowell both acquired land along the river. The railroad opened through here in 1908 and a depot was built near the bridge over the Middle Fork. Construction stopped here for several months as digging on the nearby large cut took longer than planned, and it didn't open until summer 1908.

Soon a town began to grow and a post office opened in 1909, the Town of Sherley appeared on the Arkansas Railroad Commission map in 1910, and the town was incorporated on November 18, 1911, with a population of 350. There are several different stories about the name Shirley, but one claims that it was named after a representative of the Cotton Belt Railroad who was assigned to the area to attract M&NA business that could be routed via the connection at Fargo. The Cotton Belt representative must have been very successful, as for many years, Fargo was the number one interchange location on the railroad.

With railroad transportation available, the timber industry began to boom and ten to fifteen sawmills were built in the surrounding area. One of the first timber companies was the L. L. Bucklew Lumber Company, based in Kansas City, Missouri. In the February 15, 1912, issue of *The St. Louis Lumberman*, the company advertised its "Soft Short Leaf Yellow Pine from our Shirley, Arkansas mill." A large finishing mill was later built in Shirley, and then a furniture factory. The area also raised and shipped cotton, cattle and hogs. The town peaked in the 1920s with almost 400 residents, three hotels, a dozen stores, an ice plant, a stave mill, four doctors, and a bank. The *Arkansas Marketing and Industrial Guide* of 1921 listed a number of businesses at Shirley. These included the National Cooperage Company, Shirley Milling Company, and a half-dozen lumber mills (Duncan & Harness, Highgrade Mill & Lumber Company, James Kinser, Patton & Whillock, M. Ramsey, and Williams Lumber Company).

At the time, Shirley was a typical mountain community serving the needs of area farmers, but it also had the advantages that a railroad created, as well as the troubles created by a logging boom. In the years before prohibition, Shirley had a wild-west reputation with a number of saloons. The town built a small jail to handle the worst of the trouble makers, and the jail still stands today. The town suffered greatly when the railroad closed, and it wasn't until nearby Greers Ferry Lake was built that the town began to recover. Today the town serves both area farmers and residents as well as tourists drawn by the many lake activities, but many of the downtown buildings still stand unused. The population was 223 in the 2010 census.

While many of the buildings in Shirley stand unused, one features this mural of the railroad and the nearby Little Red River Bridge. Photo by Barton Jennings.

Shirley was a busy station for the railroad with a large number of tracks, producing 459 carloads of freight in 1945 (sixth most on the railroad). In 1936, freight #211 departed at 1:30am, while #212 was scheduled to leave Shirley at 9:55pm. The 20' x 72' depot (telegraph call "SN") was on the east side of the mainline with a 14-car spur to the south. To the west, there was a 57-car siding (1850 feet) with a crossover near the center. An 11-car spur cut off the north end of the siding, with several spur tracks breaking off near the crossover. The water tower was originally to the north of the station, but was moved immediately south of the station by the late 1920s. Across the tracks from the depot was a cotton platform, stock pen, and section house. The depot stood until 1964, when it was sold and dismantled for the lumber.

Signs of the railroad can be seen in Shirley. From the River Road bridge, the tracks passed through downtown between Brown Road and River Road/Arkansas Highway 9. Look for Depot Road at the south end of town. The elevation at this location is 542 feet.

This sign for Depot Road in Shirley is a reminder that it was once a railroad town. Photo by Barton Jennings.

You can walk about a mile of the former railroad grade at Shirley, using the Cottrell Wilson Historic Trail, also known as the Sid Burgess Historic M&NA Railroad Trail. The trail starts at the former depot

Harrison (AR) to Heber Springs (AR)

location and heads east (railroad-south) to the Cottrell Wilson cemetery. The cemetery contains an estimated 40 graves, but most are unmarked. Included is a Bulgarian worker who died while making the nearby cut for the railroad. Sid Burgess was the last acting depot agent in Shirley. After the railroad was abandoned, Sid maintained the old train depot until it was dismantled in 1964.

216.5 MIDDLE FORK LITTLE RED RIVER BRIDGE – This bridge is gone except for several piers that are still in place. The bridge originally included a 154-foot through truss span in the middle with 55-foot deck plate girder spans on each end. From June 6, 1939, until July 15, 1952, there was a water-stage recorder on the downstream side of one of the bridge piers at an elevation of 483.12 feet above mean sea level. The grade is still clearly visible on either side of the bridge.

The bridges on either side of Shirley were sold to a scrapper who planned to salvage the steel. They first blew up the south bridge, but the cost never justified doing the same to the other bridge.

216.7 GORSWCH & WALLER TRACK – Early M&NA track profiles show this track. The Gorswch & Waller Lumber Company bought huge tracts of timber on Star Mountain, located southeast of Shirley. There was a spur track built here to serve a sawmill and a wood yard. Reportedly the company operated in the area from approximately 1911 until the early 1920s.

218.4 POE – Little is known about the purpose of Poe, an abandoned location, except records show it to be at an elevation of 490 feet, the spur track held five cars, and that timber was cut in the area. The station location is along the south bank of the Little Red River on Pole Ranch Spur road, once Poe Ranch Road. Poe was likely named for Richard Razy Poe, a former Confederate Lieutenant who became the sheriff of Van Buren County, and later a real estate and insurance agent.

Richard Razy Poe was the subject of an 1885 Act of the General Assembly of the State of Arkansas. The Act reimbursed Poe for costs related to a theft of tax money. The Act stated that in 1883, Poe had placed the funds in an iron safe, in the town of Clinton, which "had been provided and designated by the County Court as the repository of the county funds, and which was considered both fire proof and burglar proof." However, the safe was robbed of $741.48 on the night of June 5th, 1883. Poe spent his own time and money to track down the thieves, "and captured two of the parties engaged in the robbery, one of whom has been convicted and sentenced to the penitentiary, and the other, an escaped convict, has been returned to the penitentiary." Meanwhile, Poe had used his own money to pay the taxes, which was reimbursed by the State of Arkansas through this Act.

219.0 BRIDGE 219.0 – This bridge crossed a small stream that flowed off the top of the hill to the south. M&NA annual reports show that the bridge was worked on in 1929 and 1931. In 1929, the bridge was shortened and part of it was replaced using a 25-foot steel girder span. In 1931, another steel girder was installed in this bridge.

220.4 COUNTY LINE – The railroad crosses the county line between **Van Buren County** and **Cleburne County** just east of Deadland Hollow. **Cleburne County** was created on February 20, 1883, the last of 75 counties in Arkansas. The county was named for Confederate Major General Patrick Cleburne of Helena, Arkansas. Cleburne was Irish-born, and emigrated to the United States with two brothers and a sister. Going first to Ohio, Cleburne moved to Helena where he became a pharmacist. He formed several business partnerships and soon became quite wealthy. In December 1855, Cleburne and a partner bought the *Democratic Star* newspaper. During the Civil War, Cleburne quickly gained in rank due to his bravery and strategic combat plans, both of which earned him the nickname "Stonewall of the West." Although Cleburne fought for the Confederacy, he called for the emancipation of all slaves as a way to end the war. This call led him to be passed over for several promotions. Cleburne was killed at the Battle of Franklin (Tennessee) in 1864, while leading a charge on foot. He was temporarily buried in Mount Pleasant, Tennessee, and then his body was moved to the new Maple Hill Cemetery in Helena in 1870.

Today, Cleburne County and its county seat of Heber Springs are tourist draws thanks to Greers Ferry Lake. The area has also become a popular resort and retirement area. The county's population has tripled since 1960 when Greers Ferry Lake first opened. Its population in 2010 was 25,970.

222.1 SENDEFF – Coming into Sendeff from the west, the railroad made a 159-degree horseshoe curve using a curve of 8 degrees and 40 minutes. Sendeff, spelled Sandeff or Sandiff on most maps, was a railroad flag stop with no side tracks after 1928, but there was a spur track earlier. A mail crane was here in the 1920s to provide mail service, located approximately 200 feet north of the switch. The railroad also had a tool house here in the 1910s. Arkansas records indicate that there was a "Standiff" post office 1910-1921. Sendeff is located at the north point of another sharp bend on the Middle Fork at an elevation of 476 feet. To the north is Bliss Mountain. In this area, Sandiff Road uses the former railroad grade, which is on the edge of Greers Ferry Lake.

223.3 PARTAIN – Partian was a 20-car siding to the east with a mail crane until the late 1910s. The town of Partain is actually a mile or more to the west, but this was the closest location to the community. The name comes from the Partain family which has lived in the area since the 1800s. Note that the Middle Fork is now backed up as a part of Greers Ferry Lake. The grade can be seen as far as just north of Stewart Hollow, beyond that the railroad grade is under the lake's waters.

225.7 KARBER – Karber was a short 6-car spur track to the west with the switch on the north end. In 1945, Karber was a flag stop for the passenger trains. Today, Karber is located under the waters of Greers Ferry Lake.

The railroad continued to closely follow the Middle Fork Little Red River until cutting across to the South Fork. To take the shortcut, the Allegheny Improvement Company was forced to remove 125,000 cubic yards of rock. The cut took so long to build that a temporary shoo-fly that included a switchback was built across the ridge, requiring a temporary 1700-foot wooden trestle to be built across the South Fork. The deep cut can still be seen as it passes under Edgement Road, Arkansas Highway 16, less than one-half mile east of the Edgemont post office.

Greers Ferry Lake

When the railroad was built and operated, there was no Greers Ferry Lake. Instead, the railroad followed the Middle Fork Little Red River, crossed over the ridge that divided the Middle and South Forks, and then bridged over the South Fork to follow the Little Red River on south toward Kensett. Today's Greers Ferry Lake actually consists of two parts. The north part is where the three branches merge – South Fork, Middle Fork, and Devils Fork. From there, the Little River flowed south in a deep and narrow channel, today known simply as the Narrows.

From the Narrows, the Little Red River flowed east past Miller, made several large bends north and east of Heber Springs, and then headed east again past the communities of Red River and Snell. The railroad turned south at Miller and then curved east through Heber Springs and rejoined the river at Red River. Between Partian on the Middle Fork, and Miller on the main channel, most of the railroad grade is now under the lake.

The construction of the Greers Ferry Dam and Lake was authorized by the Flood Control Act of 1938, as modified by the Flood Control Act approved during August 1941. The stated purpose of the dam was the generation of hydroelectric power and to reduce flooding. However, since then, the management plan for the lake has added recreation, soil conservation, fish and wildlife management, forestry preservation, and even providing drinking water.

The actual construction of the dam started in March 1959, and it was finished in December 1962. A major celebration was held to dedicate the dam on October 3, 1963. President John F. Kennedy participated in the event, his last major public appearance before his trip to Dallas and his murder on November 22, 1963. The last of the project was completed in July 1964 when the powerhouse and switch yard began operations. Since then, Greers Ferry Lake has become a major Central Arkansas recreational area with a number of retirement communities. The dam and lake were named for a ferry operated on the Little Red River near where the dam was built.

227.4 EDGEMONT – After the railroad left the Middle Fork and passed through a deep stone cut, it reached Edgemont. The town started in the 1840s and 1850s when settlers claimed lands along the river bottoms and on the timbered ridges, creating a community known as Kinderhook. Farms in the valley typically grew cotton while those on the hillsides raised corn. When the railroad arrived, the town grew and a post office opened on September 19, 1908, with the name of Edgemont.

For years, Edgmont was a busy station on the Missouri & North Arkansas. Clay Lumber Company, Cotton Plant Mills Company, and J. E. Pettit all had lumber mills here. Additionally, E. L. Sherlock operated a cotton gin and there was the Globe Cooperage and Lumber Company. To serve the business, Edgemont had a 25-car spur track to the west with the switch on the south end, located just north of the depot which was also to the west. The depot has been described as a Standard #3 frame building, measuring 22' x 40' and built in 1909. Until about 1930, the station used the telegraph call "BG".

Edgemont was one of a number of stations that were closed in 1930. It, along with Arlberg, Olvey, Letona and Rondo, were closed as business dropped off and the railroad again teetered on financial failure. A hearing on October 16th of that year by the Arkansas Railroad Commission approved the closings through a process known as *nunc pro tunc*, a legal term that allows an action retroactively to correct an earlier ruling. The station at Edgemont was the subject of another hearing on December 4, 1930, along with the Elba station.

For several decades, Edgemont was really a large community, with residents on both sides of the river. To solve the problems related to high water, the local residents built a 500-foot swinging bridge across the Little Red River. Most of the businesses, such as the general store, were on the mountain sides to stay above the periodic floods. However, the elevation wasn't enough as during the 1950s, the U.S. Army Corps of Engineers announced that the new Greers Ferry Lake would flood the town with as much as sixty to eighty feet of water. Because of this, Edgemont moved to higher ground about a mile to the north. Today's Edgemont is still an unincorporated community, but it is busy serving the many needs of tourists. Some of the remains of the original Edgemont are reportedly still at the bottom of the lake.

228.6 PRAWS – This station was listed in the January 1915 *A B C Pathfinder Shipping and Mailing Guide*, and in M&NA valuation records from 1917. However, the station was not listed in the November 25, 1923, *Time Table No. 4*. One interesting note in the *A B C Pathfinder Shipping and Mailing Guide* was that Wells Fargo & Company handled shipments to and from the station.

Edgemont Cut

This is the location of one of the largest challenges to the railroad's construction, moving 125,000 cubic feet of earth to allow the railroad to cut across the ridge between the Middle and South Forks of the Little Red River. The cut took months to dig and a shoo-fly was built to allow operations to begin. According to the *Arkansas Gazette*, the shoo-fly also required a great deal of trestlework. An article on page 1 of the August 15, 1908, issue stated that the cut was the site of the most trestle work on the railroad. On the north side there was 900 feet of temporary trestle, in addition to 148 feet of permanent trestle. On the south side, another 800 feet of temporary trestle was built along with 562 feet of permanent trestle. The article also stated that the South Fork would be spanned by two 125-foot steel spans, and that a short distance away, a 150-foot steel span would cross another fork of the Little Red River. The cut can still be found as it passes under Arkansas Highway 16, Edgemont Road, not far east of the Edgemont post office.

228.9 SOUTH FORK LITTLE RED RIVER BRIDGE – The South Fork begins in the Ozark National Forest near Scotland in Van Buren County and flows east around Clinton and then into Greers Ferry Lake. The stream is known for its brook trout.

The South Fork was first spanned by a temporary 1700-foot wooden trestle while the large Edgemont Cut was completed. Later, a new bridge was built that included eleven timber pile trestle spans, two 125-foot through truss steel spans, and 40 timber frame trestle spans on the south approach. The southern-most part of the timber span was eventually filled in. The steel bridge spans were built by the Wisconsin Bridge & Iron Company, which had a contract for the bridges on the expanding Missouri & North Arkansas. Wisconsin Bridge & Iron was formed in 1870 and was a major manufacturer of bridges built across the Midwest, but also sold bridges and participated in projects as far away as Alaska, Hawaii and Florida. Based in Milwaukee, the company was a significant competitor to the larger American Bridge Company, which was created by J. P. Morgan when he consolidated almost 30 bridge and steel fabricators in 1900. The Wisconsin Bridge & Iron Company was sold in the 1970s.

The railroad had a small "watchman's house" just south of the bridge and west of the tracks.

229.6 HIGDEN – Higden is another small town that was impacted by the building of Greers Ferry Dam. Higden was once located closer to the river, but was moved to the nearby hilltop before the lake was formed. Today, the small town (population of 120 in 2010) is at the tip of the point on the west side of the "Narrows." Some area residents claim that some of the homes and buildings of the original Higden are still underwater today in the lake.

The Little Red River was an early draw for settlers. In September 1820, Major Stephen Harriman Long was sent to survey the area, and he reported that settlers were already living along the river. Stephen Long was one of the most important government explorers of the early 1800s. It is claimed that he covered more than 26,000 miles in five expeditions. He is best known for his scientific expedition of the Great Plains, an area he called a "Great Desert," leading to the term "The Great American Desert." Long's career began as a lieutenant of engineers in the U.S. Army Corps of Engineers in 1814, and he was assigned in 1816 as a topographical engineer to the Southern Division under Major General Andrew Jackson. Long later helped to survey and build the Baltimore & Ohio Railroad, and then received his first patent for railroad steam locomotives in 1826. He eventually patented a number of locomotive designs, some so advanced that they couldn't be built at the time.

The current Higden is actually the third location of the town, and is using its third name. The community started as Salt Springs Barrens as settlers moved into the area along the Little Red River. Although it was alongside the river, the area was given the name Barrens because the soil was rocky and poor. However, the land was thick with pine trees which grew well in the soil. A post office opened on June 14, 1894, as Channel, named for the long and narrow channel that the river used to pass through a ridge. On April 9, 1895, the post office was renamed Higden after Thomas Geoffrey Higdon, an early resident. The difference in spelling is explained by an error made on the post office application.

The town moved about a mile to the northeast when the railroad was built, locating next to the tracks. The town prospered with its new location, and it was incorporated in November 1909. The

1910 census reported 336 residents, although reports claimed that more than a thousand people lived and worked in the area. Like many of the new towns along the Missouri & North Arkansas, the initial business was timber, although there was also a grist mill, drugstore, cotton gin, and several stores. A fire in 1916 changed the look of the town from boomtown to permanent construction.

By the 1920s, Higden was a large lumber town. Lumber mills were being operated by Baker & Son Lumber Company, Alexander Lumber Company, Samuel Bradley, B & D Sawmill Company, Ward & Fleetwood, O'Bannan & Son, and J. W. Ward. The Doniphan Lumber Company also had a mill at Higden that supported its main mill near Searcy. The company's own railroad, the Donipan, Kensett & Searcy, connected to the M&NA and operated trains over the M&NA to serve the company's different mills and operations. Samuel Bradley also sold hardwood and A. S. Alexander sold railroad ties at Higden. A grist mill was operated by John Riley. The railroad also had a cotton dock and stock pens on the siding south of the depot.

As the timber was cut, the population of Higden steadily dropped, so that by the 1950s there were fewer than 100 residents. The town moved to its third location in the late 1950s as Greers Ferry Lake was filled. It was reported that only five families did not have to move to higher ground. The core of the new town was on a thirteen-acre site that was once the location of the Higden schoolhouse. Many residents simply moved away, and the population of Higden was only 40 in 1960. However, the town has grown some due to its location on the lake and its population was 120 in the 2010 census.

The track from Shirley to Higden was turned over to the M&NA on October 1, 1908. While the Allegheny Improvement Company didn't turn over the Higden to Kensett railroad until December 1, 1908, trains began running over the track on October 19. Higden siding was 28 cars long and was on the east side of the mainline. The depot was on the west side and there was a 22-car spur track that curved off to the northwest just north of the building to serve a sawmill. An interesting design characteristic of the railroad was that the mainline had a six-panel frame trestle just north of the spur track switch, and the spur crossed the same stream on a four-panel frame trestle.

As the tracks headed on to Heber Springs, they went down the Narrows following the Little Red River. The tracks once crossed Salt Creek, where there was a flag stop, and then went on to a location just north of Miller where the route turned south around Millers Point to reach the siding at Miller. Near the Narrows Marina, the old grade can sometimes be seen.

232.7 **SALT CREEK BRIDGE** – Salt Creek drained the area that is today just north of the Pryor Mountain Quarry, to the southwest of the railroad.

234.0 **SALT CREEK** – Original valuation maps of the railroad show a 265-foot spur track here with a wood platform on the mainline. In 1925, the railroad timetable showed that Salt Creek was a flagstop. M&NA records show that the 9-car track was retired in 1927.

For a few years after the railroad was built, timber was loaded at Salt Creek. Reports from several local sources say that the timber was cut on the mountain tops and then slid down to the tracks using one of several chutes. There are also some reports that a small coal mine was worked here for several years, selling the coal to the railroad for fueling locomotives. The primary lumber company listed as being at Salt Creek was the W. B. Baker Lumber Company, who had their main facility at Heber Springs, Arkansas.

236.8 MILLER – Miller is another former railroad town that is now under the waters of Greers Ferry Lake. Located just east of Millers Point, this area was settled by the 1860s, but was never a large town. Maps from the 1890s show the community as Goffs Cove, although many birth records from the time used Miller. Miller Bottoms was another name used for the area. For a number of years, there was a one-room schoolhouse. The railroad built through here in 1908, following the Little River to just north of Miller before turning south to follow Cove Creek through Miller.

When the railroad turned south, it began to follow Arkansas Highway 16. Where the railroad left the river, Arkansas Highway 16 continued north, crossing the Little Red River using a cable swing bridge known as the Miller Bridge. This bridge was built in 1912 by contractor Harry Churchill. Churchill built several cable swing bridges in the area, all of which are now gone. This one is gone and its location is under the lake.

Miller had a 33-car siding, located to the west of the mainline. A Standard #3 22' x 40' depot stood here until 1930. There was a mail crane from the late 1920s until the end of the railroad. A new cotton platform was built here in 1926, while the water station was retired in 1927. The town was platted with Front Street along the railroad, and then West 2nd and West 3rd Streets. Running east-west was Main Street, with two more streets to the north and three to the south.

J. E. Chilton operated a lumber company here, and the Searcy Cotton Seed Oil Company also once had a facility here. Miller also had a school, a cattle dip, a small coal mine, and a logging slide for bringing timber down from the top of nearby hills. There are some reports that the hotel behind the station was a popular place and was reported to be a house of ill repute. Some legends state that the hotel was never closed because the women were Indian and not white women.

Old Cherokee Boundary Line

Located just north of Miller is the Old Cherokee Boundary Line, running northeast to southwest. Before the arrival of white settlers, this area was primarily inhabited by the Osage, although other tribes sometimes hunted in the area. In 1808, the United States purchased the land from the Osage and the first American settlers entered the area. As the eastern tribes were moved west, part of the land northwest of here was given to the Cherokee. The boundary was defined as being from near Morrilton, on the Arkansas River, northeast to the White River west of Batesville. The Old Cherokee Boundary Line, also sometimes known as the Old Indian Treaty Boundary, still shows on many maps and is often used on land descriptions in Cleburne County.

243.3 **HEBER SPRINGS** – From Miller, the railroad once continued south and then turned east, crossed a low ridge which is now covered by a dam known as Big Dike, and then followed Sulphur Creek into Heber Springs. The line along Sulphur Creek can today be seen at the Bittle Road entrance to the Cleburne County Fairgrounds. At Heber Springs, the railroad passed through the south part of town through what is today the E-Z Mart convenience store on South 7th Street and then north of the former hardware complex. The tracks then went just north of the Heber Springs City Cemetery, and the grade is now a paved walking trail known as the Sulphur Creek Trail. The railroad then continued to the northeast before curving to the southeast, still following Sulphur Creek. Parts of the grade and a few foundations, including parts of the former coaling dock, can be found in this area.

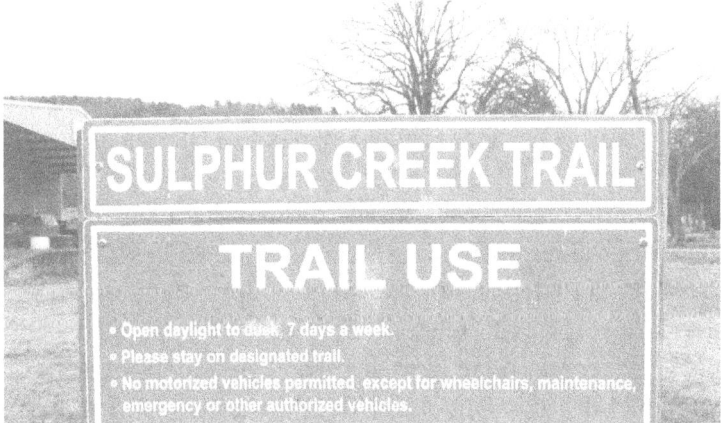

A short distance of the former M&NA grade is now the Sulphur Creek Trail, marked by several signs along its route in Heber Springs. Photo by Barton Jennings.

The remains of this concrete coaling tower still stand east of 7th Street and just north of the original mainline grade. This structure allowed coal cars to be rolled over the structure and unloaded into a small hopper basin, where a small conveyor was used to lift the coal up and dump it into a steam locomotive's tender. Photo by Barton Jennings.

For many years, Heber Springs was a busy railroad town as it was the division point between the Second District (Harrison to Heber Springs) and the Third District (Heber Springs to Helena). Between Joplin and Heber Springs, trains #211 and #212 operated daily in 1936. #211 was scheduled to arrive in Heber Springs at 3:15am, while #212 was scheduled to depart northward at 8:05pm. Between Heber Springs and Helena, #211 and #212 operated daily except Sunday, and provided mixed train service – both passenger and freight service. #211 departed southward at 7:00am while northward #212 was scheduled to arrive at 6:15pm. These schedules indicated that the trains were switched at Heber Springs, explaining many of the railroad facilities that once stood here.

The train station (telegraph call "HB") once stood where the convenience store on South 7th Street now stands. Serving passengers, the Heber Springs Hotel was behind the 21' x 91' depot. An elevation benchmark at the station showed it to be 337 feet above sea level.

The tracks through Heber Springs basically ran east-west, causing some confusion in describing the area. Because of this, actual compass directions will be used. Heber Springs had a three-track yard to the south of the mainline, with a 17-car siding to the north, just west of the station. East of the station was a wye to the north, along with several spur tracks for local industries. There was a unique 13' x 24' wooden 40,000-gallon water tank, supported by a pump house moving water from Sulphur Creek. Water could also be obtained from the city water supply system. The water tank was damaged, along with a locomotive, by strikers in July 1921.

Many of the facilities were built in 1913 when Heber Springs was made a division point, as well as the location of a number of railroad shops. For example, a new engine shed, several small shop buildings, a coaling platform, and 5000 feet of new track were built at the time. For many years, Heber Springs was also the dividing point between freight and passenger service to Joplin and Helena, before much of this activity moved to Kensett in the late 1920s. In 1929, the engine house was retired and that work was also moved to Kensett.

Sanborn Fire Insurance Map from Heber Springs, Cleburne County, Arkansas. Sanborn Map Company, April, 1918. Library of Congress, Geography and Map Division. https://www.loc.gov/item/sanborn00264_002/.

The Heber Springs area was very busy for the railroad, and the 1918 Sanborn map shows a number of tracks and several hotels around the M&NA passenger station. To the east (railroad south) was the shop complex, including the motor car house. To the west (railroad-north) was a large railroad tie yard and several small facilities for cotton seed, fertilizer, coal, and other products.

Heber Springs was also a good source of freight revenue for many years. In 1921, the *Arkansas Marketing and Industrial Guide* listed almost a dozen companies in the town. This included the flour and feed mills of Heber Springs Milling Company and Bridewell Mercantile Company, the handle factory of W. E. Bruner & Company, and five lumber companies. These lumber and timber companies included Cleburne County Lumber Company, Doniphan Lumber Company, Heber Springs Milling Company, W. B. Baker Lumber Company, and Western Tie & Lumber Company. Later, the Manda Corporation helped fund the creation of a rock crusher near Heber Springs. In 1926, the railroad built a new cotton platform to handle the product from area farmers. Even in 1945, the last full year of the railroad, Heber Springs reportedly was responsible for 1120 carloads, the most of any station on the line.

A 1928 Sanborn map showed how the railroad and its customers were situated in Heber Springs. From the depot and heading west, there were a number of railroad facilities. To the south of the depot and across the tracks, was a cotton gin operated by the Heber Springs Gin Company. On the north side of the many tracks, from east to west, was a freight house, a cotton platform, a stock pen, and then the Gay Oil Company. Heading east, the west leg of the wye was approximately where South 6th Street would have been. On the west leg was a spur track into the Job Phillips potato warehouse. Just east of the wye was the W. E. Bruner & Son handle factory. Further east was the warehouse of the Bridewell Mercantile Company. On the south side of the mainline and just northeast of the cemetery was the W. B. Baker Lumber Company planing mill. Finally, further east and on the north side of the tracks was a spur into the Arkansas Power & Light Auxiliary Station and Ice Plant.

Soon after the Missouri & North Arkansas built through Heber Springs, there were proposals for other railroads to connect the town to the outside world. The July 17, 1915, issue of *Railway Review* had a short article about a railroad from Heber Springs, which was mistakenly placed in Missouri by the magazine. "A movement is reported under way at Heber Springs, Mo. [sic], and at Memphis, Tenn., to extend the Bald Knob branch of the St Louis, Iron Mountain & Southern Ry. from Bald Knob to Heber Springs, about 30 miles, and thereby make a direct railroad to Memphis. Heber Springs is on the Missouri & North Arkansas R.R., which runs southeast direct to Helena, on the Mississippi river, while the proposed line would run directly east to Memphis. William C. Brown, Heber Springs, and others are interested."

The City of Heber Springs

This community began in 1881 when Max Frauenthal bought land from John T. Jones, a circuit court judge in Helena, and created the Sugar Loaf Springs Company. The Sugar Loaf Springs Company had a town platted and Sugar Loaf was incorporated on October 4, 1882. The original plan was for a resort town centered around the springs, but with the new county of Cleburne being created, Frauenthal donated land for the courthouse square and Spring Park. He even built a frame courthouse to attract the new county seat. With the goodwill earned by the donation, Frauenthal was reportedly given the opportunity to help name the new county and he pushed the name Cleburne for Confederate General Patrick Cleburne.

With the title of county seat, the town began to grow. The post office opened in 1881. The use of the name Sugar Loaf was a problem as there was already a post office with that name. The post office, therefore, took the name Heber Springs, often quoted as just Heber. The name came from Dr. Heber Jones, the son of John T. Jones. Heber Jones was a physician in Memphis, Tennessee, where Frauenthal later moved. In 1910, the town of Sugar Loaf also became Heber Springs.

Today, Heber Springs is still the county seat of Cleburne County, and its 1914 brick Jeffersonian Revival style courthouse was listed in the National Register of Historic Places in 1976. The house of Clarence Frauenthal, the son of Max Frauenthal, was also built in 1914 and is now in the hands of the family again after being owned by the Cleburne County Historical Society. It too is listed on the National Register. Much of downtown Heber Springs is listed as the Heber Springs Commercial Historic District, listed on the National Register in 2009. Heber Springs has benefitted greatly from the tourism brought by Greers Ferry Dam, located just northeast of town.

Heber Springs is seeing a growth in population. According to the 2010 census, the population was 7165. Over the years, several well-known people have been born in Heber Springs. Johnnie Bryan (J. B.) Hunt, founder of J. B. Hunt Transport Services, was born in Heber Springs in February 1927. Golfer Stan Lee, five-time Arkansas State Golf Association Match Play champion, three-time Arkansas high school golf state champion, and the 2007 USGA Senior Amateur champion, was born in Heber Springs in September 1952. Laurell Kaye Hamilton (Laurell Kaye Klein), the author of the *Anita Blake: Vampire Hunter* series and *Merry Gentry* series was born in Heber Springs in February 1963.

The two-story Ruland Junction Toy Train Museum is located in Heber Springs at the corner of South 12th and West Walnut Streets. The museum features two floors of model trains, the collection of the Ruland family. The model trains are as old as 100 years, and include standard gauge on the first floor. Upstairs are HO- and O-gauge trains, mostly Lionel. In addition, the walls are covered with train memorabilia and photographs.

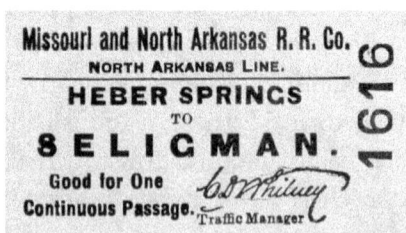

Missouri and North Arkansas R. R. Co. ticket for passage from Heber Springs to Seligman. From the collection of Barton Jennings.

Missouri & North Arkansas Route Guide
Third District –
Heber Springs (AR) to Helena (AR)

The Third District of the Missouri & North Arkansas/Missouri & Arkansas, defined as being from Heber Springs to the end of the line at Helena, included the track built by the Missouri & North Arkansas in 1908 and 1909. This part of the railroad had the most connections with other railroads, such as Missouri Pacific, Rock Island, Cotton Belt, Yazoo & Mississippi Valley, and the Doniphan, Kensett & Searcy Railroad.

This part of the railroad included few grades and even fewer curves. However, it included track through the White and Cache River bottom lands, an area of almost yearly flooding. Much of this part of the railroad was described as being little more than one to two feet above the surrounding land, and a line that badly needed to be raised and leveled. It also includes the last stretch of track operated by a common carrier railroad – the six miles of track from Cotton Plant to Fargo.

Reports show that this part of the railroad was built from each end, with a great deal of construction working north from Helena, and in both directions from the connection with the Rock Island at Cotton Plant. At least one of the contractors building the line used convicts as labor. In 1907, it was reported by the *Arkansas Gazette* (November 19, 1907) that "Thirty-five convicts were taken from the camp of the Arkansas Brick and Manufacturing Company yesterday and sent to Cotton Plant. The men are to be used in Woodruff county in cutting out the right of way for the North Arkansas road from Cotton Plant to Helena." Two weeks later, the newspaper reported that six of the convicts had "escaped from a stockade" on the east side of the Cache River, west of Cotton Plant.

The mileposts presented are from *Missouri & Arkansas Railway Company Time Table No. 7*, dated Sunday, February 25, 1945, and a June 28, 1925, timetable of the Missouri & North Arkansas. However, it should be noted that mileposts for many of the station locations have changed slightly over the years.

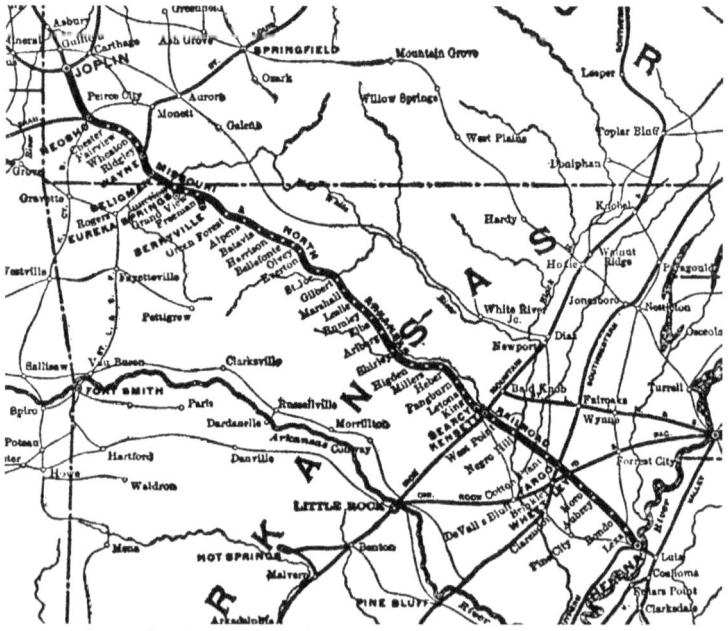

From *The Official Guide of the Railways and Steam Navigation Lines of the United States,* January 1910, page 950, enlarged portion of map.

Missouri and Arkansas Railway Co. Cash Fare Receipt and Seat Check both from the the collection of Barton Jennings.

THIRD DISTRICT

SOUTHWARD

TIME TABLE No. 7

Effective 12.01 A. M. SUNDAY February 25, 1945

THIRD CLASS	SECOND CLASS	FIRST CLASS		Siding Capacity		Distance from Joplin	Maximum Grade	STATIONS
327 Local Freight	11 Freight	1 Passenger	5 Passenger Motor	Pass.	Other			
Daily Except Sunday	Daily	Daily	Daily Except Sunday					
Lv 6.00AM	Lv 7.00AM	Lv 5.12PM		Yd.		243.32	0.45	DN.....HEBER SPRINGS....CWY
							6.29	
6.25	7.20	f 5.26		53B		249.61	0.50	RED RIVER.........X
							1.70	
6.31	7.25	f 5.29		28B		251.31	0.70	SNELL.............
							5.03	
6.56	f 8.03 M2	s 5.40 M12		27B	12	256.34	0.60	D........PANGBURN.........
							4.82	
7.15	8.18	s 5.52		44B		261.16	0.60	LETONA............
							5.62	
7.39 M2	8.33	f 6.04		17B		266.78	0.60	....ARMSTRONG SPRINGS... *
							7.00	
7.54	s 9.18	s 6.18		42B	122	273.78	0.05	D..........SEARCY........WX
							0.60	
						274.38		.....C. R. I. & P. CROSSINGS.....
							3.32	
8.15 / 8.50	s 9.50	Ar 6.30PM	Lv 7.30AM	55NB / 23SB	63	277.70		DN..........KENSETT......CWY
								Mo. Pac. 3.50 Crossing
0.00	f 10.00		s 7.40	17D		301.20	0.40	.....WEST POINT.........
							7.28	
			f 8.01		5N	288.48		ENRIGHT............
							3.33	
9.35	s 10.35		s 8.10	45B	43	291.81	0.25	........GEORGETOWN.....
							1.23	
						293.04		.......WHITE RIVER......W
							2.06	
9.50	f 10.50		s 8.20	43S		295.10	0.00	........McCLELLAND.....
							3.10	
9.59	f 10.59		s 8.29	23S		298.20	0.00	.........DIXIE........*
							3.81	
			f 8.39		12S	302.01	0.12	.......DAGGETT........
							3.87	
10.29	s 11.45AM M328		s 8.49	31B	92	305.88	0.00	D.......COTTON PLANT......X
							4.04	
						309.92		........DEVUE.........W
							1.67	
11.10 M328	s 12.25PM		s 9.04	14B	5	311.59	0.30	D...........FARGO.........
								S. L. S. W. 4.73 Crossing
11.30AM	s 1.00 M12		s 9.16	41B	46	316.32	0.30	D........WHEATLEY.......
								C. R. I. & P. 2.76 Crossing
			f 9.24		10S	319.08	0.30	......WEATHERBY........
							7.80	
12.15PM M12	s 1.54 M6		s 9.45	45B	18	326.88	0.25	D..........MORO........
							7.55	
12.40	s 2.30		s 10.05 M328	44B		334.43	0.20	.........AUBREY........W
							5.86	
1.20 M6	s 2.55		s 10.21	38B		340.29	0.10	.........RONDO.........
							4.91	
1.35	3.15		f 10.35		5N	345.20	0.50	......NORTH LEXA........
								Mo. Pac. 7.80 Crossing
2.00	s 3.50		s 10.57 M12	24B	47	353.00	0.00	D......WEST HELENA.......
							0.68	
						353.68		.....MO. PAC. CROSSING.....
							2.57	
2.25	4.10		f 11.05			356.25	2.50	.......OUTER YARD.......T
							0.66	
						356.91		....MO. PAC. CROSSING.....
							1.22	
						358.13		....MO. PAC. CROSSING.....
							0.70	
						358.83		....MO. PAC. CROSSING.....
							0.29	
						359.12		....MO. PAC. CROSSING.....
							0.24	
Ar 2.50PM	Ar 4.30PM		Ar 11.20AM	Yd.		359.36		D...........HELENA......CWX 2..
Daily except Sunday	Daily	Daily	Daily Except Sunday	End Connected B—Both N—North S—South				116.04
327	11	1	5					

Missouri & North Arkansas Railway Company Time Table No. 7, Sunday, February 25, 1945. Third District, southward. Courtesy Boone County Historical & Railroad Society.

Third District – Heber Springs (AR) to Helena (AR)

THIRD DISTRICT   8

TIME TABLE No. 7
Effective 12.01 A. M. SUNDAY February 25, 1945

NORTHWARD

Maximum Grade	STATIONS	Maximum Grade	Station Numbers	Telegraph Call	FIRST CLASS 6 Passenger Motor Daily Except Sunday	FIRST CLASS 2 Passenger Daily	SECOND CLASS 12 Freight Daily	THIRD CLASS 328 Local Freight Daily except Monday
12 0.45	DN.....HEBER SPRINGS....CWY 6.29	0.60	243	HB		Ar 8.31AM	Ar 6.40PM	Ar 4.10PM
11 0.50	..........RED RIVER..........X 1.70	0.55	250			f 8.17	6.19	3.46
11 0.70	..........SNELL.......... 5.03	0.50	251			f 8.14	5.55	3.40
14 0.60	D..........PANGBURN.......... 4.82	0.05	256	BU		s 8.03	f 5.40 M11	3.25 M1
6 0.60	..........LETONA.......... 5.62	1.00	261			s 7.51	5.15	3.05
8 0.60	....ARMSTRONG SPRINGS...* 7.00	0.60	267			f 7.39 M327	4.55	2.45
8 0.05	D..........SEARCY..........WX 0.60	0.60	274	DE		s 7.25	s 4.35	2.25
8	....C. R. I. & P. CROSSINGS..... 3.32							
0	...DN..........KENSETT.....CWY Mo. Pac. 3.50 Crossing	0.30	278	KS	Ar 4.10PM	Lv 7.15AM	4.15 s 3.35	2.05 1.25
0 0.40	..........WEST POINT.......... 7.28	0.20	281		s 4.01		f 3.25	1.15
8	..........ENRIGHT.......... 3.33		288		f 3.40			
1 0.25	..........GEORGETOWN.......... 1.23	0.15	292		s 3.30		s 2.55	12.45
4	..........WHITE RIVER..........W 2.06							
0 0.00	..........McCLELLAND.......... 3.10	0.30	295		s 3.20		s 2.35	12.25
0 0.00	..........DIXIE..........* 3.81	0.04	298		s 3.11		f 2.25	12.15PM
1 0.12	..........DAGGETT.......... 3.87	0.10	302		f 3.00			
8 0.00	D......COTTON PLANT......X 4.04	0.10	306	CN	s 2.50		s 1.55	11.45AM M11
2	..........DEVUE..........W 1.67							
9 0.30	D..........FARGO.......... S. L. S. W. 4.73 Crossing	0.10	312	FR	s 2.34		s 1.30	11.10 M327
2 0.30	D..........WHEATLEY.......... C. R. I. & P. 2.76 Crossing	0.20	316	WY	s 2.21		s 1.00 M11	10.45
3 0.30	..........WEATHERBY.......... 7.80	0.30	319		f 2.14			
3 0.25	D..........MORO.......... 7.55	0.30	327	MO	s 1.54 M11		s 12.15PM M327	10.25
3 0.20	..........AUBREY..........W 5.86	0.20	234		s 1.34		s 11.50AM	10.05 M5
3 0.10	..........RONDO.......... 4.91	0.15	340		s 1.20 M327		s 11.30	9.40
3 0.50	..........NORTH LEXA.......... Mo. Pac. 7.80 Crossing	0.40	345		f 1.05		11.15	9.25
3 0.00	D......WEST HELENA.......... 0.68	0.15	353	WS	s 12.45		s 10.57 M5	9.00
1	..........MO. PAC. CROSSING.......... 2.57							
2.50	..........OUTER YARD..........T 0.66	0.50	356		f 12.35		10.30	8.25
	..........MO. PAC. CROSSING.......... 1.22							
	..........MO. PAC. CROSSING.......... 0.70							
	..........MO. PAC. CROSSING.......... 0.29							
	..........MO. PAC. CROSSING.......... 0.24							
	....D..........HELENA..........CWX	2.50	359	HU	Lv 12.20PM		Lv 10.00AM	Lv 8.00AM
	116.04				Daily Except Sunday	Daily	Daily	Daily Except Monday
					6	2	12	328

Missouri & North Arkansas Railway Company Time Table No. 7, Sunday, February 25, 1945. Third District, northward. Courtesy Boone County Historical & Railroad Society.

Missouri & North Arkansas R.R. Co.
NORTH ARKANSAS LINE.
LESLIE
TO
PANGBURN.
Good for One Continuous Passage.
Traffic Manager
948

Missouri and North Arkansas
Railway Company
EUREKA SPRINGS, Ark.,
TO
KENSETT, Ark.
Good for One Continuous Passage, commencing not later than one day after date of sale. Subject to tariff regulations.
Asst. Gen'l Pass. Agt.
A 2489

Missouri and Arkansas
RAILWAY COMPANY
COTTON PLANT, Ark.
— TO —
HELENA, Ark.
Good for One Continuous Passage commencing not later than one day after date of sale. Subject to tariff regulations.
Gen. Frt. & Pass. Agt.
57

Missouri and North Arkansas
Railway Company.
AUBREY, Ark.,
TO
WHEATLEY, Ark.
Good for One Continuous Passage, commencing not later than one day after date of sale. Subject to tariff regulations.
Asst. Gen'l Pass. Agt.
A 748

Missouri and North Arkansas
Railway Company
AUBREY, Ark.,
TO
RONDO, Ark.
Good for One Continuous Passage, commencing not later than one day after date of sale. Subject to tariff regulations.
Asst. Gen'l Pass. Agt.
6736

Missouri and Arkansas
RAILWAY COMPANY
HELENA, Ark.
— TO —
SOUTHLAND, Ark.
Good for One Continuous Passage commencing not later than one day after date of sale. Subject to tariff regulations.
Gen. Frt. & Pass. Agt.
440

Tickets from the collection of Barton Jennings.

Heber Springs (AR) to Helena (AR)

243.3 HEBER SPRINGS – For information about Heber Springs, see Heber Springs in the Second District.

Heading south, the railroad headed to the northeast and looped around the north end of Round Mountain, near where the intersection of Arkansas Highways 110 and 25 exists today. The railroad then turned to the southeast. At the river bend near Libby Bluff, the railroad again came along the south bank of the Little Red River. This was the station of Red River.

Part of the grade heading south from Heber Springs is now the Sulphur Creek Trail, a paved walking and biking trail. The route provides an opportunity to see what some of the route was like as the railroad left town. Photo by Barton Jennings.

249.6 RED RIVER – Red River was a 53-car siding, located to the railroad-east (river-side) of the mainline, as well as a passenger train flag stop with a platform. In 1945, records show that Red River was the second largest source of shipments on the railroad, with 734 cars of traffic.

Red River is named for the adjacent Little Red River. The Little Red River was once created by the merger of the South Branch, Middle Branch, and Devils Branch near Edgemont, Arkansas. Today, this is all part of Greers Ferry Lake, and the river is considered to start at the base of the Greers Ferry Dam. Approximately 100 miles downstream, the river flows into the White River north of Georgetown, Arkansas.

Because the river comes out of the dam, it is a cold river for many miles. Trout were introduced to the river starting in 1966, when the Greers Ferry National Fish Hatchery was opened just below the dam. The hatchery produces rainbow trout and brook trout for suitable streams below U.S. Army Corps of Engineers dams located in Arkansas and eastern Oklahoma. On the Little Red River, trout are stocked and caught as far downstream as Pangburn. Three types of trout are stocked – rainbows, browns, and cutthroats. Rainbow trout are the dominant fish population. Brown trout are popular and the world record 40-pound, 4-ounce fish was hauled from the Little Red River.

For the next mile, Libby Road, Arkansas Highway 337, is built on the former railroad grade. Where Libby Road turns to the south at the intersection with Little Dunham Road, the railroad grade continues straight. The name Libby was also used for this community, and at one time the railroad called this Libbie Spur, and showed it to be eleven cars long during the early 1920s.

Heber Springs (AR) to Helena (AR)

251.3 SNELL – Snell was located at the east end of Libby Bluff, a feature along the Little Red River. The original name came from the Snell family who settled in the area in the 1800s, and who operated the J. L. Snell General Store starting in 1907. A post office opened at Snell in 1907, but its name was changed to Libbie in 1921. The name Country Settlement was used earlier for the community. While the post office changed its name to Libbie, and many locally used Libby, the railroad used the name Snell until the end. The M&NA had a mail crane about 1200 feet railroad-north (compass west) of the passenger platform on the west (compass-south) side of the mainline. The post office closed in 1928 and mail service was moved to Heber Springs.

There was a 28-car siding to the west at Snell until the end of the railroad. This track served the Arkansas Crushed Stone Company. For many years, there was a water station here, too. It was destroyed by strikers in 1921, but rebuilt. It was retired in 1930.

Heading south, the railroad grade is used for a short distance by Ryan Drive and then loops around a series of hills, squeezes between a bluff and a sharp bend of the Little Red River, and then curves around the north side of Mount Zion to enter Pangburn.

Doniphan Lumber Company Trains

As previously written, the Doniphan Lumber Company had logging railroads at Snell and Letona. A Supreme Court of Arkansas Case, *Doniphan, Kensett & Searcy Railroad Company v. Missouri & North Arkansas Railroad Company*, with an opinion delivered on July 1, 1912, provides a good review of these operations. The legal issue was that the trackage rights agreement stated that the Doniphan, Kensett & Searcy Railroad (DK&S, owned by the Doniphan Lumber Company) could only move pine for their Searcy mill in their trains, yet the DK&S wanted to move all timber and company products. However, the agreement clearly stated that the DK&S "will handle no traffic, whether passenger, freight, mail and express, or of any other character" to any stations at or between Searcy and a "point three miles north of water tank at Snell."

The Arkansas Supreme Court stated that the DK&S was owned by the Doniphan Lumber Company, "which operates a mill at Doniphan and owns large bodies of timber lands situated chiefly in Cleburne County." The trackage rights agreement involved was for "a period of ten years from and after January 1, 1911" and was for the use of the M&NA tracks "between the present connection of the tracks of the Arkansas Company (M&NA) and the Doniphan Company (DK&S) at the town of Searcy, White County, Arkansas, and a point three miles north of the water tank at Snell, as now located in the county of Cleburne." The fee for these rights was "the sum of one dollar per mile for each mile its trains moved over these tracks."

An agreement was eventually reached whereby the DK&S could haul additional timber and products, but only if the finished product eventually moved as freight on the M&NA.

255.5 COUNTY LINE – The grade of the Missouri & North Arkansas passes from **Cleburne County** into **White County** north of Mount Zion. **White County** is the second largest county in land area in Arkansas, and the 31st county created. It was created on October 23, 1835, by taking land from Independence, Jackson, and Pulaski Counties. The name White is not from the nearby White River. Instead, the county was named for Hugh Lawson White, a Whig candidate for President of the United States in 1836 and earlier a Senator from Tennessee. The county seat is Searcy, and the county's population was 77,076 in 2010.

White County is one of a number of borderline counties that are half delta and half mountainous. The southeastern half of the county is alluvial land used for farming and timber production. Meanwhile, the northwestern half of the county is higher rocky ground used for dairy and beef cattle ranching. From 1890 to 1950, White County was the largest producer of strawberries in the United States. Most moved by rail to northern markets as some of the first strawberries of the season. This made them some of the most valuable berries each year. Many years, more than 1500 railcars were shipped annually, bringing $1,600,000 to the county. Additionally, many growers also produced strawberry plants for producers around the world. The A. W. Hoofman farm sold almost six million plants in 1935 alone to producers in places such as China, Mexico and Cuba, as well as all across the United States.

256.3 **PANGBURN** – The Missouri & North Arkansas Railroad operated their first train to Pangburn on Friday, April 3, 1908, the day after the construction crew arrived here. The former grade entered Pangburn from the north and traveled through town between 1st Street and Oak Street. From the north, the grade of the railroad passed through today's ballpark, once the site of a large lumber complex. It then headed south and crossed Main Street (Arkansas Highway 16) between the Pangburn post office and the adjacent gas station. Heading further south, the line stayed east of Marsh Mountain, crossed Big Creek, and entered Letona from the north.

Pangburn had a 27-car siding on the west side of the mainline, with a 12-car spur heading north off the south end of the siding. The Pangburn Cotton Gin was located on the west side of the mainline, south of today's Main Street. The railroad also had a cotton platform in that area. The Standard #3 depot (22' x 40') used the telegraph code of "BU" and was located on the east side of the mainline. The Pangburn depot is another one that was turned into a house after the building was sold. Unfortunately, the building deteriorated and required major work by 2010. The owners offered it to several organizations, but after the city council turned down the offer, the building was torn down and the timber salvaged during late 2012.

After the railroad shut down, the Pangburn depot was used as a home. Unfortunately, it was torn down in 2012. This view shows the distinctive bay window that made the depot easy to locate. Photo by Barton Jennings.

Trains #211 and #212 provided daytime service between Heber Springs and Helena. Pangburn provided a great deal of business, and trains #211 and #212 were scheduled to depart at 7:45am and 5:40pm respectively.

Before white settlers arrived, the Pangburn area was the location of an Osage village. However, the village was abandoned when the first settlers arrived about 1817, but some of the structures were used as protection for the settlers' livestock. The first family to arrive were the Kings, who had used a flatboat to travel up the Little Red River. As the community grew, the Judson family arrived and opened a small store, and when the post office opened in 1856, it was located in their store and used the name of Judson. In 1880, the post office and the community changed its name to Pangburn as the town moved a short distance south to avoid flooding. The name Pangburn came from Dr. William David Pangburn, who with his family, moved from Schenectady, New York, to here about 1860. Pangburn had bought several small farms, and the new community was located on his land, at an elevation of 348 feet.

During the 1800s, Pangburn was a port town on the Little Red River. While the river levels prevented regular service, crops, timber, and other products were held here until water was high enough to allow the arrival of small steamboats. The boat service ended when the Missouri & North Arkansas Railroad arrived in 1908, but the timber industry provided a large boost to the community. Reportedly the first lumber company to arrive was the Western Tie and Timber Company from Linn Creek, Missouri, which supplied ties for the railroad construction and also floated ties down the river for other railroad projects.

From when the railroad was built until the Great Depression, Pangburn was a center of lumbering. Some of the companies that operated at Pangburn included the Arkansas Soft Pine Lumber Company, Baker Lumber Company, Eskew Lumber Company, Lewis Brothers, N. Schimdt, and the Dan Shepard Lumber Company. All of this activity led to the incorporation of Pangburn on April 8, 1911. As the timber was cut, open land was planted with cotton, and soon three cotton gins were operating around Pangburn. The population peaked at 706 in 1920, and then the end of the timber industry and changes in the cotton industry led to a slow reduction. By 1960, the population was 489.

Things began to change after 1960. First, the Greers Ferry Dam led to an increase in tourism, especially fishing for trout. Next, Pangburn became the location of Titan II Launch Complex 373-4, assigned to the 308th Strategic Missile Wing (SMW) based out of the Little Rock Air Force Base. This was the first launch facility to be built in Arkansas, and was also the location of fifty-three deaths on August 9, 1965, when an accident caused a massive fire in the silo. Another economic boom occurred shortly after the start of the 21st Century when natural gas drilling began in what is known as Fayetteville Shale. By 2010, the population of Pangburn was 601, down from 654 in 2000.

Pangburn prides itself as being the home of Luther G. Presley, the writer of the song *When the Saints Go Marching In*. Presley was inducted into the Southern Gospel Hall of Fame on October 11, 2008. As the sign honoring his work says, "may his memory remain immortalized for his enlightening contributions to musical history and notability of his hymns."

Several markers stand in Pangburn to honor Luther G. Presley, the writer of the song *When the Saints Go Marching In*, including this one near the town's offices. Photo by Sarah Jennings.

259.2 DRAKE – Located at an elevation of 279 feet, this 3-car spur track was generally known as Drake Spur and served the Drake sawmill. During the early 1900s, the area's population was enough to support the Drake Spur School, a one-room schoolhouse serving several dozen students. The track was removed when the sawmill closed, and the area is now known as Mountain Home, with most of the community located to the east on Arkansas Highway 16.

260.1 BIG CREEK BRIDGE – Big Creek, also once known as Big Indian Creek, forms in the hills south of Heber Springs where Sexton Creek, Waters Creek, and

Candlestick Creek all merge to form a larger stream. Big Creek flows to the east and eventually enters the Little Red River. Approaching Big Creek from the north, the M&NA was forced to build a long raised grade across the lowlands. The bridge used large concrete piers to carry the three deck plate girder spans (two were 40 feet long while one was 90 feet long) required to cross the stream.

260.8 DK&S JUNCTION – Letona was a base for a sawmill and a logging railroad operated by the Doniphan Lumber Company. The mill was open by 1900, but plans for the logging railroad were announced in 1910. The March 2, 1910, issue of *Engineering-Contracting* had a short article about the plans. It stated: "Surveys have been made, right-of-way secured and some of the material bought for a new railroad to be built by the Doniphan Lumber Co. from Letona, in White County, on the Missouri & North Arkansas, west into Cleburne County, for a distance of about 15 miles. The road, as planned, will touch within a few miles of Quitman and later will be extended to that place."

The logging railroad was operating by 1911, and Letona was listed as a connection with the Doniphan, Kensett & Searcy Railroad in the September 1912 *Official Railway Equipment Register*, with early M&NA documents showing it to be here at DK&S Junction. From near Letona, the railroad ran up Big Creek to south of Heber Springs. It had branches to Sexton Creek and Candlestick Creek, while the main route followed Bush Creek over a ridge just south of Cross Roads Church. A major logging camp named Raywinkle was once located in that area. Later a line was built to the Stacey Springs area. This line was abandoned in 1915 and a new logging line was built from near Pangburn to the Little Red River. Some sources state that this line actually crossed the river to allow the company to log parts of eastern Cleburne County. The Little Red River spur closed during January 1917.

As previously covered, the Doniphan Lumber Company's Doniphan, Kensett & Searcy Railroad had trackage rights from Searcy to this area over the M&NA. Until 1917, these trains were shown in the timetables of the M&NA, operating daily except Sunday. Train #40 departed Searcy at 5:00am and arrived at Letona at 5:55am. The return train, #41, was scheduled to depart Letona at 4:50pm and arrive at Searcy at 5:40pm.

The peak of operations was reportedly 1914 when the DK&S paid the M&NA $7424 for trackage rights. During this time, the rates were $1 per mile for one locomotive and 20 cars, plus $0.10 per car-mile for each additional car. As a part of the agreement, 25% of the manufactured goods from timber that moved using the trackage rights was to be shipped over the M&NA. The Doniphan Lumber Company received a rebate when more than 25% was shipped. As the last of the lumber was being cut, an agreement in 1916 allowed the movement of a maximum of 100 carloads of rough cut pine from sawmills at Snell and Pangburn. The last movement of a DK&S train over the M&NA was in 1917.

261.1 LETONA – John and Nancy Magness arrived in the Letona area in 1815, reportedly the first settlers in what became White County. Through the 1800s, the area was just a collection of farms. Possibly the most excitement of the century took place on May 27,

1862, when Confederate forces, Company A of the Thirty-second Arkansas Infantry, attacked a forage train being operated by the First Missouri Infantry, a battle known as the Skirmish at Big Indian Creek.

This isolation changed when the Doniphan Lumber Company built a lumber mill nearby, and the community received a post office in 1900 named Cox for the first postmaster, Asa Cox. Some reports from the time show that the post office was also called Coxey. The M&NA arrived in early 1908, and soon a depot near the sawmill was built and named Letona, reportedly for a railroad employee. However, other sources say that the name came about by combining the words "Leto" (the name of the mother of the Greek god Jupiter) and "na" for North Arkansas. The Cox post office also changed its name to Letona in 1908.

To house visitors, the Letona Hotel was built in 1910 across the street from the railroad depot. The 2½ story wood frame structure is located on North Hotel Street just north of Arkansas Highway 310. The building is now used as a private residential duplex and was placed on the National Register of Historic Places in 1991. The years 1910-1911 were important for Letona as plans were announced for a logging railroad and the town was incorporated on September 23, 1911. The population reached 300 in 1913. Further promotions by the Letona Realty Company, owned by the family of Letona mayor Z. M. Walker, brought in more industry and residents.

The closure of the Doniphan Lumber Company operation in the late teens was a major setback, but other companies continued to operate. In 1921, J. E. Hughes, B. F. Lawrence, and the Premium Hardwood Lumber Company all operated lumber mills or dealt in hardwood. J. M. Neighbors operated a corn meal and feed business. There was also a cotton gin and a growing agricultural trade featuring peaches, strawberries, and radishes. The peach trees were reportedly part of a plan by the Doniphan Lumber Company to plant 8,000 acres of peach trees on land that had been cut by the company.

This structure was once the Letona Hotel, located across the street from the M&NA depot. Photo by Sarah Jennings.

The number of residents made a slow drop until 1960 when the census reported that 141 people lived in Letona. Since then, the number of residents has slowly increased as jobs in nearby Searcy can easily be reached by highway. The population of Letona in 2010 was 255

In 1940, the railroad had a 44-car siding on the west side of the mainline at Letona. The depot was on the east side close to the Letona Hotel. According to Kubat, the station measured 22' x 40' and was a

Standard #3 frame building. During the 1910s and 1920s, there were a number of industry tracks also in the area. The railroad agency closed about 1920 when Doniphan Lumber Company moved away. However, Letona was still a source of traffic for the railroad, being the source of 149 cars of traffic in 1945. The depot building was sold on November 11, 1945, when the railroad sold off much of its unneeded property.

262.3 MAGNESS CREEK BRIDGE – The creek is named after the Magness family who settled in the area in 1816. The bridge had timber approaches to a 50-foot-long deck plate girder span across the creek. This was one of many bridges burned during the second week of January 1923 (January 12th), during the peak of the railroad labor strike. The night before, the timber bridge at Milepost 263.1 was also burned.

263.4 MT. PISGAH – Mount Pisgah was a short 2-car spur track to the east with the switch on the south end, retired in 1929. There was also a small frame shelter that was used as a flag stop for the passenger trains. The railroad made a slight curve and then headed south toward Armstrong Springs. Mount Pisgah is named for the mountain located just to the west. The community was first settled in 1816 when the Magness family started a farm at the base of the mountain. The Magness family cemetery still exists. The earliest listed grave in the Mount Pisgah Cemetery is for Mary Teer, who died on August 16, 1858.

The top of the mountain, at 660 feet, is the highest point in White County. For years during the 1820s, it was a landmark on one of the major routes of the

Southwest Trail. This trail, also known as the Old Military Road, was a route from the St. Louis area to Fulton, Arkansas. There, connections were made with several trails that led to Natchitoches, Louisiana, and directly to Texas. At the time, the Red River at Fulton was the border between the United States and Mexico, and the route was popular with those heading to the Texas area at the invitation of Mexico. The trail was improved as a military road during the 1830s, and even today the route is used by several major highways.

During the years of the Southwest Trail, the town was an important stop and supply base. It was noted for having doctors, and the Mount Pisgah Mason lodge was well known. A post office opened in 1872, but it closed in 1914 when the mail service moved to Searcy. County maps from the 1930s show most of the town just to the east of the tracks, with a number of churches. In 1938, the "New Mount Pisgah School" was built using fieldstone. However, little remains today at the intersection of Mt. Pisgah Road and Morris School Road.

266.7 ARMSTRONG SPRINGS – This railroad station has a complicated story. First, while it is named Armstrong Springs, it is actually in the town of Crosby, and was first known as King. However, Armstrong Springs was a popular health resort about a mile to the west. Since more passengers used the stop than freight shippers, the railroad station was named for the resort.

The general area of Armstrong Springs started as the Homestead Plantation. In 1851, Jacob Douglas Armstrong led his family through the area and camped at the springs, waters that had been used by

Native Americans and early settlers to cure illnesses. Jacob recovered from an illness while at the springs and immediately made plans to stay in the area. He quickly bought the local farm and springs and soon opened a hotel for visitors, promoting the location as Armstrong Springs. To support visitors, a number of businesses were started such as stores, a blacksmith shop, farms, a school and churches.

Crowds came for the cures and the family advertised the location across the country. In 1908, the Armstrong family sold the resort to Bishop John B. Morris and the Brotherhood of St. Paul. The Catholic organization built a hospital near the springs and members of the order took care of the patients. Part of the facility also became a school taught by the Olivetan Benedictine Sisters. However, by 1915, the springs began to dry up. The Benedictine Sisters' school closed and the hotel was turned over to E. W. Kettler and his wife of nearby Crosby, where the station for Armstrong Springs was actually located. Most of the resort and hotel closed the next year.

Change came quickly. The facility was briefly used as a school for troubled boys, and then in 1922, the Franciscan Brothers of Cincinnati turned the facility into a Catholic boys' school. The hotel became the school while the hospital became the residence hall for the Brothers. The school was known as the Morris School for Boys in honor of Bishop John Morris. It closed in 1993, and then became the Center Hill School in 2000.

The post office here also went through a number of changes. According to the Arkansas History Commission, the first post office opened in 1901 with the name Quinton. It was named for Quinton Straud Armstrong, the grandson of the founder of

Heber Springs (AR) to Helena (AR)

the community and resort. Records indicate that the names Strand and Neal were also proposed. In 1912, the name was changed to Armstrong Springs. Meanwhile, another area post office was named Crosby, which opened in 1909 on the railroad. This post office was originally to be known as King Station after the name of the railroad station. The railroad changed the station's name to Crosby in 1909. This post office merged with Armstrong Springs in 1917, and the combined station became known as Crosby. Starting by 1912, the station was shown as "Crosby (Armstrong Springs)" in railroad timetables. Later in 1917, the post office again became Armstrong Springs to match the new name of the railroad depot. It finally closed in 1951.

For the railroad, there was a 17-car siding to the west known as Armstrong Springs. The Standard #4 station (20' x 40') was a telegraph station until 1920 and used the telegraph call "BY". The depot was reportedly removed during the early 1920s. A mail crane was installed sometime in the 1910s and operated until the end of the railroad. The railroad had stock pens and a cotton platform here, both retired in 1927. The only major industry was the Ben Filtrip Lumber Company, but the Acme Box Company was also here in the early 1920s. There was a public school at Crosby starting in 1907.

From Armstrong Springs, the railroad headed south for approximately 1.5 miles before turning east toward Searcy.

268.5 ACME – This spur track came and went several times. It was shown as the two-car spur track of Acme as early as the November 25, 1923, *Time Table No. 4*. It was shown as a flagstop for local freights

#221 and #222, but was gone by *Time Table No. 7* (September 4, 1927). The 1928 M&NA annual report stated that the railroad installed White Spur at this location that year. In *Time Table No. 9*, dated May 11, 1930, a seven-car spur track was shown here. The 1930 annual report stated that the track was retired that year.

271.2 KEYS CREEK BRIDGE – On modern maps, this stream is shown as the Key Branch of Deener Creek. The railroad crossed Keys Creek just east of today's Rose Lawn Apartments.

Coming in from the north, the Missouri & North Arkansas crossed today's Arkansas Highway 36 near the intersection with Joy Drive, just southeast of here. Chapel Lane, located just to the west, uses the old railroad grade. The shopping center on the south side of the highway also uses much of the old right-of-way. The grade can be seen as the tree line east of South Sawmill Road. Heading east, the grade is now used by Mulberry Street and the Beebe Capps Expressway.

273.8 SEARCY – Searcy is the county seat of White County and has a population of approximately 25,000. Searcy is the home of Harding University, a private liberal arts school associated with the Church of Christ. Harding College was founded in 1924 at Morrilton, Arkansas, and was named for James A. Harding, a minister and Christian educator. The school moved to Searcy in 1934 and used the campus of the recently closed Galloway Female College. Today, Harding University is the largest private university in the state of Arkansas.

During the early 1800s, the area was known as White Sulphur Springs for the healing springs now located in Spring Park. In 1837, the Arkansas State Legislature declared that White Sulphur Springs would be the county seat of the new White County. In 1838, the community was renamed Searcy after Richard Searcy, an early settler of Arkansas and a prominent legislator. Searcy served on the Fourth Circuit Superior Court of Arkansas until his death at the age of 36 in 1832. Israel Moore, a surveyor from Philadelphia, was contracted to plat the new town and to lay out the streets and to name them. He used many of the names from his hometown, and most still use the names that he assigned. Despite the survey, for some time, there was actually a legal battle over who owned the land where Searcy was sitting, with Moore one of the parties involved.

A post office known as Frankfort opened here in 1837, but it was changed to the current Searcy the next year. Searcy grew due to the county offices, but also due to its location on the Little Red River, earning the name Searcy Landing for its steamboat docks. The economy allowed schools to be open by the 1850s, and many of the first buildings were made with brick, unusual for a frontier town. With the growth, Searcy was incorporated on August 6, 1851. A third economic factor were the health resorts that grew around the springs. The decade's long impact of the Civil War hurt, but by the 1880s, Searcy was a booming community.

By the 1920s, Searcy was a consuming city, with most businesses catering to the local residents. There were bottling plants such as the Searcy Bottling Works and Walter Luffman, the Searcy Ice Company, the White County Warehouse Company, and the

Searcy Electric Light & Power Plant. There were still several companies in the timber industry, such as the Kelley Lumber Company, the Black Brothers Lumber Company, Brown & Company, and the Southern Red Cedar Post Company. A few other companies included the Searcy Cotton Oil Mill, the Searcy Concrete Block & Paving Company, Henry Wrape Cooperage, and Kaye Brothers broom factory.

A firm with a deep history in Arkansas also dates to this time. In 1923, Grisham's Ice Cream Company was created in Searcy. In 1932, Grisham's was acquired by one of its best salesmen, Ray Yarnell. Renamed Yarnell's Ice Cream, the company became regionally famous and grew to serve most of the state. For years Yarnell Ice Cream was the largest privately-owned ice cream company in Arkansas. The firm eventually failed and closed on June 30, 2011. In November 2011, the Schulze & Burch Biscuit Company bought the recipes and real estate for $1.3 million and restarted the company during April 2012.

Another unique job creator in Searcy was Wal-Mart's first distribution center outside of Bentonville. This facility today is a Sam's Club distribution center, while a newer and larger facility for Walmart stores is located a short distance to the south. Searcy has also been in the center of much of the oil and natural gas boom in Arkansas, and several drilling companies have been based here.

The Railroads

At one time Searcy was served by three different railroads: the Chicago, Rock Island & Pacific; the Doniphan, Kensett & Searcy; and the Missouri & North Arkansas. Little of these three railroads remain today, although rail can be found in streets and some of the grades are still obvious. The former Doniphan, Kensett & Searcy wooden station still stands at 412 South Main Street. The former grade can still be seen here, but new construction is quickly removing it. Searcy's Pioneer Village, located on the south side of town near the baseball and softball field complex, also houses the former Missouri Pacific depot from Garner, Arkansas. The Village has become the home for a number of late 19th century buildings from around White County.

Nothing remains of the east-west running M&NA facilities in Searcy, but a 1919 Sanborn map shows that there was a small yard and freight house, a combination passenger station with two waiting rooms, and several additional tracks. By 1936, trains #211 and #212 provided both passenger and freight service at Searcy. #211 was scheduled to depart at 8:55am, and #212 had a scheduled departure time of 4:55pm, although times could vary based upon traffic volumes and track conditions.

Searcy was another M&NA town with a large number of side tracks. The large 20' x 80' depot (telegraph call "DE") was located between South Main and South Spring Streets on the north side of Mulberry Street, just a block north of the Beebe Capps Expressway. West of the depot, on the north side of the mainline, was a 21-car siding, plus several yard tracks, a scale track, and a freight shed and platform. To the south was a 42-car siding with a scale on the west end and a crossover near the depot. Across these tracks was the Roberts Hotel, which served patrons from both the M&NA and DK&S passenger trains. Around the depot was a 38-car spur track with the switch on the east end. At the east siding switch was a connection to the Doniphan, Kensett & Searcy Railroad and an industrial lead that served several industries, both to the north of the mainline. After the Missouri & Arkansas abandoned in the late 1940s, the DK&S operated several former M&NA industry tracks to maintain service for shippers. However, the tracks in the area are now gone, and the west end of the DK&S is at the Bryce Corporation complex at East Park and Benton Avenues.

This is M&NA passenger car #57, converted many times over the years to handle passengers, mail, baggage and express freight. It was retired in 1945, sold, and turned into a residence located on the east side of Oak Street in Searcy, near the former main line of the M&NA. In 2007, the car was moved to Bald Knob, Arkansas, for restoration. Photo by Barton Jennings.

Ticket for passage on the Missouri and North Arkansas between Searcy and Leslie. From the collection of Barton Jennings.

Heber Springs (AR) to Helena (AR)

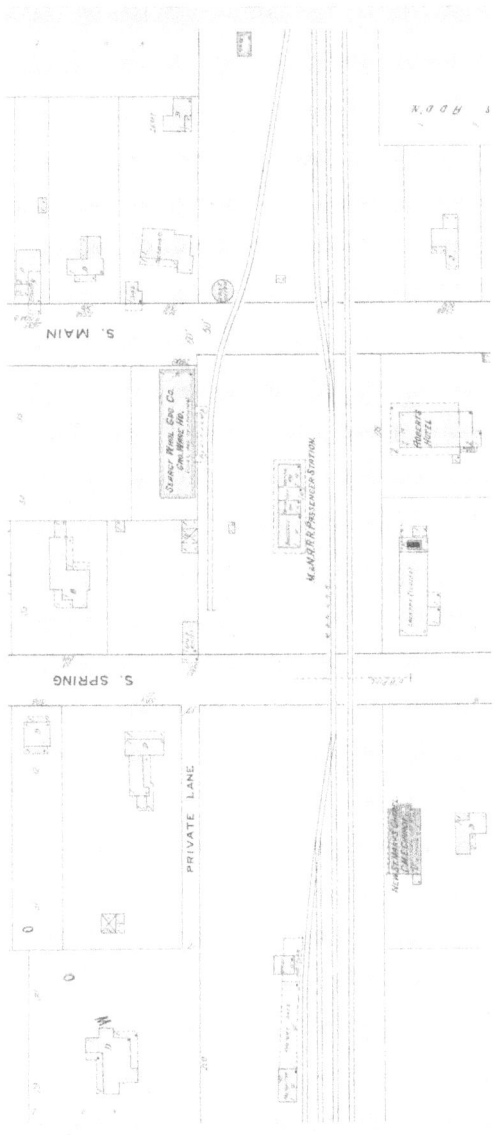

Sanborn Fire Insurance Map from Searcy, White County, Arkansas. Sanborn Map Company, Feb, 1919. Library of Congress, Geography and Map Division. https://www.loc.gov/item/sanborn00341_007/.

The Searcy Branch Railroad

The first railroad in Searcy was the Searcy Branch Railroad. In 1870, the Cairo & Fulton was building their line across Arkansas, and the route was to go several miles to the east of Searcy. The Searcy town council met with the railroad to attempt to get them to change their route, even offering to pay for a depot and any additional costs required to route the tracks through their town. Managers of the Cairo & Fulton examined the route, but hills located between Searcy and Bald Knob made construction of the line difficult, and the high costs created a controversy within Searcy about the possible expenses.

To solve the problem, during April of 1871, Searcy voters supported a plan to extend $20,000 in credit to connect Searcy with the C&F main line. On July 21, 1871, nine citizens of Searcy signed articles of association to create a a railroad to connect Searcy with the Cairo & Fulton at Kensett. This, according to the *Reports of Case at Law and in Equity, Argued and Determined in the Supreme Court of the State of Arkansas* (1887), started The Searcy Branch Railroad Company. The company quickly built a wooden tramway from Searcy to the Cairo & Fulton road at Kensett, using coaches pulled by horses. Reportedly the line cost $18,000 to build and equip with one passenger car and one freight car.

By 1877, the line was deteriorating and was sold to the Yarnell brothers, W. A. and A. W. Yarnell. The agreement for the purchase required that the Yarnells pay the sum of five hundred dollars in cash, and then extend the railroad to West Point. In 1882, the brothers incorporated the Searcy & West Point

Railroad Company, which eventually became a part of the Searcy & Des Arc Railroad.

Doniphan, Kensett & Searcy Railway

In 1906, the Doniphan Lumber Company located a large sawmill to the north of Kensett. The same year, the lumber company built a 1½ mile railroad from the mill to the southeast to a junction with the St. Louis, Iron Mountain & Southern at Kensett. To build the railroad, the Doniphan Lumber Company incorporated the Doniphan, Kensett & Searcy Railroad Company on March 20, 1906. In 1907, the railroad was extended when approximately five miles of track was built from Kensett to Searcy, where the line connected with both the Rock Island and the Missouri & North Arkansas Railroad. On May 22, 1909, the Doniphan, Kensett & Searcy Railway was created to acquire the assets of the old railroad company, and to acquire trackage rights over the Missouri & North Arkansas to reach the Doniphan Lumber Company timber near Letona.

The Doniphan, Kensett & Searcy Railway (DK&S) was part of a series of hearings by the Interstate Commerce Commission which evaluated a number of railroads owned by logging companies called "Tap Lines." These lines were essentially industrial railroads serving only their owners, but were established as common carriers to obtain a share of the shipment rate revenue. Many of the lines were found to not be common carriers, and they lost their ability to charge a part of the rate for their services.

The Tap Line Case report included a number of details about the DK&S. It stated that the "lumber company and the tap line are identical in interest, their stock being held by the same individuals. The tap line is also indebted to the lumber company in a sum exceeding $35,000." The report stated that the track from Doniphan to Kensett was used "exclusively for the traffic of the lumber company and its employees." However, the line from Kensett to Searcy was "used chiefly for the movement of logs for the lumber company." There was some outside traffic over it, but that traffic accounted for less than 15 percent of the total.

The report also stated that the DK&S owned 2 locomotives, 21 flat cars, and 2 cabooses, all having safety appliances. The Doniphan Lumber Company was reported as owning no rail equipment of its own. The employees of the DK&S include two train crews, one section gang, two station agents, and two general officers, who also were officers of the lumber company. The DK&S was described as a profitable company and the Interstate Commerce Commission established a switching charge for the Doniphan to Kensett line, as well as a division of the rates on traffic moved over the line to Searcy.

A valuation report from the Interstate Commerce Commission later stated that the Doniphan, Kensett & Searcy Railway owned "5.805 miles of first main track and 1.316 miles of yard tracks and sidings." The railroad continued to operate at the need of the Doniphan Lumber Company, later the Carter Bloxonend Flooring Company. During December 1931, the railroad was sold to the Missouri Pacific, which later became part of Union Pacific. For years, the railroad has operated as a subsidiary and was used to train managers in train operations.

Heber Springs (AR) to Helena (AR)

The Doniphan, Kensett & Searcy and its owner played an important role in the history of the M&NA. This is the Searcy depot of the DK&S in 1988. Nearby, there was once an interchange track between the two railroads. Photo by Barton Jennings.

At Kensett, a short part of the Doniphan line still exists to serve an industry. The Searcy line also still exists, although cut back from Milepost 300.40 at Searcy, to Milepost 299.12 in 1999. The rail line follows Searcy Street west from Kensett, which becomes Park Avenue. The line now ends at Benton Avenue, and the grade on west is now a paved sidewalk.

The mill and community at Doniphan are now the Doniphan Lumber Mill Historic District. It was placed on the National Register of Historic Places in 1991.

274.1 GIN CREEK BRIDGE – Gin Creek was a popular stream during the early days of Searcy and White County development. Several mills were on the stream, which is spring fed, and reportedly the first cotton gin in the area was located on it in the 1850s between Searcy and the Little Red River. It is fished regularly for largemouth and smallmouth bass, bream and bluegill.

274.5 C.R.I.&P. CROSSING – The M&NA crossed the Chicago, Rock Island & Pacific (Rock Island) and then had an interchange track and spur track in the northeast quadrant of the diamond. Many timetables show that there was a gate that was normally set against the M&NA. Just to the northwest, the M&NA had a track that served Federal Compress. The location today is not recognizable, but it was near the current intersection of E. Beebe Capps Expressway and Dr. Jimmy Carr Street. This Rock Island line has a complex history involving four smaller railroads that each built a part of the line.

The oldest part of the Rock Island property is the Searcy & West Point Railroad Company, incorporated on July 3, 1882, to "commence at the town of Searcy and run from thence via Kensett, on the St. Louis, Iron Mountain & Southern Railway, on the most direct and practicable route, to West Point, on the Little Red River; the termini and the line thereof being about nine miles." An 1896 Sanborn map showed the Searcy facilities of the Searcy & West Point Railroad. The railroad started at the corner of West Pleasure Avenue and Spring Street. On the northeast corner, across the street from today's White County Public Library, was the express and freight depot. From here, the railroad ran eastward down the middle of Pleasure. There was a cotton platform on the north side of Pleasure just east of Oak Street, with the 2-stall shop complex further to the east, just west of Charles Street.

On August 26, 1897, the Des Arc & Northern Railway Company was incorporated to build and operate a railroad and telegraph line between Searcy and Des Arc, as well as an extension on to Bee Rock on the Little Red River. The company built the 24 miles between Des Arc and Searcy. On June 29, 1899, the Searcy & Des Arc Railroad Company was incorporated to consolidate the two railroads "to form a continuous line of railroad from Searcy, in White County, to Des Arc, in Prairie County, in the State of Arkansas – 25 miles." At the same time, the route of the Searcy & West Point Railroad was abandoned, leaving just the line south of Searcy.

On November 28, 1902, the next part of the railroad was incorporated when the Hazen & Northern Railroad Company was created to build a railroad and telegraph line from a connection with the Searcy & Des Arc Railroad southward to the Choctaw, Oklahoma & Gulf Railroad (CO&G) near Hazen, Arkansas. The railroad was built further east than planned and connected to the CO&G at Mesa, five miles to the east. The plan for the railroad also included a line from Searcy to Heber Springs. This line was never built and the route became the Missouri & North Arkansas. The CO&G supported the completion of the railroad.

The *Third Annual Report of the Railroad Commission of the State of Arkansas* (1903) included a statement that the Searcy & Des Arc Railroad Company was a part of the Rock Island System, and that the Choctaw, Oklahoma & Gulf "took possession of the road on May 1, 1902, and upon taking charge found that there were neither books nor records to show what had been done prior to that date." On March 24, 1904, all of these lines were sold to the Chicago, Rock Island & Pacific Railway Company. Initially the railroad handled a great deal of timber, but then slowly saw a reduction in freight traffic to just handling the spring and fall agricultural moves. In late 1959, the line between Searcy and Des Arc was abandoned. The line between Mesa and Des Arc was abandoned in 1980 when the Rock Island shut down.

There is one additional story related to this line that involves the Missouri & North Arkansas. Several times when the route across the White and Cache River bottoms was examined, there were proposals that the M&NA use the Rock Island from Searcy to Mesa and then east to Wheatley. This would have avoided some of the most expensive track to maintain. While the Rock Island favored the agreement, the M&NA never felt that it could afford the change.

277.7 **KENSETT** – Until the early 1870s, this area was simply a number of scattered farms working the land between the Little Red and White Rivers. A small town about a mile north of here attracted a post office in 1837 by the name of Franfort. In 1838, the post office closed and moved to Searcy. However, during the early 1870s, a railroad was built through the area and towns were created. One of these was Kensett, named for Thomas Kensett, a member of the railroad's board of directors. Thomas Kensett's family had made their money in the canning business, and he was involved with a number of railroads, including later the Iowa Central Railway. On October 4, 1872, the Kensett post office opened. About this time, the Searcy Branch Railroad connected Kensett to Searcy. The railroad later became part of the Searcy & Des Arc Railroad and was abandoned in the late 1890s.

The first decade of the Twentieth Century was a time of big growth for Kensett as both the Doniphan, Kensett & Searcy and the Missouri & North Arkansas built through town. This gave Kensett shippers a number of competitive options, and industry moved to the area. The M&NA also provided some employment as the railroad built a small yard and shop complex just west of the Missouri Pacific line. Kensett was finally incorporated on October 16, 1911. During the late 1920s, the connection with the Missouri Pacific at Kensett was the third largest interchange point on the M&NA. During the period 1926-1928, the M&NA delivered 5307 cars to Missouri Pacific and received 3837 cars, out of a total of 36,863 and 35,095 cars. This was 14% of the outbound traffic and 11% of the inbound traffic. Because of the traffic, a siding was added at Kensett in 1926 as part of the system upgrade of the railroad.

Although Kensett was just four miles from Searcy, southbound #211 wasn't scheduled to depart Kensett until 10:00am, more than an hour after it departed Searcy. This was due to the great deal of interchange business that took place at Kensett. Northbound #212 was scheduled to depart at 4:30pm.

Like many small towns, the Great Depression was hard on the town, and the robbery of the Kensett Bank in 1934 didn't help. The population started to drop as industry closed and war jobs in big cities attracted workers off the farms. The closing of the Missouri & Arkansas in the late 1940s also cut the connections with several sources of business. The 1950s saw some return to prosperity as jobs were created nearby in Searcy. Additionally, the first all-electric cotton gin in White County opened at Kensett during the early 1950s.

Kensett was actually the home of a number of important and famous people during the Twentieth Century. Among these are Bill Dickey, National Baseball Hall of Fame catcher for the New York Yankees during the Babe Ruth era; Lonnie Glosson, known nationally as the "Talking Harmonica Man" and frequently billed as the "Best Harmonica Player in the World;" Georgia Holt, an actress and singer best known as the mother of pop superstar Cher; and Wilbur D. Mills, who served in Congress for thirty-eight years, including seventeen years as chairman of the powerful Ways and Means Committee.

Today, the population of Kensett is slightly less than 2000, and it is noted as having the lowest sales tax rate in White County. The natural gas industry has offices in the area and the landscaping and nursery business is big here. Among these nurseries are the Double Springs sod farm and the Two Rivers Nursery. The downtown Cowen Park contains Missouri Pacific Caboose #11345 on what was the location of the Hotel Bevil. The grade of the Missouri & North Arkansas can clearly be seen at the south end of the park.

Missouri & North Arkansas Shops

When the railroad was built through Kensett, construction stopped for some time here. Rail service from the north started on October 19, 1908. A small shop complex was planned to do minor work and to store equipment. During 1910-1911, the Searcy-Kensett Transportation Company operated a former Rock Island gasoline motor car between the two towns to serve the many Missouri Pacific passenger trains, often using the shop for minor repairs.

A full evaluation of the railroad in the late 1920s determined that the shops at Kensett were insufficient, requiring a great deal of expense to move equipment to Harrison for repairs. Improvements began in 1926 when a siding was added at Kensett. In 1929, plans were announced for a new shop complex. The October 26, 1929, issue of *Railway Age* reported: "Missouri & North Arkansas – The receiver for this company has acquired seven acres of land adjoining the company's property at Kensett, Ark., for the purpose of constructing a roundhouse, a machine shop and a storage shed for passenger cars."

This land was railroad-north of the Missouri Pacific diamond. The facility included a siding to the south (railroad-west), and a complex of tracks and a wye to the north (railroad-east). There was a standard 16' x 24' wooden 50,000-gallon water tank which obtained its water from the Kensett city water system. East of the wye was a track to the north that served a three-track shop complex. The new shop included a 3-stall engine house measuring 70' x 120'. While the original plan was for a full repair shop, the equipment was never purchased and no major repairs were ever conducted here. However, the remains of the Heber Springs shop were closed and much of the minor repair and inspection work was moved to Kensett.

For many years, Kensett was the dividing point between the north and south end of the railroad. Passenger trains often began and ended here. For example, in 1937, a gas-powered Brill motorcar operated the passenger service between Kensett and Helena, while a streamlined American Car & Foundry car operated Kensett north. The yard and shops were used to collect equipment from the south end of the railroad in 1946. They were soon torn down. However, some of the foundations can still be found just west of downtown Kensett. Three service pits are clearly visible, with the two to the west shorter than the eastern pit.

Missouri Pacific Crossing

This line today belongs to Union Pacific, and is the primary route for moving chemicals, automobiles, lumber and other products between Texas and Mexico to the markets in the north and northeast. The railroad still functions much as the builders planned. The railroad started as a 5' 6" gauge railroad known as the Cairo & Fulton Railroad, chartered by the State of Arkansas on February 9, 1853. The Cairo & Fulton, designed to build track across Arkansas from Missouri to Texas, was part of a series of incorporations between St. Louis and southern Texas. The Civil War delayed the construction, and work didn't start until 1871. Because of the delays and changing finances, the company was reorganized on May 21, 1872, as the Cairo, Arkansas & Texas Railroad Company (CA&T). By January 7, 1873, the railroad had completed approximately 70 miles of track from the Arkansas-Missouri border to the White River at Newport, Arkansas.

Construction sped up in 1873, and by summer the tracks had reached Kensett from the north. On December 22, 1873, trains began to operate between St. Louis and Little Rock. As a part of the line's consolidation, the CA&T and other lines were leased to the St. Louis, Iron Mountain & Southern Railway.

On June 28, 1879, the gauge of the entire line was changed to the standard gauge of 4' 8½". In 1883, the St. Louis, Iron Mountain & Southern was acquired by Jay Gould as part of his plans to create a national rail network. The railroad entered receivership on August 19, 1915, and was merged with the Missouri Pacific on May 12, 1917. The line became the heart of the Missouri Pacific system, moving some of the most valuable shipments on the railroad. In 1982, Missouri Pacific was part of a merger that created a larger Union Pacific. This route still serves the Texas and Louisiana petrochemical industry, and hosts daily Amtrak *Texas Eagle* trains, passing through Kensett in the middle of the night if they are on schedule.

A joint depot (telegraph call "KS") was located here on the west side of the Missouri Pacific mainline and on the north (railroad-east) side of the M&NA. The station was the former 106' x 21' Missouri Pacific passenger and freight depot, which was moved almost 1000 feet to the new diamond south of today's intersection of Southwest 1st and West Dandridge Streets. Reports from 1910 state that the station was moved to prevent the Arkansas Railroad Commission from ordering the move and establishing the required services. The move was completed by April of that year.

The station area featured several platforms to exchange passengers, including one M&NA spur track and platform to handle the gas-electric motorcars that operated north of Kensett. With the M&NA on the edge of failure during the Depression, the railroad moved out of the Missouri Pacific station and into a small 12' x 18' depot built by the M&NA in 1933. Earlier in 1927, the railroad had built its own freight room from a retired freight car. Just east (railroad-south) of the diamond was a siding to the south with an interchange track that connected with the Missouri Pacific mainline. In this same area was the Chess & Wymard Stave Mill.

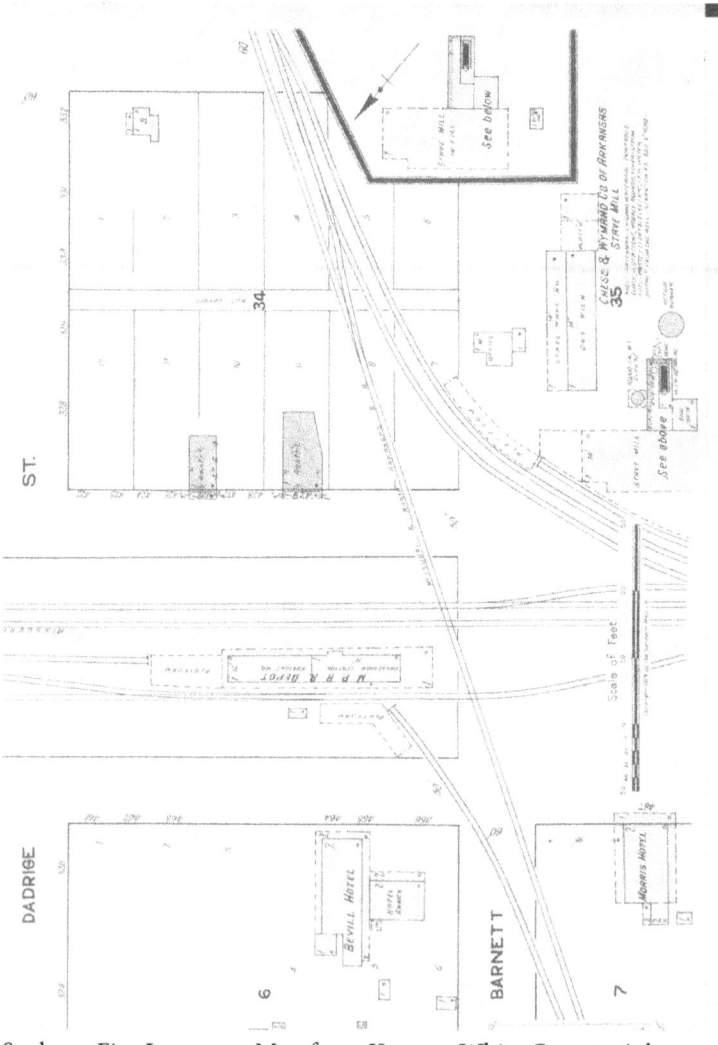

Sanborn Fire Insurance Map from Kensett, White County, Arkansas. Sanborn Map Company, March, 1919. Library of Congress, Geography and Map Division. https://www.loc.gov/item/sanborn00276_002/.

This 1919 Sanborn map shows the diamond and station arrangement between the M&NA and Missouri Pacific. Note the platform and spur track used by the M&NA motorcar.

The diamond was controlled by a gate that was normally lined against the Missouri & North Arkansas. To cross the Missouri Pacific, the M&NA would get authorization and then swing the gate open, blocking the Missouri Pacific. Also to protect the diamond, there was apparently a ball signal for many years. A ball signal was an older form of traffic control where the number of balls (during daylight hours) or lanterns (during night time) raised on the pole indicated which route had priority. Later, the ball signals were replaced by more modern signals.

Heading east from the Union Pacific mainline through Kensett, the M&NA grade is initially Luttrell Street. This street sign shows the intersection with Depot Street, the street immediately to the east of Union Pacific. Photo by Barton Jennings.

Heading from Kensett to West Point to the southeast, the abandoned Missouri & North Arkansas Railway grade is now Old Railroad Road. The track from Kensett to Cotton Plant was the last part of the railroad completed due to the White River bottom lands, an area with almost seasonal flooding.

Several street signs mark the old M&NA railroad grade heading south from Kensett as the grade is now known as Old Railroad Road. Photo by Barton Jennings.

280.0 SPUR 280 – The November 25th, 1923, employee timetable showed a 5-car spur at this location with the name Spur 280.

281.2 WEST POINT – West Point was in the middle of a long straight stretch on the Missouri & North Arkansas. The railroad followed the same route as used by Old Railroad Road from Kensett, passed through the southwest side of town, and continued to head to the southeast. The grade is easy to see between

West Point and Arkansas Highway 36. From there to Pryor, the railroad was immediately to the north of Highway 36. West Point had a Standard #4 20' x 40' depot to the east and a 17-car siding to the west. The growing of strawberries and other similar berries was attempted around West Point, and a railroad-owned berry shed stood here until 1926. West Point also hosted some track crews, but the "section dwelling" was retired in 1932.

The location of West Point was long a native hunting and fishing area, and was one of the first places settled by white explorers in 1789. When steamboats began to serve the Little Red River, this was the normal high point of navigation. The town of West Point was first surveyed in 1850, and lots were sold the same year by local businessman J. M. West. The population immediately boomed to 350 citizens. In 1852, a post office opened at West Point, making it the second oldest existing post office in White County. In 1858, West Point was incorporated, and several sources state that it was once in the running to be the capital of Arkansas. Because West Point was an important river port, it was the destination of several military movements during the Civil War. Two historical markers that are part of the Arkansas Civil War Sesquicentennial Marker Program are located in West Point. They read as follows.

Naval Combat at West Point

The U.S. gunboat Cricket steamed up the Little Red River Aug. 14, 1863, hunting the Confederate steamboats Kaskaskia and Tom Sugg. She captured the vessels at Searcy Landing and de-

stroyed a pontoon bridge. While the flotilla steamed downriver, 500 Confederate cavalrymen led by Col. G. W. Thompson attacked. The Kaskaskias pilot was wounded, and Confederate troops tried to board her, but were repelled. The Cricket fired her cannons at the attackers and some rounds hit West Point, damaging several houses as the vessels struggled downstream.

Combat on the Little Red River

The Confederates pursued the Cricket and steamers down the river, attacking again about four miles below West Point without success. The Cricket met the U.S.S. Lexington farther downstream, and the Confederates struck again as the fleet steamed down the Little Red. The Lexington opened fire with her 8-inch guns, and Thompson called off the attack. The Confederates suffered 8 casualties, including Maj. L. A. Gilkey, who fell mortally wounded. Union troops lost 2 men killed and 6 wounded in the only naval engagement of the 1863 Little Rock Campaign.

When the Cairo, Arkansas & Texas Railroad built through nearby Kensett, West Point lost much of its importance as a trade and transportation center. In 1879, West Point became the end of a short branch line of the Searcy & Des Arc Railroad Company. Known as the West Point Division, the line stretched

3.2 miles from Kensett to West Point, according to the Railroad Commission of Arkansas. In 1880, the census showed West Point's population as 123, and estimates for later in the decade are about 150. An article in the *Memphis Avalanche* covered the town's bygone era of prosperity, mentioning vacant store buildings and empty houses. However, the town also had three general stores, a drugstore, a blacksmith, a grist mill, a cotton gin, a wood shop, a school, and a church.

The Searcy & Des Arc Railroad, later the Choctaw, Oklahoma & Gulf Railroad and then the Chicago, Rock Island & Pacific, abandoned their line to West Point about 1900, although the *Third Annual Report of the Railroad Commission of the State of Arkansas* (1903) still showed the Kensett to West Point route. Attempts were made to save the branch and several local businessmen even tried to incorporate a new company to operate the line. Things began to look up in 1908 when the Missouri & North Arkansas built through town, but the railroad's poor condition didn't allow the town to compete with nearby Kensett. However, timber firms such as the Acme Box Company, Kelley Lumber Company, and L. A. Pryor all operated near West Point.

In 1923, the last steamboat arrived and departed West Point, ending that source of business. Next, the Missouri & Arkansas abandoned their line through town in 1946. Over the years, West Point advertised itself as "The Town with a Heart" because of the shape of the nearby Little Red River. Today West Point is a town of about 200 residents, consisting mostly of homes and a post office, with few local businesses.

282.0 MISSISSIPPI RIVER FUEL – South of West Point was a short spur track to the east that served the Mississippi River Fuel facility. The Mississippi River Fuel Corporation operated pipelines from Monroe, Louisiana, to St. Louis, Missouri. The firm was connected to several petroleum and natural gas companies, such as Standard Oil of New Jersey, United Gas, Columbian Carbon, United Carbon, and Electric Power & Light. This plant was built in 1935, providing an economic boost to West Point during the peak of the Depression. The pipeline company later acquired a sizeable interest in the Missouri Pacific Railroad, and established a pipeline subsidiary known as the Mississippi River Transmission Company. After Union Pacific merged with Missouri Pacific, the company sold the pipeline subsidiary.

While many records show that the plant was built in 1935, M&NA records show that a spur track was built here in 1929.

284.2 ANDREWS – The railroad had a small frame shelter located here starting during the 1910s. A post office was open 1909-1912. There were several early families with the name Andrews who settled in the area and created large farms. Today, Andrews, an unincorporated community in White County, is a cluster of a few rural homes at an elevation of 212 feet.

Heading toward Georgetown, the railroad grade can be seen on the north side of Arkansas Highway 36.

285.5 PRYOR – Heading to the southeast, look for where Arkansas Highway 36 starts to make a loop to the south, following the route of Taylor Slough. This location was known as Cunningham in 1925, and later was known by the railroad as Pryor. There was a short 9-car spur track to the west with the switch on the north end. L. A. Pryor sold lumber out of this location, according to the *Arkansas Marketing and Industrial Guide* of 1921. There is nothing here today except for a road into several large farm fields.

At the southeast end of the loop along Taylor Slough, Highway 36 comes back alongside the former grade of the Missouri & North Arkansas, which cut straight through the slough. The railroad once crossed the highway where Hubach 1 Road heads north, near the farm complex with a large two-story red brick house with six tall white columns. From here to Georgetown, the former railroad grade can now be seen to the south.

287.2 BARBER'S LAKE – Barbers Lake was shown as a flag stop in the 1945 timetable of the Missouri & Arkansas Railway. Barbers Lake was located on Barbers Lake Slough, part of a chain of streams in the area. There was a small passenger shelter here from 1909 until the late 1920s. In 1926, the railroad replaced a bridge just north of here at Milepost 287.1 with a culvert and fill.

287.6 BARBER LAKE SPUR – During the early 1900s, there was a small spur track here that used the name Barber Lake.

287.8 WRAPE – Henry Wrape and his Wrape Stave and Heading Mill Company operated several mills in east and northeast Arkansas. One of these was the Henry Wrape Company plant at Searcy. Over the years, Henry Wrape bought several blocks of land in this area. Later, the Wrape Company became part of the Searcy Flooring and Lumber Company. The location was listed as a flag stop and 669-foot spur track in 1925. The track was retired in 1927.

288.5 ENRIGHT – Enright is located where Hubach 2 Road heads north from Arkansas Highway 36. This area is a mix of tree farms and traditional farms as of 2018. Enright was a short 5-car spur track to the west with the switch on the north end. It was listed as a flag stop for much of the railroad's life, and there was a small shelter here until 1927. There was a mail crane here during the 1930s, and a post office was at Enright 1919-1955.

The *Arkansas Marketing and Industrial Guide* of 1921 showed that E. E. Stone and the White County Lumber Company both had operations at Enright, selling pine, red oak, and white oak. Products specifically mentioned included railroad ties, wagon and car parts, and smaller wood cuttings.

289.1 WATKINS – Watkins was a short 8-car spur track to the west with the switch on the south end. It was listed as a spur track but not a scheduled or flag stop for passenger trains. The name Watkins is very familiar in White County. The name White was also once used for this location, probably for the White County Lumber Company which operated in the area.

291.8 GEORGETOWN – Georgetown may be the oldest existing town in Arkansas, and the second settlement only after Arkansas Post. This claim is based upon a settlement that began nearby by Francis Francure on almost 1400 acres in 1789. The community went through a number of names. According to

The Encyclopedia of Arkansas History and Culture, Georgetown was "previously called Francure Township, as well as Negro Hill or Nigger Hill, probably indicative of the first slaves in the area being offloaded at the town's landing on the White River. It is also likely that an early black community located on a hill near the river was composed of runaway slaves from Louisiana, thus lending Negro Hill its name."

A key to the location was the White River and the access to steamboat service. A post office opened here in 1870 with the name Negro Hill. It became Georgetown in 1909, when three men from Clarendon, Arkansas, all with the surname of George, acquired land in the area and sold lots as part of an effort to create a town on the newly built Missouri & North Arkansas.

With the arrival of the railroad, industry boomed for a short time. The Thomas-Bowman Cooperage Company, the Dultmeier Manufacturing Company, and the Perry Hall lumber mill were examples of timber-related companies that located here. The need for workers also attracted other businesses such as four stores, a hotel, a movie house, three fish docks, a school, a drugstore, a barber shop, a doctor's office, a dentist's office, and two churches. Other manufacturing companies included a mattress factory and a hammer and ax handle mill. The population increased to almost 500.

However, the location of Georgetown also had its problems as the area routinely floods. Once the timber was cut, most of the mills shut down or moved away. The 1945 flood was a major part of the death of the Missouri & Arkansas Railway. In that year, the floods greatly damaged the nearby White River bridge and the line was abandoned the following year. While efforts to restore the line were considered, the cost of bridge repairs kept anyone from preserving the rail service.

Georgetown is located at an elevation of 203 feet, more than the number of residents which has held steady at about 125 for the past several decades. An interesting feature about the town is that it was incorporated on December 27, 1985. The town still covers about sixteen blocks, but houses are spread out. There are also a number of foundations that demonstrate how large the town used to be.

Coming in to Georgetown from the northwest, the railroad grade is just south of Highway 36, often visible in the woods. The railroad grade continued straight where the highway curves to the north, curved slightly as it crossed Deep Bank Slough, and then bridged across the White River. The Georgetown depot was located to the east of the mainline, with a long spur track curving off to the southeast. There was also a 45-car siding to the west of the mainline. The depot, shown as a Standard #3 structure measuring 22' x 40', was sold, moved and used as a house. It was flooded in 2011 while its owners were away and was eventually burned by the local fire department as part of a training exercise. There was a standard 16' x 24' wooden 50,000-gallon water tank near the bridge. There were two pumping stations, designed to supply water from the White River no matter the river level.

292.3 DEEP BANK SLOUGH BRIDGE – Much of the area around Georgetown is the Hurricane Lake State Wildlife Management Area. Deep Bank Slough drains the area south and southwest of Georgetown. The slough has one of several area boat ramps with

Heber Springs (AR) to Helena (AR)

access to the White River. The former M&NA bridge was located approximately where the boat ramp is now.

293.0 WHITE RIVER BRIDGE – This is the same White River that the railroad crossed at Beaver, Arkansas. However, it has changed greatly after the river started as several branches in the Ozark/Boston Mountains in northwest Arkansas, flowed north into Missouri, and then east and southeast back into Arkansas. At Beaver, the White River is still a small mountain river, but here it is a wide and muddy delta river. The river is navigable from the Mississippi River as far upstream as Batesville, Arkansas. At one time, Locks #1, #2, and #3 in the Batesville area allowed barge movements even further upstream, but in May 1952, Lock and Dam #1 was leased to the City of Batesville for recreation and hydroelectric purposes. On June 20, 1952, the lock gates at dams #2 and #3 were made inoperative by securing them closed. During April 1957, Lock #1 was heavily damaged by flooding and the lower gate was destroyed, ending any ability to navigate further upstream.

This bridge was one of the last items completed on the Missouri & North Arkansas Railroad. Construction of the bridge wasn't approved until February 4, 1908, when "An Act Authorizing the construction of a bridge across White River, Arkansas" was approved by Congress. The Act approved a bridge "across the White River at or near Negro Hill Landing, Arkansas, in township six north, range four west, at a point suitable to navigation interests, in the State of Arkansas." Apparently the railroad was ready for the approval as little time was spent in designing the bridge and beginning construction, with the railroad opening on March 1, 1909.

The bridge was built by the Wisconsin Bridge & Iron Company and the base of the rail was located at an elevation of 205.53 feet. Because of the navigation requirements, the bridge featured, from north to south, two 125-foot through truss spans, a 300-foot through truss turn span, plus a 60-foot deck plate girder span. There were timber trestles off each end. The bridge was long an issue for the railroad as the various piles often settled in the weak soils, and speeds were often limited to as little as 5 miles per hour for freight trains. For the train crews, the White River bridge was also listed as an overhead obstruction that would not clear a man riding on top or side of a car. Concerns about how the bridge would impact navigation can be seen by the work to make it one of the first truss bridges removed between Leslie and Cotton Plant after the railroad was abandoned. Documents show that plans for the bridge's removal were underway in September 1952. An interesting part of these communications was that they involved officials of the Arkansas & Ozarks Railway.

The 1927 floods affected much of the United States. April flooding along the White River impacted the railroad and many of the communities. However, this was actually the second flood of the year. A letter from H. J. Armstrong, Chief Engineer of the M&NA, to the Weather Bureau, U.S. Department of Agriculture, says that something else happened around the first of the year.

In his letter of March 17, 1927, Mr. Armstrong wrote about the pivot pier settling on the White River bridge at Georgetown, Arkansas. The Weather

Bureau had a river flood gauge on the pier and was worried about the accuracy of recent readings. The letter stated that the pier settled all at once after the January flood, and thus the measurements during the flood were accurate. Mr. Armstrong also wrote that the gauge was extended higher from 22 feet to 30 feet, placing this extension on the concrete base of the water tower and was to be used only for water over 22 feet – apparently for flood waters above the top of the pier. The letter finally stated that the pivot pier was being straightened and the gauge would be reinstalled.

After the April 1927 flood, the center pier again was leaning. A plan was created to drive piling both upstream and downstream of the failed pier, and then install five steel girders connecting the two pile clusters. The end of the through truss and the pivot span then rested on the girders instead of the old failed pier, which was eventually removed. Even with this work, completed in 1929, the pier never seemed to be right after the floods. The 1946 ICC report on the line indicated that the pier again needed to be repaired or replaced.

While the bridge was active, and even after, the Code of Federal Regulations (33 CFR, Section 117.583 – *White River, Ark., Missouri and Arkansas Railway Co. bridge near Georgetown, Ark.*) had specific requirements for river traffic and the bridge. It stated that the railroad was not required to keep a draw tender at the bridge to raise and lower it for traffic, but instead "[w]henever a vessel, unable to pass under the closed bridge, desires to pass through the draw, at least 48 hours' advance notice of the time the opening is required shall be given to the authorized representative of the owner. Upon receipt of such notice the authorized representative shall arrange for the prompt opening of the bridge at the time specified in the notice for the passage of the vessel." This regulation was still in the Code of Federal Regulations as late as at least 1969.

East of the river, the railroad headed straight through McClelland except for a small loop around a deep lake, staying north of a large horseshoe bend in the White River. Over the years, the railroad faced regular flooding in these White River bottoms, often leading to the railroad temporarily shutting down, and even detouring. One of the most cited detour routes was from Kensett to Fair Oaks on the Missouri Pacific, and then back to the Missouri & Arkansas at Fargo using the Cotton Belt.

County Line

Here, the White River is the county line between **White County**, to the west, and **Woodruff County** to the east. **Woodruff County** is a small and rural county. It is the 13th smallest county in Arkansas and the second least populated with only 7260 residents in 2010. The county had a population of 22,682 in 1930, showing the great loss due to the end of logging and manual farming. The county only has one incorporated town and four incorporated cities.

The county was created on November 26, 1862, with Augusta as its county seat. The name Woodruff honors William E. Woodruff, founder of the state's first newspaper, the *Arkansas Gazette*. The county is almost all bottomland of the White and Cache Rivers. Today, one of the main economic activities is hunting, especially duck and deer.

294.4 BEAR SLOUGH BRIDGE – This is a branch of Bear Slough that drains the area to the southeast, an area known as Peach Orchard Bluff. This is former swamp that has been drained and protected from White River flooding by a large levee.

295.1 MCCLELLAND – McClelland is an unincorporated community in Woodruff County, located at an elevation of 180 feet above sea level on Arkansas Highway 262. While it once was a small town, today it is simply a cluster of farms and private grain storage facilities. A post office opened here in 1912, and closed in 1957, with mail service moved to nearby Augusta, the county seat. A mail crane was reportedly here during the teens and twenties, and again during the mid-1930s. A 12' x 46' depot was built here about 1911 when Chicago Mill & Lumber built their logging line, but there is some question whether the railroad ever used it as an agency.

The name McClelland honors vice-president R. L. McClelland of the lumber company that bought land in the area. The land was bought from Dr. B. A. Fletcher and his brother Dr. T. M. Fletcher, members of one of the first families to settle in this area. As a town grew, the company needed to name their town, and they chose the name of the company officer. The lumber company at McClelland was the Chicago Mill & Lumber Company, established in 1881 by Hermann Paepcke as the Paepcke-Wagner Company. The company had mills and land all across the region, with facilities also in West Helena, Arkansas; Tallulah, Louisiana; Cairo, Illinois; and Greenville, Mississippi. The company was known for their box-making operations, manufacturing boxes for everything from watermelons to automobile parts.

The Chicago Mill & Lumber Company also operated a number of railroads as a part of their operations. According to Interstate Commerce Commission records, the lumber company once operated a number of logging lines connected by trackage rights over several railroads. The Helena Southwestern Railroad Company was incorporated on November 7, 1913, and acquired the rail properties of the Chicago Mill & Lumber Company, although the lumber company also owned the railroad. The railroad included "trackage rights over 57.80 miles of track owned by the Missouri and North Arkansas Railway Company from West Helena, Ark., to McClelland, Ark." The volumes were initially enormous for the railroad, with one report stating that more than 2660 carloads of logs moved from McClelland in the year ending on June 1, 1914. In 1916, the Helena Southwestern Railroad acquired the railroad property in Prairie and Woodruff Counties from the lumber company, and the ICC reported that the logging railroad at McClelland, whose grade northward is now Arkansas Highway 262, was retired in 1920. However, trackage rights over what was called the McClelland Division existed until January 1938 when the last of the company's timber was cut in Woodruff County.

The former M&NA railroad grade is clearly visible where it heads north toward the White River, crossing Arkansas Highway 262. Parts of the old grade are now used as access roads into nearby fields. In addition to the logging railroad, McClelland was the location of several industry tracks. Later maps show a 43-car and a 13-car spur track to the northeast. Just to the southeast, the railroad once crossed Bear Slough where Highway 831 now crosses.

Heber Springs (AR) to Helena (AR)

295.2 BEAR SLOUGH BRIDGE – This is the main channel of the slough. Bear Slough stretches between Sevenmile Lake to the north, and the Cache River to the south. Sevenmile Lake is an old horseshoe lake that once connected the Cache and White Rivers. The railroad crossed the slough just to the west of County Road 831.

295.8 KRAMER – This location was originally known as the American Co-op Company track, but the track was removed in 1929 after it became Kramer. A few foundations can still be seen at Kramer, located where the railroad grade crosses Highway 262 for the second time. The old grade heads to the southeast across farmland, used as a farm access road. Much of this land is today planted in rice, although cotton was a popular early crop. Heading southeast towards Dixie, the railroad crossed Roaring Slough for the first of three times.

297.7 ROARING SLOUGH BRIDGE – Heading south, the railroad is a straight line from McClelland to near Wheatley. However, the curvy Roaring Slough is crossed three times. The slough has as many names as there were bridge crossings. Nothing remains of this timber trestle.

298.2 DIXIE – Dixie is today a small group of farm buildings and houses located on Highway 33, situated close to Roaring Slough. A post office opened at Dixie in 1918 and closed in 1954, with all mail service moved to nearby Augusta. There is no clear source of the name of the community, but it is likely because of its location in the South. Early M&NA

records show a McLean Hardware Company track here.

The *Arkansas Marketing and Industrial Guide* of 1921 listed the Dixie Plantation Company as a shipper at this location, and the railroad built a new 16' x 56' cotton platform here in 1926, retiring the old structure. The railroad had a 23-car industry track that curved off to the northeast, and there was a mail crane from the early 1920s until the end of the company's operations. There was a small passenger shelter here until the end of the Missouri & Arkansas.

Over the next two miles, the railroad crossed Roaring Slough twice as the stream meanders through this area.

298.5 WILLOW SLOUGH BRIDGE – Willow Slough and the Willow Slough Drainage District are to the north and east of Bald Knob, Arkansas. Over the years, the various waterways that once mingled have been broken apart by drainage canals and the creation of large farms. This stream is today known as Roaring Slough. A 1995 study by Louisiana State University stated that Roaring Slough is a tributary of the Cache River, and is actually a large crevasse channel of the White River which was probably formed 4000 to 7000 years ago. Put more simply, Roaring Slough is basically "an abandoned White River meander belt." Before levees were built in the area, water often flowed into the slough during White River floods, connecting the White River and Cache River basins. Today, Roaring Slough functions more as a storage area for backwater flooding from the Cache River.

Heber Springs (AR) to Helena (AR)

299.7 SLASH & BUCK BAYOU BRIDGE – This interesting name was found in early Missouri & North Arkansas documents, but no record can be found elsewhere of the name. Today, this stream is Roaring Slough, which has made several tight horseshoe bends, forcing the M&NA to cross it three times in a single long tangent. As the stream has been channelized over the years, the remains of the trestle have been removed to help with water flow.

300.1 COWAN – The former flag stop of Cowan is located where a field access road crosses the railroad's grade. This station was shown as Cow Mound in the railroad's 1925 timetable, and shown as being 21 cars long in 1923. It was again listed as a flag stop in the 1945 timetable, this time named Cowan and with no side tracks shown, as they had been retired in 1929. There is some evidence that a platform did exist here, and there was a mail crane here for the post office, on the east side of the tracks 150 feet north of the platform, until the late 1910s or early 1920s.

301.3 CACHE RIVER BRIDGE – The Cache River, slightly longer than 200 miles, drains much of northeast Arkansas before flowing south to join the White River at Clarendon, Arkansas. The river was originally a slow and muddy river. Parts of the river's watershed include sloughs, swamps, and oxbow lakes. Little of the river could ever be called straight or swift flowing. However, the river was used as part of a drainage system to make farmland from area swamps. Because of this, parts of its upper channel have been channelized and straightened. During the 1970s, there were plans for the U.S. Army Corps of Engineers to dredge and straighten more of the river, but duck hunters and other groups fought the plan. In 1986, much of the lower part of the river, more than 90 miles of channel, was saved by the creation of the Cache River National Wildlife Refuge. This refuge includes the largest tract of contiguous bottomland hardwood forest remaining in the United States.

While the Cache River was a mix of flooded swamp land and meandering channels, it was an important food source for early natives, and a number of Indian mounds were built along its course. As white settlers arrived, the heavy swamps discouraged development. However, as some land was cleared and drained, cotton and other cash crops became common in the area. This led to steamboat service during the early 1800s and the creation of several river towns along its route. However, more reliable water conditions on the nearby White River prevented any major development.

On February 1, 1908, three days before Congress approved the construction of the M&NA White River bridge, approval was received to "construct, maintain, and operate a bridge and approaches thereto, across the Cache River at a point suitable to the interests of navigation, in section twenty-one, township five north range three west, in Woodruff County." The railroad originally used 530 feet of timber pile trestle to cross the Cache River, but later parts were replaced by deck plate girder spans, which included a 96-foot-long turn span. Reportedly, the turn span was replaced by a traditional deck plate girder span about 1925.

The area on the east side of the river is the Rex Hancock Black Swamp State Wildlife Management Area. The area includes almost 7000 acres of land used for wildlife food, hunting, and camping.

Heber Springs (AR) to Helena (AR)

There is no clear source of the name Cache, but some sources state that in the Picardie language, the word for hunt is similar to Cache. Picardie is a part of northern France, historically speaking a unique form of French. Several early French explorers who visited Arkansas were from Picardie.

302.0 DAGGETT – Daggett is actually a short distance to the southwest on Highway 790, also known as Daggett Road. Gale Street heads to the northeast to reach the location of the 12-car railroad spur track, which headed to the west from the mainline. The track, located at an elevation of 190 feet, once served a slack barrel stave mill owned by the Daggett Stave Manufacturing Company, shown as the H. A. Daggett Stave & Heading Company by some news sources at the time. The mill opened by 1912 and was owned by H. A. Daggett and J. G. Tarkington, and closed in 1938. A slack stave is used to make a slack barrel, used for transporting dry goods and foodstuffs.

From the small frame shelter that was once here, the railroad continued to head to the southeast, through Gum Flat Bayou, and straight to Cotton Plant, Arkansas.

305.9 COTTON PLANT – The Cotton Plant Railroad, the first railroad at Cotton Plant, came into town from the southeast, along the route that is now Railroad Road, in 1879. It curved through town and turned north along what is today Vine Street. The railroad was known as the Gunn & Black Railroad for the partners who originally built the route to support their mill. The railroad was later the Batesville & Brinkley Railroad (1882) and then the White &

Black River Valley Railroad (1890). The railroad later became part of the Rock Island through a lease.

The Missouri & North Arkansas crossed the Chicago, Rock Island & Pacific (CRIP) just southeast of Cotton Plant. From there, the former M&NA grade heads straight to Bayou De View and to Fargo, the last operating section of the old Missouri & North Arkansas. The Cotton Plant-Fargo Railroad (CP-F) was established as a six-mile railroad in 1952, after the Helena & Northwestern was abandoned in November 1951, as an attempt to preserve service to Southwestern Veneer and other rail users in Cotton Plant. The railroad used a small 20-ton Plymouth, built in 1928 (serial number 2932) for the Ohio Seamless Tube Company. The railroad was finally abandoned in 1977.

As stated, Cotton Plant, telegraph call "CN", was the last station on the route of the Missouri & North Arkansas to receive freight service from a descendent of the railroad. The M&NA Cotton Plant depot, built in late 1909 for a cost of $5,000, was unique in that it was one of the few built with an integral pavilion (Eureka Springs was the only other station built with a pavilion). The building measured 20' x 76', plus the 14-foot-long pavilion. The station was once located just southwest of the intersection of Lynch and 1st Streets. The waiting room faced the intersection while the freight room was to the north. The Cotton Plant station survived the end of the railroad, was used by a church, but later burned, with only the foundation and porch pillars remaining. The area has recently been cleaned up and little remains.

Heber Springs (AR) to Helena (AR)

While long gone, the Cotton Plant depot still stood in May, 1984. This view shows the unique patio on one end. Photo by Barton Jennings.

The railroad passed through the southwest side of Cotton Plant, being built as some of the last tracks completed between Joplin and Helena in 1908. Cotton Plant was an important station on the railroad due to the lumber and agricultural shippers, and there were historically a number of tracks. Cotton Plant was busy enough to require padding in the schedule. Train #211 had a scheduled departure time of 12:05pm, and #212 was scheduled to depart at 2:30pm.

To handle some of the local work, a boxcar body warehouse was installed in Cotton Plant in 1926. By the beginning of World War II, there was a 31-car siding on the west side of town with several industry tracks into the Cotton Plant Compress & Warehouse Company, then a 14-car siding and a track to downtown from a wye near the southeast part of town near the Southwestern Veneer facility. The track to downtown served some of the industries once served by the Rock Island. This difference in original ownership was shown in the environmental impact statement (EIS) of the Cotton Plant-Fargo Railway Company abandonment application. The EIS stated that the former M&NA route had a right-of-way width of 100 feet, while the former Rock Island right-of-way from Ash Street to Main Street was 200 feet wide.

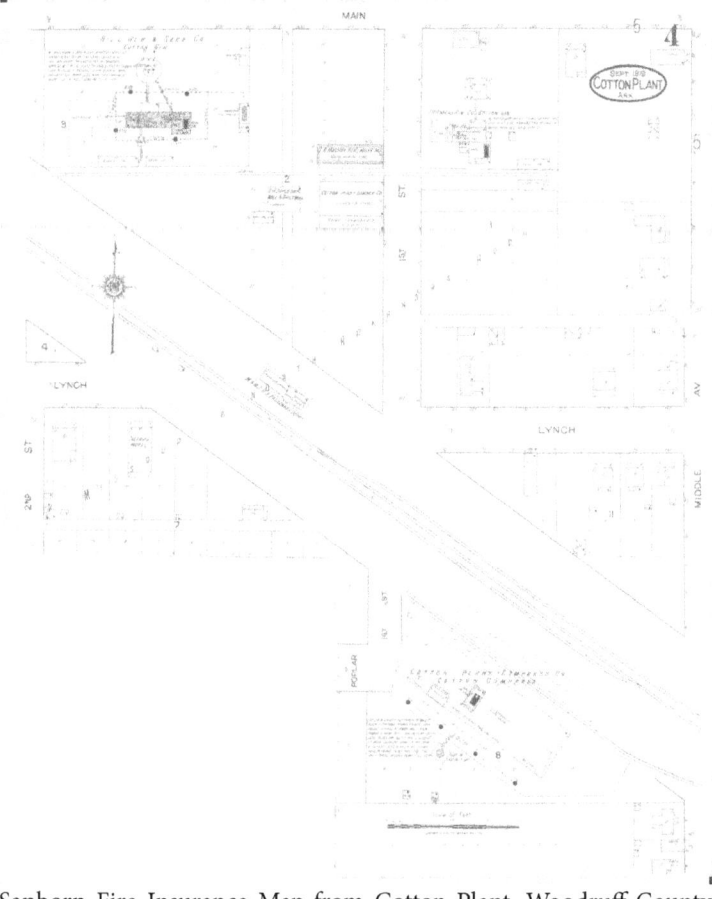

Sanborn Fire Insurance Map from Cotton Plant, Woodruff County, Arkansas. Sanborn Map Company, September, 1919. Library of Congress, Geography and Map Division. https://www.loc.gov/item/sanborn00224_003/.

Heber Springs (AR) to Helena (AR)

Cotton Plant was a busy and important station for the M&NA in 1919. To the south of the depot was a cotton compress, and to the north were several cotton gins, a lumber company, grist mill, and several seed houses.

Even though many of the buildings are gone at Cotton Plant, a few still demonstrate the importance of the community to the railroad. This is the former Cotton Plant Warehouse, used to store and ship cotton for local farmers. Photo by Barton Jennings.

For years, the end of the CP-F was the Farmers Gin Cooperative, located at 7906 Arkansas Highway 38, just east of where the M&NA crossed the highway. The Cooperative closed in 1974. The other major industry for the railroad during the later years was the Southwestern Veneer Company, located at the southern edge of town. The 1976 abandonment EIS stated that the only shippers were the Delta Plywood Corporation and the Cotton Plant Warehouse.

When the M&NA was first built, the Southwestern Veneer Company operated a motor car over the railroad to and from Georgetown to transport employees. An early advertising ink blotter stated that the mill had a capacity of 300,000 feet per day, and that it manufactured three- and five-ply boards. The blotter, which listed both the Southwestern Veneer Company and the Eastern Arkansas Veneer Company, included a photo of a long train of logs loaded on flat cars. A 1941 book (*Arkansas – A Guide to the State*, by the Writer's Program of the Works Progress Administration) stated that the plant was "housed in a group of long, low, corrugated-iron buildings. Here tupelo, gum and other hardwoods taken from the Cache and White River bottoms are cut into workable lengths, soaked in vats for several hours, and then cut into thin sheets. The finished plywood is shipped to furniture manufacturers in Northern states."

In 1984, an old motor car shed still stood in Cotton Plant, as shown here on May 22nd. Photo by Barton Jennings.

State of Arkansas records indicate that the plant later became the Cotton Plant Plywood Corporation, which closed in 1978. It later was the DeQueen Plywood Corporation which dissolved in 1983. Today, a few of the buildings still stand, but are covered in vegetation along Gus Avenue.

City of Cotton Plant

Until the mid-1800s, this area was swamp, consisting of dense timber and cane. The first settlers arrived about 1820, attracted by free land. Some of the initial settlers made a living by trading with the local tribes, including the Quapaw and Choctaw. The trading post acquired the name of Richmond. In 1832, a survey of the area was conducted at the order of President Andrew Jackson. Legend has it that in 1846, William Lynch brought cotton seeds from Mississippi, a variety that grew well in the former swamp land. As the town grew, it was forced to change its name because there was already a Richmond in nearby Little River County, so the new name of Cotton Plant was chosen to honor the new crop. A post office opened in 1852 with the new name.

During the Civil War, Cotton Plant was the site of the Battle of Cotton Plant, also known as the Battle of Hill's Plantation or Battle of the Cache. This battle on July 7, 1862, was an early part of the Vicksburg Campaign, a Union effort to control the Mississippi River. Union Major General Samuel Curtis was moving on Helena to supply area forces. A number of Confederate units, plus local guard forces, attempted to stop the march, but were defeated. Curtis later took Helena, creating a supply base for General

Grant and his move to take Vicksburg, Mississippi. Because of the importance of the campaign, the battlefield has been recognized as one of the Civil War's 384 principal battlefields by the Civil War Sites Advisory Commission.

After the war, Cotton Plant, like many southern agricultural communities, suffered from a mix of high taxes, low crop prices, and a shortage of adult labor. Things improved in 1881 when the Batesville & Brinkley Railroad was built to Cotton Plant. The railroad allowed warehouses, cotton gins, and a cotton compress to be built and have their products shipped to market. The *Arkansas State Gazetteer and Business Directory*, Volume 1, 1884-5, stated that Cotton Plant was a "post village on the B & B RR in Woodruff county, 86 miles northeast of Little Rock, 20 miles southeast of Augusta, the county seat. Searcy is the nearest banking point. Settled in 1854, it contains a steam grist mill and a cotton gin, and ships cotton. Population, 160. Mail daily." The town incorporated in 1887.

A report from 1890 stated that Cotton Plant produced 1500-2000 tons of cottonseed and 4000-7000 bales of cotton each year. The construction of the Missouri & North Arkansas opened up more markets, especially for the timber industry. Almost immediately, the Standard Stave and Hoop Mill opened, as did several sawmills, woodworking factories, and the Southwestern Veneer Mill, the largest veneer plant in Arkansas. In addition, there were four cotton gins, a cotton compress, several large warehouses, and the Cotton Plant Oil Mill. Weekly paychecks from companies such as Pioneer Stave Mill, the Eckhart and Leonard Mill, Home Stave Mill, Daggett Stave Manufacturing Company, and

Southwestern Veneer kept Cotton Plant busy on Friday nights.

Like many places, the Depression was not kind to Cotton Plant. Many of the mills closed during this time. Southwestern Veneer, which managed to stay open, had its own problems. According to the July 15, 1930, issue of the *Dallas Morning News*, "Fire believed due to spontaneous combustion badly damaged two plants of the Southwestern Veneer Company here Sunday. The loss was estimated at between $100,000 and $150,000." At the same time, Cotton Plant became known as the birthplace of the first woman elected to Congress from Arkansas. Pearl Peden Oldfield was elected to the United States House of Representatives in a special election to replace her husband, and she served from January 9, 1929, to March 3, 1931. A major excitement was the construction of a city water and sewer system in 1935, built by the Works Progress Administration. A large parade and celebration was held when the systems were turned on.

Cotton Plant experienced some of its best times immediately after World War II, and the population peaked at 1838 residents. However, the population began to move away and the cotton gin closed by the late 1970s. By the 2000 census, the population was 969, and then 649 in 2010. Today, Cotton Plant includes as many empty buildings in its Cotton Plant Commercial Historic District, listed on the National Register of Historic Places, as operating businesses. Most of the buildings date from the 1920s after the major fires of 1901 and 1924.

Cotton Plant is also known for its black community that has produced several well-known singers and musicians. This includes Sister Rosetta Tharpe, a highly influential gospel singer, and Katie Bell "Ma Bell" Nubin, a mandolin player who played with Dizzy Gillespie's band. Rosetta Tharpe was also known for her mix of black spirituals, hillbilly, and boogie woogie music, and her use of an electric guitar. She was one of the first to perform in dyed flame-red hair, crazy clothes, and a complete stage show. Known as "the original soul sister" and "the Godmother of rock and roll," she is also a member of the Rock and Roll Hall of Fame.

Cotton Plant has several markers about its music history, including this one for Sister Rosetta Tharpe. Photo by Sarah Jennings.

Cotton Plant & Western Railroad

This is another railroad that was built to reach timber. Several magazines such as the *Texas Trade Review and Industrial Record* (July 15, 1915), *The Southern Lumberman* (July 3, 1915), and the *Railway Review* (July 17, 1915) reported on the creation of the company. According to the *Railway Review*, the railroad was "chartered in Arkansas to build a line from Cotton Plant to Des Arc, about 15 miles." E. C. Nelson of Helena, Arkansas, owned 991 of the 1000 shares of the stock. Nelson and the others involved were officers of the Chicago Mill & Lumber Company, and the line was turned over to the Helena Southwestern in 1916. The logging spur was abandoned in 1920.

307.4 CHICAGO, ROCK ISLAND & PACIFIC CROSSING – Until 1940, the Missouri & Arkansas Railway crossed the Rock Island Railroad here, near the Ash Grove Cemetery. The Rock Island route dates back to the 1870s when the partnership of Gunn & Black built a sawmill at Brinkley to support their door, sash and blind factory in Memphis, Tennessee. They built a private 3' 6" gauge railroad north from Brinkley to Cotton Plant by July 1, 1879. In 1881, the Texas & St. Louis Railroad, later the Cotton Belt, built a 3-foot gauge railroad through Brinkley. In response, Gunn & Black changed their railroad to the same gauge and incorporated it as the Cotton Plant Railroad.

On June 22, 1882, the Batesville & Brinkley Railroad was created with the intentions of buying the Cotton Plant Railroad and extending it north to Newton, on what became the Missouri Pacific main line, and then up the White River to Batesville, Arkansas. The railroad was extended 19 miles to Patterson, and then the Augusta & Southeastern Railway Company was purchased to further extend the line. During late 1886, the St. Louis, Arkansas & Texas Railway (Cotton Belt) rebuilt its line to standard gauge, and the Batesville & Brinkley Railroad did the same by 1888.

On January 10, 1890, the White & Black River Valley (W&BRV) was incorporated to consolidate the various lines. The route was expanded further to the two White River ports of Newport and Jacksonport. On July 1, 1900, the railroad was leased for 80 years by the Choctaw, Oklahoma & Gulf Railroad Company, which connected to the company at Brinkley. *The Commercial and Financial Chronicle* (January 25, 1902) provided a list of the railroad equipment acquired with the W&BRV. It listed 4 locomotives, 8 passenger cars of various types, 47 box cars, 32 flat cars, 1 stock car, 1 caboose, and 3 miscellaneous cars.

The Chicago, Rock Island & Pacific leased the Choctaw, Oklahoma & Gulf on March 24, 1904. Not long after, the Interstate Commerce Commission provided a description of the White & Black River Valley Railway, stating that it "is a single-track, standard-gauge, steam railroad, located entirely in Arkansas. The main line extends from Brinkley to Jacksonport, 56.472 miles, and a branch line extends from Wiville to Gregory, 5.963 miles, a total of 62.435 miles of main tracks owned. Other tracks wholly owned aggregate 7.182 miles, making a total of 69.617 miles of all tracks wholly owned. The White & Black River Valley Railway also owns jointly with the St. Louis, Iron Mountain & Southern

Railway Company 0.112 mile of yard tracks and sidings at Brinkley."

As river traffic was replaced by railroads, towns like Jacksonport lost their importance, and the four miles of railroad from there to Newport was abandoned by June 1928. The rest of the railroad was abandoned on March 9, 1941, with a track or two in Newport being sold to the Missouri Pacific, and a few tracks in Cotton Plant going to the Missouri & Arkansas.

In 2018, one of the best preserved remaining structures from the local industries in Cotton Plant is this grain elevator scale house. Photo by Sarah Jennings.

307.5 COUNTY LINE – Just east of the Rock Island diamond, the Missouri & Arkansas went from **Woodruff County** to **Monroe County**. **Monroe County** was created on November 2, 1829, by the Arkansas territorial legislature, and was named for James Monroe, the fifth President of the United States. The county seat is Clarendon, originally known as Mouth of the Cache. The county is generally a mix of rural farmland and bottomland hardwood forest. The county's population peaked at 21,601 in

1920, stayed level until the early 1940s, and has now dropped to about 7000.

309.7 BAYOU DE VIEW BRIDGE – The name Devue, or De View, is used for a number of features in the area. This is Bayou de View, a part of the Cache and White River basins. The stream is less than 100 miles long and drains parts of Woodruff, Monroe and Prairie Counties. There are efforts to expand the Cache River National Wildlife Refuge to include more than 30 miles of Bayou de View.

The remains of a long timber trestle can still be seen crossing the bayou. According to the environmental impact statement (EIS) of the Cotton Plant-Fargo Railway Company abandonment application, this bridge was a key reason for the railroad's abandonment. The EIS stated that the Corps of Engineers had begun an improvement plan in the Cache River Basin and that the bridge would have to be reconstructed at an estimated cost of $250,000.

309.9 DEVUE – In 1945, the Missouri & Arkansas timetable showed Devue as a flag and water stop; in 1923 the Missouri & North Arkansas showed the water stop as Deview. The water station was supplied from a standard 16' x 24' wooden 50,000-gallon tank, filled from nearby Bayou De View, shown as Devue Bayou in a 1940 report. This Devue is at the crossing of the Bayou De View, located deep within the bottomland hardwood forest.

Local legend says that the area received its name when a French settlement was started about two miles south of here. The name has also been spelled Deview, and was considered to be a thriving village before the Civil War. When the village was missed by both the Cotton Plant Railway Company and the Missouri & North Arkansas, it began to suffer and is now just a collection of a few homes and a church.

311.6 FARGO – Fargo, railroad telegraph call "FR" and also shown as SLSW Crossing, was little more than a grade crossing with the St. Louis Southwestern, better known as the Cotton Belt. For the Missouri & Arkansas, there was a 14-car siding on the west side of the mainline, located just north of the Cotton Belt diamond. There was an interchange track between the siding and the Cotton Belt tracks to their south. During the late 1920s, Fargo was the number one interchange location on the railroad. During the period 1926-1928, the M&NA delivered 7394 cars to the Cotton Belt and received 4948 cars, out of a total of 36,863 and 35,095 cars. This was 20% of the outbound traffic and 14% of the inbound traffic. Train #211 was scheduled to depart Fargo at 12:45pm, providing time for it to interchange traffic with the Cotton Belt. Train #212 also had a great deal of time for switching here, not scheduled to depart until 1:55pm.

The Cotton Belt was here first, being built through the area during the early 1880s. The line was built by the Texas & St. Louis Railway as a three-foot gauge railroad, with the goal of connecting the locations in the railroad's name. The line was located by Samuel W. Fordyce of Hot Springs, Arkansas, who rode the route by horse multiple times before construction began. The line was completed on August 12, 1883. The railroad became the St. Louis, Arkansas & Texas on April 29, 1886, after the various parts of the line were consolidated. Plans were made to standard gauge the railroad, with work beginning on October

18, 1886. The railroad grew by absorbing a number of connecting railroads, but the company soon entered receivership. The St. Louis Southwestern Railway Company (Cotton Belt, or SSW) was created and acquired all of the properties by June 1, 1891. By 1930, the Cotton Belt was controlled by Southern Pacific, which became a part of Union Pacific in 1996.

No station or town was created at this location. In 1898, a post office opened nearby with the name Fargo. When the Missouri & North Arkansas was built through the area in 1908, the crossing between the two railroads took the name of Fargo. In 1911, the M&NA built a joint depot to provide connecting passenger and freight service. The depot was on the northwest side of the diamond and was L-shaped to fit along both railroads. The two wings were reportedly 20 feet deep and 30 feet and 49 feet along on the track sides.

The Missouri & Arkansas Railway ended service through Fargo in 1946, but the line between Helena and Cotton Plant was sold to the Helena & Northwestern Railway. The Helena & Northwestern was created by a number of local businessmen, including Ben C. White, the traffic manager of the Southwest Veneer Company at nearby Cotton Plant. The railroad began service late in 1949 in response to a strike on the Missouri Pacific, switching industries in the Helena area. The railroad closed in late 1951, and the Cotton Plant-Fargo Railway was created by the Southwest Veneer Company to protect service to its Cotton Plant facility. Service began on April 1, 1952. The line applied to the Interstate Commerce Commission in 1976 to abandon the railroad.

Fargo was never a large town, never seeing more than a few hundred full-time residents. However, it was the home of the Fargo Agricultural School, a school created by Floyd Brown, a graduate of the Tuskegee Institute in Alabama, and his wife Lillie Epps. The school opened in 1919 and taught African-American students both vocational skills such as carpentry, plumbing, and farming, as well as English, mathematics, science, history, and music. The school was sold to the State of Arkansas in 1949. The school became the Fargo Negro Girls Training School, and eventually merged with a similar school in Alexandria, Arkansas, due to desegregation requirements. In 1960, the Fargo property became the Floyd Brown-Fargo Agricultural Museum. In 1981, the school property was acquired by the Arkansas Land and Farm Development Corporation, an organization that provides financial assistance to rural African-American families in Monroe County.

As the town got smaller, the Fargo post office closed in 1976. Despite this, Fargo incorporated in 1987 as part of an effort to obtain state and federal funds for roads and a water system. In 1990, the population was down to 140, 118 in 2000, and 98 in 2010. The former school is now part of the Fargo Training School Historic District, a part of the National Register of Historic Places since May 27, 2010.

Heading south from Fargo, the grade is easy to follow as it passes the site of the Fargo Agricultural School. The grade is the M and A Road leaving Fargo, then Weaver Road, and finally a farm road before the driveable grade ends in heavy woods just north of Interstate 40.

313.5 COUNTY LINE – Heading towards Helena, the railroad exited **Monroe County**, located to the west, and entered **St. Francis County** to the east. **St. Francis County** was formed on October 13, 1827, by the Arkansas territorial legislature, and named for the St. Francis River. The St. Francis River drains much of southeastern Missouri and northeastern Arkansas along its 425-mile route. The new county included land that was once part of Phillips County, the seventh county created in what would become the State of Arkansas. The county seat moved about a number of times, first meeting in the home of William Strong, and then moving to Franklin. In 1840, the county seat moved to Madison, and then to Mount Vernon in 1855. The new county courthouse burned in 1856 and the county seat moved back to Madison. In 1874, the county seat moved to Forrest City, created by Nathan Bedford Forrest as a construction camp and commissary while he completed the construction of the Memphis & Little Rock Railroad, later the Chicago, Rock Island & Pacific.

313.6 PUTTY – Putty was listed as a 2-car spur with the switch at the south end in the 1945 employee timetable. The location of Putty is approximately where the lone farmhouse still stands on Weaver Road, sitting just north of a small lake.

316.3 WHEATLEY – The town of Wheatley has gone through a number of name changes since it was first settled in the mid-1800s. The town was originally known as Dennis Station, named for Wheatley Dennis. The first post office in the area opened in 1870 as Britton, named for the nearby railroad station. It was changed to Wheatley in 1872. Some early spellings also used Wheetley. The town was originally in Monroe County, but a redrawing of the county line moved it to St. Francis County. The arrival of the Missouri & North Arkansas led to the incorporation of Wheatley in 1907. In 1909, the Wheatley Rice Milling Company was built at Wheatley, with a rice dryer and storage facility near the railroad crossing.

During the 1920s, the Lee Highway, later U.S. Highway 70, was built alongside the Rock Island Railroad through Wheatley. The rice dryer burned and then was enlarged in 1929, and became a part of Riceland Food in 1945. Besides the rice mill, the Wheatley Spoke Company and the Ark-Mo Lumber Company also operated facilities here in the early 1900s. The town's population peaked at more than 500 during the 1980s, but has declined to approximately 350 for the past decade. However, the large rice elevator still marks the location of Wheatley.

The large Riceland Food elevator at Wheatley can be seen for miles and marks the location where the M&NA once had a diamond and interchange track with the Rock Island Railroad. Photo by Barton Jennings.

Passing through Wheatley, the Missouri & North Arkansas grade is now the mill access road on the west side of the complex. The railroad crossed the Rock Island near the Dennis Street grade crossing, and closely followed today's Union Street. It then followed Arkansas Highway 78 to the southeast. Highway 78 was designated as one of the original state highways on April 1, 1926.

Rock Island Diamond

The Missouri & North Arkansas Railroad crossed the Rock Island Railroad here, and for many years it was an important connection as many shippers had their cargo sent through Helena to avoid the high terminal fees at Memphis, Tennessee. This importance could be seen by the M&NA yard that was located just south of the CRIP line. The yard was used for interchange business and featured a 28-car siding to the east and a 40-car track to the west. The west track connected directly to a Rock Island interchange track to the west. There was also an interchange track in the northeast quadrant of the diamond, as well as stock pens that were retired in 1927. Both railroads used a joint depot near the diamond, with the Missouri & Arkansas using the telegraph code of "WY" for the station. The station was once a boxcar body that was replaced in 1929. Later, a larger frame building was built.

Wheatley was another significant interchange point for the M&NA. In 1936, both trains #211 and #212 had a great deal of time in their schedule to handle this work. Southbound #211 and northbound #212 were both scheduled to leave Wheatley at 1:25pm. This meet between the two trains required the two sidings and rail yard that the railroad maintained.

The Rock Island line was originally the Memphis & Little Rock Railroad Company. It was originally chartered on January 11, 1853, "for the purpose of establishing a communication by railroad between the City of Memphis, in the State of Tennessee, and Little Rock, in the State of Arkansas." The goal was to build the railroad to move Arkansas produce to the Memphis & Charleston Railroad at Memphis for eastern markets. The firm received 438,647 acres of federal land grant on February 3, 1853, and was the only operating railroad in Arkansas at the start of the Civil War. The Eastern Division of the railroad, Hopewell (near West Memphis) to Madison (east of Forrest City), was completed in 1859. The Western Division, Argenta (North Little Rock) to DeValls Bluff on the White River, saw construction begin in 1860 and in 1862. The railroad was built to a track gage of five feet.

After the Civil War, the company received another federal land grant of 365,539 acres on July 28, 1866. Construction connected De Valls Bluff and Madison by April 4, 1871. The expense of the construction forced its sale under foreclosure to Stillman Witt, et al., Trustees on March 17, 1873. The company was then sold to the Memphis & Little Rock Railway Company on December 12, 1873. This railroad didn't last long as it was sold under foreclosure to William S. Pierson, Watson Mathews and R. K. Dow, Trustees on April 27, 1877, who sold it the next day to the Memphis & Little Rock Railroad Company. On May 23, 1887, the railroad was again sold, this time to George B. Rose, Trustee, who sold it to a the Little Rock & Memphis Railroad Company on September 1, 1887.

The railroad again failed and was again sold by foreclosure, again to a trustee, this time Fredric P. Alcott on October 25, 1898. The railroad then became the property of the Choctaw & Memphis Railroad Company later the same day. The Choctaw & Memphis had been created to "acquire the property of the Little Rock & Memphis Railroad Company, and also to construct a railroad between the City of Little Rock and the Arkansas-Indian Territory State line." The railroad then became the property of the Choctaw, Oklahoma & Gulf Railway Company on June 30, 1900. While already under the control of the Chicago, Rock Island & Pacific Railroad, it was consolidated with many other lines into the main company on January 1, 1948.

While the M&NA no longer exists at Wheatley, Union Pacific still operates the former Rock Island Railroad mainline. This station sign marks the location. Photo by Sarah Jennings.

After the failure of the Rock Island in 1980, the Cotton Belt, part of Southern Pacific, acquired the line from Memphis through Wheatley to Brinkley. The Cotton Belt had operated on this line since 1912 when it negotiated trackage rights for its passenger trains, and then its freight trains in 1921. Union Pacific acquired the Southern Pacific on September 11, 1996, and still operates this route.

317.5 COUNTY LINE – **St. Francis County** is to the west and north, while **Lee County** is to the east. At the county line, the railroad was immediately to the west of Arkansas Highway 78. Lee County includes the base survey point for the entire Louisiana Purchase, meaning that all locations from Louisiana and to the north and west as far as Minnesota and Montana are measured from Lee County. This location is where the Louisiana Base Line and the Fifth Principal Meridian cross in the southwest corner of Lee County.

Lee County is a relatively new county in Arkansas, created on April 17, 1873, from parts of Phillips, Monroe, Crittenden, and St. Francis Counties. The county was named for General Robert E. Lee, one-time Superintendent of the United States Military Academy, General in Chief of the Armies of the Confederacy, and president of Washington College (later Washington and Lee University). The eastern border is the Mississippi River, and the St. Francis National Forest, the smallest national forest in the country, covers the southeastern part of the county. While the northern part of the county includes some rolling hills, most of the county is flat delta farmland.

Lee County is primarily agricultural, with rice, cotton and similar products grown throughout the county. The emphasis on farming has caused a large drop in population as machinery has taken over many of the traditional farm jobs. In 1920, the population of the county was 28,800 while it was 10,400 in the 2010 census. The county seat is located in Marianna, reportedly the birthplace of the first non-native American born west of the Mississippi, John Patterson.

Not far south of here, at Milepost 318.2, was one of the bridges that was destroyed during the strike of the early 1920s. On January 10, 1923, this bridge was dynamited by unknown individuals.

319.1 WEATHERBY – Weatherby was located at what is today known as Nash Corner, a few farm buildings where Arkansas Highway 78 turns to the east. Until the end of passenger service, this was a flag stop for passenger trains with a small frame shelter. There was also a 10-car spur track to the east, with a switch on the south end. The railroad continued across farmland to the southeast to West Helena.

A. P. Weatherby operated a number of timber operations in northeast Arkansas, generally handling hardwood timber. The company's main mill was at Pocahontas, Arkansas, which opened in 1919.

321.3 HOPPER – For years, there was a 4-car spur track at this location. By 1945, Hopper was shown as having no tracks, but was listed as a flag stop for passenger trains. It was located where Lee County Road 918 crossed the railroad. Today, north of Lee County Road 918, the former railroad grade is used as a farm access road. During the 1920s, Hopper Brothers operated a small lumber and shingle mill here.

Heber Springs (AR) to Helena (AR)

325.0 LITTLE PRAIRIE – This station was located on Lee County Road 915 north of Lee County Road 904. There was a 4-car spur track to the east, with a switch on the south end. There is no town or houses here today.

The September 11, 1910, issue of the *Arkansas Democrat* had an article on the new rice crops growing at Little Prairie. The article mentioned that rice was new to the area and showed much promise. It also stated that the rice from Little Prairie, located "about two miles north of Moro, on the Missouri and North Arkansas Railroad," would mostly be handled by the rice mill at Wheatley, Arkansas.

326.9 MORO – Like a cat, Moro, sometimes shown as Moreau, has lived a number of lives. The first began in 1850 when Dr. James A. Sullivan created the community, naming it after Moro Bay, England. The doctor had arrived from Virginia, and then encouraged his former neighbors to join him. To help the community grow, Sullivan offered each family two acres of land, a house, and a mule. Moro's growth resulted in a post office in 1855, and about 700 residents by 1861.

The second life of Moro was during the Civil War. On November 7, 1862, well-armed Federal troops seized the town and established a temporary camp. On November 8, Confederate troops attacked the community, but were repulsed. As the focus of Union forces moved towards Vicksburg, Moro was abandoned by Federal forces and occupied by Confederate troops attempting to retake Helena. Confederate General John Marmaduke, and later General Sterling Price, used Moro as their base of operations. The shift in military control of Moro resulted in many residents fleeing the area and the destruction of a number of homes and businesses.

The third life of Moro followed the Civil War as the town rebuilt thanks to the timber business, and later farming. The post office closed for much of 1867, but returned as the economy improved. Over the next several decades, cotton, livestock, feed grains, and other products were bought and sold at Moro. By the late 1800s, the population of Moro was approaching 1000, but a 1900 tornado devastated the community.

The arrival of the Missouri & North Arkansas Railroad kicked off the community's fourth life. However, the railroad was located a short distance from the original Moro, so the town moved to the M&NA. With the arrival of a railroad, business was able to locate again in the area. Almost immediately, the Moro Mercantile and Gin Company and the Moro Mercantile Company opened next to the railroad. Reports from the time indicate that the town included several churches, a bank, a blacksmith, a machine shop, and a number of other businesses typical of a town of its size. Moro also soon became the center of area education as three school districts combined and a new brick schoolhouse opened at Moro in September 1911.

As the town grew, it was incorporated on May 22, 1914. The 1921 *Arkansas Marketing and Industrial Guide* listed a number of companies at Moro. This included J. M. Campbell & Company (cooperage); Brown Brothers and the Moro Handle Company (handles and spokes); and J. A. Hooper and H. Jordan (lumber mills). This was about the peak of the community. Much of the town burned in 1925, and the railroad replaced its cotton platform in 1926 with a 32' x 50' structure. The Depression caused the closing of many area businesses, and as with other area communities, many residents moved away to better jobs. In 1946, the next disaster struck the community as the Missouri & Arkansas Railway closed. However, in late 1948, the railroad between Helena and Cotton Plant was sold to the Helena & Northwestern Railway, temporarily saving rail service through Moro. This railroad soon failed and was abandoned officially on November 2, 1951. Soon after, the mercantile and gin operations closed. By the 1980s, the school was also closed and consolidated with nearby Marianna.

Cotton has always been big business in southeast Arkansas, and this gin building still stands at Moro, Arkansas. Photo by Barton Jennings.

Today, Moro is still the second-largest incorporated community in Lee County, with only the county seat of Marianna being larger. In the 2010 census, Moro's population was 216. The town still serves the area farms, but generally by providing mechanical services and agricultural supplies. Also look for signs about first baseman Ben Waltrip, chosen by the Colorado Rockies in the 2012 Major League Baseball draft.

The railroad had a small wooden depot at Moro, using the telegraph call of "MO". According to Kubat, the building measured 20' x 40' and was a Standard #4 building. There was a 45-car siding to the east and an 18-car siding to the west. The station was important during the early 1930s as it was used by the post office as part of their Railway Post Office (RPO) operations. During this time, RPO clerks worked the mail from Kensett to Moro on Mixed Train #203, and then caught Mixed Train #204 back north.

From Moro to the south, the abandoned grade still follows Arkansas Highway 78 until the intersection with U.S. Highway 79. The grade continues straight to the southeast, visible in some places as a tree line or the edge of a field. This route is easy to see in aerial photos as most roads in the area run either north-south or east-west.

327.6 HOG TUSK CREEK BRIDGE – Hog Tusk Creek, like many in the area, has been straightened and is essentially a canal today. It moves water to the southwest where it merges with Little Hog Tusk Creek and then flows to the southeast and eventually enters Big Creek.

331.7 THOMASVILLE – In 1945, Thomasville, or Thomas, was listed as a flag stop, and there were no side tracks. There was apparently a large 12' x 36' frame shelter. Maps show that Thomasville was never more than just a few houses. A post office opened at Thomasville in 1911, and closed in 1922, but the railroad showed a mail crane here through 1930. The community was located on what is today Lee County Road 116.

334.4 AUBREY – Aubrey was created when the Missouri & North Arkansas built through the area. The name Aubrey comes from the name of the son of Dr. W. B. Snipes, an early resident of the area. The opening of the railroad and the sale of lots was celebrated by a community barbeque and celebration on Wednesday, August 19, 1908. In 1909, a post office opened at Aubrey, and the next year a two-story school was built and the first church started services. Within several years, Aubrey consisted of a hotel, several stores, a saw mill, and a cotton gin. In 1922, the Chicago Mill & Lumber Company operated a facility here, joining more than a half-dozen other timber operations. The Marianna Cotton Oil Company also had a plant here. The town peaked by the 1940s. The Aubrey High School closed in 1963, and the elementary school closed in 1981. Students now travel to Marianna for their education.

Aubrey wasn't incorporated until 1966, done to obtain funding for a water and sewer system. In 2010, the population was only 170. However, Aubrey is the home of the Farmers Supply Aubrey Elevator, a busy new grain complex. Aubrey is also the home of what appears to some to be a large tractor junk yard. However, that is not the case as the firm is actually Bennett Tractor Parts. The company advertises itself as having "the largest selection of used parts in the mid-south!" The firm sells parts from many manufacturers, including John Deere, Case IH, and Ford New Holland. Note their inventory in several locations throughout Aubrey.

This tractor and gin building mark where the M&NA used to pass through Aubrey. Used farming equipment can be seen all over town, thanks to Bennett Tractor Parts, based here. Photo by Barton Jennings.

The railroad used to run through Aubrey between Front and Trilby streets. There was a 44-car siding on the west side of the mainline, as well as a 22' x 40' Standard #3 depot (telegraph call "XD" until the early 1930s). There was a standard 16' x 24' wooden 50,000-gallon water tank, supported by a railroad well and pump house. This area is now occupied by Bennett Tractor Parts and Farmers Supply.

336.5 CHAPPELLE – Guy Chappelle operated a lumber company out of Wynne, Arkansas, and used a number of locations for timber loading. Census records also show several members of the Chappelle family living near here. The spur track here was retired in 1929, but was still a flag stop in 1945. Today, the location is east of Lee Road 325 near where several drainage and irrigation canals come together.

340.3 RONDO – If you follow Lee County Road 342 and Front Street through Rondo, you are following the grade of the Missouri & North Arkansas. According to several sources, there was a 38-car siding to the west at Rondo. There was a 22' x 40' Standard #3 station here that was sold in November 1945. The agency, which originally used "MU" and later "RO" as its telegraph call, closed in 1931.

During the 1980s, the former Rondo station sat next to a cotton field and was used as a house. Photo by Barton Jennings.

Things have changed greatly since the town boomed with the arrival of the railroad. The town had several businesses and homes, and gained a post office in 1909, which closed in 1959. Rondo was incorporated in 1918, and featured a general store, bank, funeral parlor, a movie theater, and several churches. A school was also soon built.

The closed Rondo School stands just north of town and to the east of the abandoned grade of the M&NA. Photo by Barton Jennings.

Rondo was another small town that initially relied upon the timber business, and then farming as the land was cleared. In 1921, the *Arkansas Marketing and Industrial Guide* listed a timber company – the W. B. Howard lumber mill – as well as agricultural companies such as the Rondo Milling Company and the Marianna Cotton Oil Company. Later, Rondo also had a Nehi soda bottling plant.

In the 2010 census, the population was 198, a steady drop since a peak of 379 in 1970. There are no longer any businesses at Rondo, and the town is a residential community for nearby Helena and Marianna. According to the *Encyclopedia of Arkansas History & Culture*, there "appears to be no record of the origin of the name Rondo."

The Marianna Cotton Oil and the Rondo Milling Companies once operated at Rondo, but this gin complex is all that remains. Photo by Barton Jennings.

The Rondo City Hall building stands near the former M&NA. Photo by Barton Jennings.

342.1 COUNTY LINE – As the railroad headed toward Helena, it exited **Lee County** at this location and entered **Phillips County** to the south. **Phillips County** was created from land along the Mississippi River on May 1, 1820, making it the second oldest county in Arkansas. The county is part of the Arkansas delta area, located where the St. Francis River flows into the Mississippi River. The county was named for Sylvannus Phillips, who arrived here from North Carolina by 1797 and is claimed to be the first white settler in today's county. He was also later a representative to the first Territorial Legislature of the Arkansas Territory. The county today is working to attract more tourism and industrial development, especially after the 1990 U.S. Census called Phillips County one of the sixteen poorest counties in the United States. The county seat is the combined city Helena-West Helena.

343.0 EDGEWOOD – Edgewood is located near the junction of Phillips County Roads 248 and 201, just west of Arkansas Highway 1. The grade is visible as it passes just north of a rural home. The name Edgewood came from the Edgewood Plantation. Edgewood was another flag stop listed in the 1945 Missouri & Arkansas timetable. It reportedly had a 12' x 36' frame shelter, and earlier a 4-car spur track.

344.2 VAN – This was listed as a spur track in early Missouri & North Arkansas documents. It was soon gone from the timetables.

344.8 CANAL BRIDGE – This small bridge crosses a canal that drains into the Lick Creek Canal to the east.

This bridge was burned on June 20, 1922, soon after the railroad again resumed operations.

345.2 NORTH LEXA – The Missouri & North Arkansas built a diamond across the Missouri Pacific at this location, known as North Lexa since it is on the north side of the town of Lexa. Today there is a dirt road crossing at the location that crosses two tracks. A third track that is the north yard lead has its switch just south of the road crossing. The grade of the interchange track can be seen to the southwest of the crossing, where Missouri Pacific tracks were once used for any interchange business. A small frame shelter was here for many years.

Lexa was created when the Iron Mountain & Helena Railroad Company built through the area. The railroad used the land of Nathaniel Lexington Graves, and a small town developed on the plantation land. A post office opened in 1880, using the middle name of Graves. Because the name was somewhat common, it was shortened to Lexa in 1885. The town of Lexa grew when the St. Louis, Iron Mountain & Southern (former Iron Mountain & Helena) built a small shop complex for repairing engines, cars, and equipment at Lexa in 1908.

According to the *Encyclopedia of Arkansas History & Culture*, "by 1911, Lexa had five general stores, three hotels, a restaurant, a drugstore, several boarding houses, and more than 100 private residences. Three schools were built – two for African-American students and one for white students." However, as the railroad was merged into the Missouri Pacific, the shops were closed and moved to other locations. Many businesses also moved away, starting a steady decrease in population. As an attempt to end the loss, Lexa was incorporated on April 15, 1925, but few things improved.

Today, Lexa is a town of approximately 300 residents at an elevation of 213 feet. The town has few businesses and primarily serves as a residential community for the Helena area. The Arkansas Midland Railway operates the Helena Branch between Lexa and Helena, and bases many of its operations in the small metal railroad office and yard in downtown Lexa.

Missouri Pacific Crossing

This location was shown in Missouri & Arkansas employee timetables as a Missouri Pacific Crossing. This route was originally the 3' 6" gauge Iron Mountain & Helena Railroad Company, originally created in Arkansas on December 31, 1860. Construction did not start until the late 1870s with the line completed from Barton northward to Marianna, for 18 miles, by 1879. The unique 3' 6" gauge was chosen as it connected with the Arkansas Midland's line into Helena which used the same gauge. The original plans for the Iron Mountain & Helena was a 140-mile line from Helena to the St. Louis, Iron Mountain & Southern at Peach Orchard, in northeast Arkansas. In 1881, the line was converted to standard gauge, and then sold to the Kansas City & Southern Railway Company on February 21, 1882. On October 26, 1882, the line was sold to the St. Louis, Iron Mountain & Southern Railway.

On November 7, 1901, the Memphis, Helena & Louisiana Railroad Company was organized to build a line from a point across the Mississippi River from Memphis, south to the Louisiana State line. Several articles in *The Railway Age* covered the initial construction. The June 6, 1902, issue reported the following information: "The Memphis, Helena & Louisiana Railway is contemplated to be constructed from a point near West Memphis, Ark., to Prippe Junction, on line of Little Rock, Mississippi River & Texas division of the St. L. I. M. & S. From this point for distance of about 4 miles the operated line of the Warren branch will be utilized to Halley. From Halley southward the road is under construction to Tallulah, La., and contract will be let in near future for the remainder of the line to Clayton, La., on the N. O. & N. W. The total distance is about 288 miles." The route was sold to the St. Louis, Iron Mountain & Southern on April 30, 1903. By 1909, 120 miles of the route was in service from Helena Junction (Latour, located just south of Lexa, Arkansas) south to the Arkansas-Louisiana state line.

The St. Louis, Iron Mountain & Southern entered receivership on August 19, 1915, and was merged with the Missouri Pacific on May 12, 1917. This was always a very rural route, but served Memphis to New Orleans rail traffic. A unique operation over the line through North Lexa was the *Delta Eagle*, the railroad's first diesel-powered streamlined train serving Arkansas. The small train, operating between Memphis and Tallulah, Louisiana, was initially successful due to the lack of roads, especially across the river bottoms of the White and Arkansas Rivers. On October 27, 1954, the route was shortened from Helena to McGehee. The train ended operations on February 27, 1960.

In 1982, the railroad was acquired by Union Pacific, which first spent large sums to rebuild it for chemical trains, but then halted service in late 1986.

The route south of Helena Junction to north of McGehee was abandoned in 1992 by Union Pacific, becoming the Delta Heritage Trail. The route northward to Marianna was kept to connect to industry in Helena, which has been switched by the Arkansas Midland Railway Company since 1992.

346.8 PEARL BRANCH BRIDGE – This bridge was just north of the Arkansas Highway 242 bridge, located 1.2 miles east of the Union Pacific Railroad tracks at Lexa. Signs do not name the stream and modern area documents do not use the name Pearl Branch. This area is part of the drainage of the Lick Creek Canal. The Beaver Bayou Drainage District was created in 1907 to drain land in the area. The Lee-Phillips Drainage District was created in 1917 to drain lands farther to the south. By the 1920s, both drainage districts had built twenty miles of the Lick Creek Canal, moving water to Big Creek.

Lick Creek, which the railroad crossed just south of North Lexa, was a major stream that drained the lands west of Helena. During the Civil War, Lick Creek marked the western limits of Federal control of the Helena area. The Union Army was worried about Confederate forces building up in the area and often sent patrols out to challenge them. One of these, known as the Skirmish at Lick Creek, occurred on January 12, 1863, and involved Powell Clayton and his Fifth Kansas Cavalry. A historical marker south of Lexa near Barton explains the action.

After the January 11, 1863, battle at Arkansas Post, General Willis Gorman led troops from Helena on a raid up the

White River. Colonel Powell Clayton and 1,200 cavalrymen went to Big Creek west of Helena when a patrol of 25 men of the 2nd Wisconsin Cavalry was sent back with messages. On arriving at Lick Creek, they found the bridge burned. As they forded the creek, around 200 Confederate horsemen attacked the patrol. The Wisconsin men, armed only with pistols, shot five or six attackers, but were quickly overrun. Only 5 of the 25 men made it to Helena.

Later in March, another large Union force spent five days along Lick Creek fighting a number of small Confederate units. The result was a number of officers from both armies killed or taken prisoner, but no significant strategic advantages were gained. Until later in the year, Federal forces were basically confined to the territory east of Lick Creek.

349.4 SOUTHLAND – The community of Southland began after the Civil War when a Quaker school and orphanage for African-American children moved here from Helena. The school was also supported by the officers and men of the Fifty-sixth Colored Regiment of the U.S. Army. Known as the Southland School, a number of freed slaves moved near the school for the opportunity of education, creating the small community of Southland. The post office of Southland opened in 1889.

During the 1920s, the New South Gin Company operated here, processing the cotton of the local farms. About the same time, a series of leadership changes led to financial issues at the school, which became the Southland College. After years of troubles, the school closed in 1925, as did the post office. By the 1940s, Southland was a simple flag stop for the Missouri & Arkansas, with a mail crane through 1930 located 130 feet north of the depot location. There was a 12' x 36' shelter here that included an enclosed freight room.

A number of scattered homes remain along Southland Road, Phillips County Road 241. The tracks crossed the road just north of the Jackson Memorial Cemetery. No sign of the old Southland School remains.

351.3 AIRPORT #2 – There was an 8-car spur track to the east, with the switch on the south end. The track was located approximately where the grade crosses today's Arkansas Highway 185, Airport Road, just south of a small residential area. This track served the Thompson-Robbins Airfield, a World War II pilot training facility. The airfield came about as an effort by the United States Army Air Corps to create pilot schools. The plan was unique in that it involved private flight schools contracted to provide the training, since the Air Corps didn't have enough instructors. As a part of the agreement, schools were built where the military provided the students and planes, built any needed buildings, and bought back any structures later not needed. After the basic training, more advanced training was conducted at regular military facilities.

To create this training facility, Helena and West Helena acquired 640 acres next to the existing West Helena airport, and opened a flight school called Helena Aero Tech on October 4, 1941. On December 6, 1941, the day before the Pearl Harbor attack, the airfield was dedicated as the Thompson-Robbins Airfield. The airfield was named for Helena residents Lieutenant Jerome Pillow Thompson and Lieutenant Jack Stewart Robbins, both of whom had died in Army Air Force flying accidents (in 1933 and 1940). Overseeing the training was the 59th Flying Training Detachment, 29th Flying Training Wing.

The Thompson-Robbins Airport still includes a few of the original World War II structures, including this aircraft hangar. The M&NA had several spur tracks that were used to serve the facility. Photo by Barton Jennings.

The facility was more than just an airfield. It included administrative buildings, housing for officers and enlisted men, a mess hall, a post exchange, and other structures. Until the facility closed on August 4, 1944, almost 4000 pilots were trained. The buildings, planes, furniture, and other items were soon sold. The airfield was also sold and became a civilian airport, classified today as a general aviation airport. It is now the Thompson-Robbins Airport, owned by the City of Helena-West Helena. Much of the facility still shows its military history, including the original hangars, the parking ramp, flagpole, foundations, and roads.

351.9 AIRPORT #1 – There was a short 7-car spur track to the east, with the switch on the north end. This track also was designed to support the nearby airfield.

353.0 WEST HELENA – Heading south into West Helena, the railroad crossed then Highway 20, today's Highway 49. It then curved to the south, passing a number of large shippers. Today, this route is Martin Luther King Jr. Drive, U.S. Highway 49. The 20' x 70' M&NA depot, telegraph call "WS", was just north of Plaza Avenue, located at the south end of a complex of tracks on the east side of the mainline.

It seems like a full day can be spent just finding all of the abandoned tracks in the West Helena and Helena areas. These former Missouri Pacific tracks cross Plaza Avenue just east of Plaza Avenue Park. Photo by Barton Jennings.

There was a spur track looping around the east side of the depot with the switch on the north end. To the north were tracks into several industries and a short siding to the east. The connecting track to the Helena Southwestern was off the mainline and to the west, located between the switches of the short siding. Photos show that after the railroad was abandoned, the depot was used by the local Head Start educational program before being removed to make way for a wider Highway 49.

West Helena is the younger of the two parts of Helena-West Helena, Arkansas. Not being on the Mississippi River and on the west side of Crowley's Ridge, this was farming and logging country. When the Missouri & North Arkansas Railroad built through the area, the land suddenly had more value, and James R. Bush bought the 2300-acre Hoggatt Clopton Plantation in 1907. The next year, the 2358 acres was sold to Edward Chaffin Hornor, who platted a town and industrial park. Soon the plat was sold to the West Helena Company (owned by Edward Chaffin Hornor, John S. Hornor, and James Tappan Hornor) which had the job of promoting and selling properties. A full town survey was completed on March 28, 1910, with the design being a completely segregated community, with parts of the town being designated for housing and businesses for whites and blacks. It was another 53 years before a post office opened in 1963.

To help with the development, the West Helena Company bought the Helena Street Railway Company and the Interurban Railway Company in October 1909 and extended the line from Helena to West Helena. Additionally, a number of entertainment centers also opened, including the Helena Country

Club, an amusement park, a theater, a band stand, and a small zoo. Industry was assisted by a series of 10-acre industrial lots along the railroad. The plan worked as numerous companies moved to West Helena and the town was incorporated on May 23, 1917. The Missouri & North Arkansas also benefitted, as there were a number of industry tracks to the north of the depot at West Helena. Most were to the east side of the mainline. The *Arkansas Marketing and Industrial Guide* of 1921 listed many of these companies, almost all in the lumber business.

- American Cooperage Company – cooperage
- Arkansas Veneer Company – boxes, box shooks, packaging material, veneer
- Buckeye Veneer Company – boxes, box shooks, packaging material, veneer
- Chicago Mill & Lumber Company – boxes, box shooks, packaging, lumber, veneer
- J. W. Denison & Company – lumber, spokes and rims for automobiles
- National Cooperage & Woodenware Company – cooperage
- Palpcke Leicht Lumber Company – lumber
- Pekin Cooperage Company – cooperage
- Penrod-Jurden Company – lumber, veneer
- Poinsett Lumber Company – lumber
- Shelly Cooperage Company – tight barrel staves
- Van Briggle Veneer Company – boxes, box shooks, packaging, staves, veneer
- West Helena Hickory Company – hardwood

Heber Springs (AR) to Helena (AR)

This smokestack and water tower mark the area where the Pekin Cooperage and Arkansas Veneer companies once operated in West Helena. Photo by Barton Jennings.

West Helena was a major industrial area for the M&NA. The 1918 Sanborn map on the following page shows the area north of Plaza Avenue where the M&NA had their passenger station. This area was full of lumber, veneer and box mills. Note that the car barn and railway repair shop for the interurban railway was several blocks east of the M&NA station.

The area south of Plaza Avenue was also full of industry, including more veneer mills, a furniture factory, cotton mill, and other rail shippers. Note how both the M&NA and Missouri Pacific served some of the industries. All of this business required a great deal of switching, and even though the M&NA operated a local switcher, trains #211 and #212 both spent quite a bit of time at West Helena in 1936. Train #211 wasn't scheduled to depart for Helena until 4:00pm, while #212 was scheduled to leave at 10:45am.

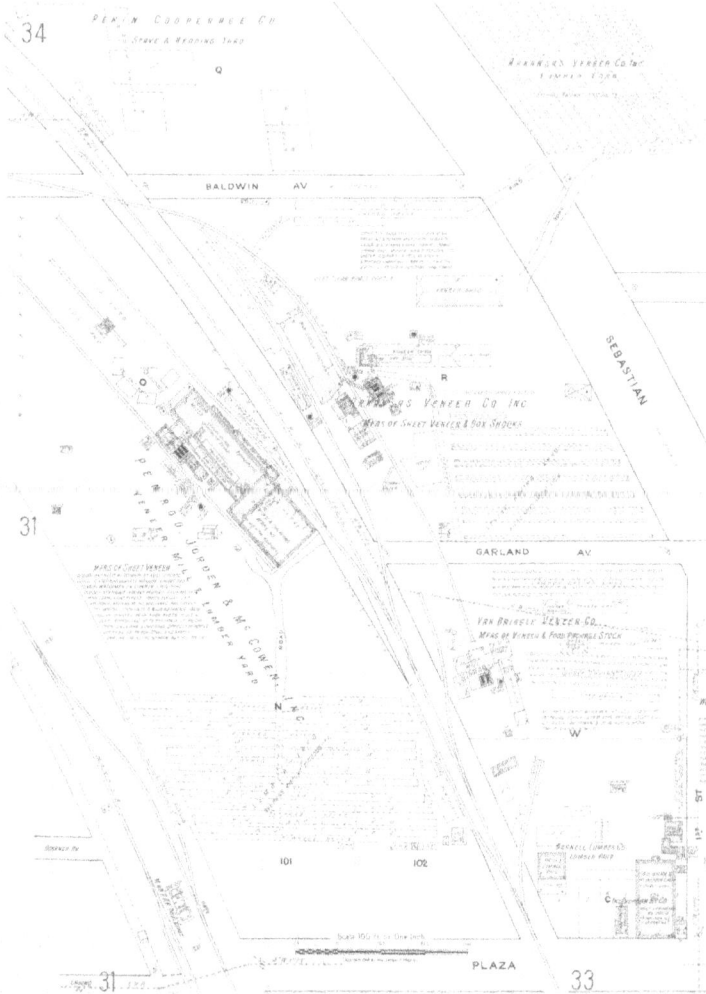

Sanborn Fire Insurance Map from Helena, Phillips County, Arkansas. Sanborn Map Company, Oct, 1918. Library of Congress, Geography and Map Division. https://www.loc.gov/item/sanborn00265_007/. Page 32 of 38.

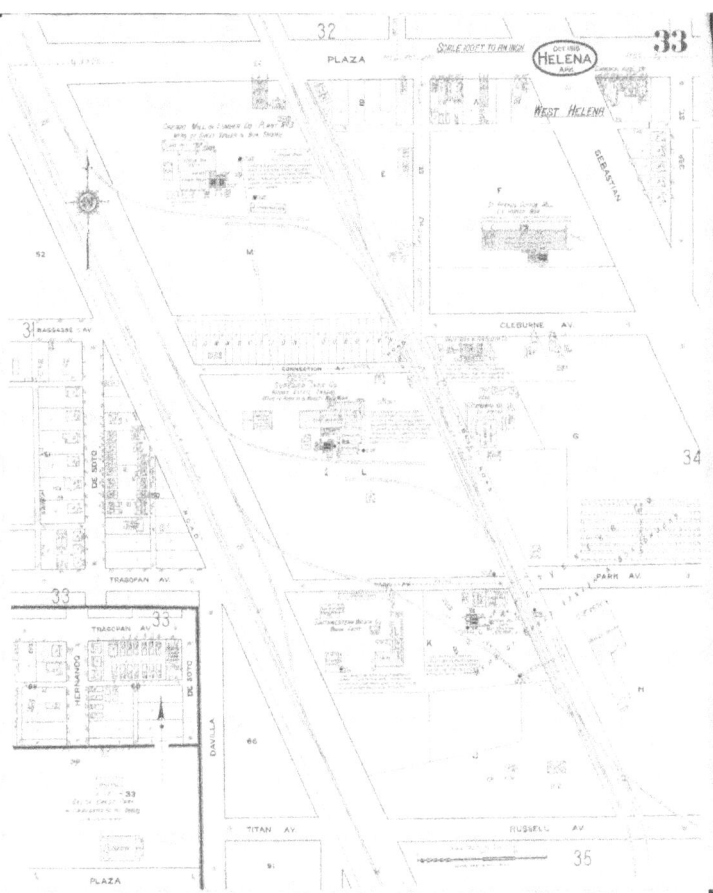

Sanborn Fire Insurance Map from Helena, Phillips County, Arkansas. Sanborn Map Company, Oct, 1918. Library of Congress, Geography and Map Division. https://www.loc.gov/item/sanborn00265_007/. Page 33 of 38.

A unique product of one of these firms was the white ash and mahogany body panels and framing for the Chrysler Town & Country and the Dodge Cornet, two famous woody automobiles of the 1940s. During the 1920s and 1930s, Pekin Wood Products, earlier Pekin Cooperage, was supplying wooden crates, boxes, and milled products to Chrysler. During the late 1930s, Chrysler acquired controlling interest in the firm. This led to Chrysler selecting the West Helena mill for the production of the car parts. Over the years, the firm also made other products, including military mortar shell boxes during the Korean War.

Another major firm in West Helena was the Chicago Mill & Lumber Company. This was a national firm that had mills and timber all across the region, with facilities also in Tallulah, Louisiana; Cairo, Illinois; and Greenville, Mississippi. The company was known for their box-making operations, manufacturing boxes for everything from watermelons to automobile parts. In particular, during the 1940s and 1950s, the mill manufactured wooden boxes for the automotive industry that were a combination of plywood with metal edges. The company's office building once stood at 129 North Washington Street in West Helena, Arkansas. It was a single-story wood frame structure built in the 1920s and added to the National Register of Historic Places in 1996, but has since been torn down.

In 1945, West Helena produced 431 carloads of freight for the M&A. While these industries are almost all gone today, there are still several industries in West Helena. One of these is the 660,000 square foot manufacturing facility of Hoffinger Industries and their Doughboy Pools. Originally Domain Industries, the firm sealed K-rations during World War I. The firm became Doughboy Industries in 1947 and entered the splash pool business. The company was eventually acquired by Hoffinger Industries and now makes ground pools, filtration systems, and many other products. The Helena Industries West Helena Manufacturing facility is also here. Owned by Helena Chemical, they are one of the largest contract chemical manufacturers in the United States. Finally, the D. B. Griffin Warehouse, a former cotton warehouse, is still in business. All of these sit on industrial land created by Edward C. Hornor.

Plaza Avenue Park

Celebrating the history of the Helena-West Helena area has recently taken on added importance to the community. Just east of U.S. Highway 49 is a small park in what is known as the "Plaza District" that features a great deal of information about the local industrial history. The park sits in the center median of Plaza Street, a right-of-way once used by the local trolley.

The park features Union Pacific caboose 25112, a Class CA-4 caboose built by Pullman-Standard Manufacturing Company at their Michigan City, Indiana, plant in October 1944. It was originally numbered UP 3812, and was renumbered to 25112 in April 1959. This was one of seven cabooses that were rebuilt in 1975 for systemwide pool service, receiving new federally approved toilets, safety windows, electric lighting and refrigerators, radios, oil heating, and improved steel platforms and steps. The caboose was eventually retired on August 20, 1986, and donated to the City of West Helena during December 1986.

Union Pacific caboose 25112 stands in Plaza Avenue Park. Photo by Barton Jennings.

Also at the park are twelve information boards that feature photos and histories of area industries. Among these are boards about the Chicago Mill & Lumber Company and Pekin Wood Products. The boards feature a number of photos and maps and are an essential stop for any visitor interested in the area's industrial history. Also a feature of the park are a number of abandoned tracks, reminders of all of the activity that was once here.

Heber Springs (AR) to Helena (AR)

Near where the M&NA once had their station in West Helena is the Plaza Avenue Park. This park includes a dozen information boards about the area's history, including several about the railroads of the community. Photo by Barton Jennings.

Helena Southwestern Railroad Company

The Helena Southwestern Railroad started as a private line built to support the Chicago Mill & Lumber Company. The 2.321-mile line, with 3.249 miles of yard tracks and sidings, was built in 1913 and then sold to the Helena Southwestern Railroad Company, which was incorporated on November 7, 1913. The sale took place in two steps on December 30, 1913, and May 1, 1914. This gave the railroad a mainline from West Helena to Helena Southwestern Junction and a connection with Missouri Pacific. There were a number of plans for expansion, and the *Railway Review*, dated February 28, 1914, stated that the railroad planned to build southwest from West Helena to Pillows Hills, Arkansas, a total of 20 miles.

The proposed line was never built, but instead other Chicago Mill properties were assigned to the railroad. During 1916, the Helena Southwestern acquired railroad property in Prairie and Woodruff Counties from the Chicago Mill & Lumber Company. To connect to these other properties, the railroad had trackage rights on other area railroads. This included almost 220 miles of Missouri Pacific track from Southwestern Junction near West Helena, to near Tallulah, Louisiana (the Main Line Division). There was also the White River Division from Barton, Arkansas, to Chimile, Louisiana. These routes connected with several other Chicago Mill properties and allowed the movement of logs and lumber. There were also 57.8 miles of trackage rights over the Missouri & North Arkansas between West Helena and McClelland, Arkansas, the McClelland Division. Most of these trackage rights and secondary operations were retired by the 1930s.

In 1990, part of the Chicago Mill & Lumber Company still stood, as shown here. Photo by Barton Jennings.

Heber Springs (AR) to Helena (AR)

The railroad operated quietly for many decades, but according to the Railroad Retirement Board, the Helena Southwestern "ceased to be an employer effective with the close of business December 31, 1986." The property was sold to P. E. Barnes & Sons, Ltd., as a private carrier in April 1987. The mill and the railroad were eventually closed and abandoned. While the Chicago Mill & Lumber Company and its Helena Southwestern is gone, there is a unique survivor of the company. Two-truck, 53-ton Heisler #10 still exists, displayed at the Railroad Museum of Pennsylvania. The Heisler was built in 1918, with serial number 1375, for the W. T. Smith Lumber Company in Chapman, Alabama. It was sold to Angelina Hardwood of Ferriday, Louisiana, and then Chicago Mill & Lumber Company in Tallulah, Louisiana.

Toward the end of its existence, the Helena Southwestern was just a private railroad serving the remains of the Chicago Mill & Lumber company. This 25-ton Plymouth powered the railroad in 1990. Photo by Barton Jennings.

353.7 MISSOURI PACIFIC CROSSING – According to Union Pacific documents, this track was built in 1936 by the Missouri Pacific to reach the many industries that grew up in West Helena; however, M&NA records show a track here earlier, with it clearly listed by 1923. A Sanborn insurance map from 1918 also shows the line already in place. The line was 2.6 miles long and connected West Helena with the original Helena Branch built by the Iron Mountain & Helena Railroad by 1880. Early M&NA timetables showed this to be a crossing with the St. Louis, Iron Mountain & Southern, and that this was the only diamond where the gate was not normally aligned against the M&NA. A 1945 Missouri & Arkansas timetable stated that this diamond had no gate, and that trains were to stop and proceed only after knowing that the route was clear.

Both tracks are gone today. However, there are still signs of the former Missouri Pacific grade where it crosses U.S. Highway 49 just north of Mooney Drive.

356.2 OUTER YARD – Because the railroad shared downtown Helena facilities with the Illinois Central, and much of the downtown property was already used by one of several railroads that became part of the Missouri Pacific system, the Missouri & North Arkansas located its yard several miles outside of town. While the yard was once designed to include a complete locomotive shop and other facilities, it never had much more than a few yard tracks, a small engine house, and a water tower. According to the Sanborn Map Company, in 1918 the railroad had a three-stall roundhouse off the north end of the turntable, plus a number of other small buildings such as a coal platform, water tank, and storage shed. For years there were also several section houses located here as well as several bunk cars installed on a track off of the turntable. The yard office was made from a freight car body, and was assigned the telegraph call "YD" until 1930.

The Helena Outer Yard engine shed burned down in 1921 and the shop work was mostly done at Heber Springs, and later Kensett and Harrison. The coaling platform was retired by 1933. About that time, there was a spur to the east, with the switch on the north end, that connected to the 80-foot turntable. Just to the south was a siding, located north of the Missouri Pacific diamond. A railroad scale was also located here for many years.

During the 1940s, the yard was located between the Missouri & North Arkansas mainline and Hill Road. Today, it is under U.S. Highway 49 near where the Helena Regional Medical Center now stands.

356.9 MISSOURI PACIFIC CROSSING – M&NA records show that this was a crossing with the former Arkansas Midland Railroad Company. This railroad company actually had a fairly complex history. It started as the Arkansas Midland Railroad, created on November 7, 1853, and chartered on January 20, 1855. The route was planned as a 115-mile line from Helena to Little Rock, and some discussion had it as a narrow gauge line. While some grading was done, the company never built any track due to a lack of funding and the Civil War. On August 31, 1870, the Arkansas Central Railway Company was organized and acquired the work of the Arkansas Midland. The firm completed track with a gauge of 3' 6" from Helena to Duncan and on to Clarendon, a total of approximately fifty miles. Train service began in 1872.

In 1872, a railroad map was published by G. W. & C. B. Colton & Company that showed the Arkansas Central as a part of a much larger network of railroads. The map was labeled as showing "the Arkansas Central, the Helena & Corinth, and the Pine Bluff & Southwestern Railways, together forming the Texas & Northeastern Railway." The map showed an existing route from Corinth (Mississippi) to Helena to Pine Bluff, and on to Shreveport (Louisiana), with projected lines and connections to places like Nashville (Tennessee), Chicago (Illinois), Houston and San Antonio (Texas), and even Los Angeles (California).

However, the railroad soon failed financially and was sold to the Arkansas Midland Railroad Company (chartered May 15, 1878) on January 3. 1880. On the same date, the Arkansas Midland acquired the Little Rock & Helena Railroad Company. The new owner of the railroad was Sidney Hornor, a member of the Hornor family that would later develop West Helena and the interurban railroad between Helena and West Helena.

When the Cotton Belt built through the area in 1883, the Arkansas Midland converted its track to 3-foot gauge. The line then converted to standard gauge in 1887. The line expanded further on August 1, 1891, when it bought the Brinkley, Helena & Indian Bay Railroad which ran from Pine City to Brinkley, and then changed its gauge to standard gauge from the original 3-foot gauge. In 1901, Jay Gould bought the railroad and then it was merged into the St. Louis, Iron Mountain & Southern on September 1, 1909. The line to Clarendon was abandoned about

1917. Because Missouri Pacific had two routes west from Helena, the Arkansas Midland route was abandoned east of Barton to near here in 1932. The line west of Barton, Arkansas, was abandoned during the 1950s.

The former Arkansas Midland Railroad route came in from the west, had a diamond with the Iron Mountain & Helena, and then with the Missouri & North Arkansas. All three routes came in from the northwest and then curved to the northeast to enter Helena. The reason for this busy location was that the railroads curved around the south end of Crowley's Ridge. Crowley's Ridge is a unique feature of Eastern Arkansas, running from here north for approximately 150 miles. The narrow ridge is normally 250 to 550 feet higher than the delta area around it. This area was known as Helena Crossing, also as Arkansas Midland Junction.

358.1 MISSOURI PACIFIC CROSSING – Early M&NA timetables showed this to be a crossing with the St. Louis, Iron Mountain & Southern (StLIM&S). This is the line that still exists today that breaks off from the original Arkansas Midland line and curves to the east to the Bunge grain elevator on the Mississippi River. The Missouri & North Arkansas grade passed through the center of the petroleum tank farm, and headed north crossing the Missouri Pacific line. It then went north through what is today a patch of thick woods staying west of a drainage ditch. The route then again crossed the Missouri Pacific line near the Bunge facility.

358.8 MISSOURI PACIFIC CROSSING – This was another crossing of the former Iron Mountain & Helena, later StLIM&S line into Helena. The M&NA crossed the Missouri Pacific route near the Bunge complex and curved toward downtown. The short route from the Bunge elevator to the Scoular elevator connected back with the Arkansas Midland and their route to their Helena depot. A short parallel route is still in service today, but it is believed to have been built by a Missouri Pacific company and not the M&NA.

During the 1910s, the area immediately north of this crossing was filled by a large Chicago Mill & Lumber complex. Sanborn showed this to be a veneer mill and a box factory. To the east, the Arkansas Oak Company had a small sawmill and sawdust piles that were noted as being 25 feet tall. To the south of the diamond, the Archer Lumber Company had a large sawmill and lumber yard squeezed between the M&NA (to the east) and the Missouri Pacific line to the west. Both railroads had a number of spur tracks into these mills.

359.1 MISSOURI PACIFIC CROSSING – Early M&NA timetables showed this to be another crossing with the St. Louis, Iron Mountain & Southern. This crossing was with the line into the Missouri Pacific depot, and it allowed the M&NA to connect to several Illinois Central tracks.

359.4 HELENA – Helena is located at the south end of Crowley's Ridge on the west bank of the Mississippi River. Local digs have unearthed pottery, various types of stone points, and large burial mounds. Many of these relics indicate that this was a trading center located on ground above the annual floods. Helena is also believed to be the location of the first non-native religious service west of the Mississippi River, conducted when Spanish explorer Hernando de Soto crossed the river near here. Other reports indicate that Marquette and Joliet visited Indian settlements in the area in 1763. The first white settlement reportedly was in 1800 when William Patterson built a dock and river terminal. His son, John Patterson, is claimed to be the first white child of American parents born in Arkansas. In 1820, Phillips County was created, being named for Sylvanus Phillips. The same year, Helena was surveyed and mapped by New Yorker Nicholas Rightor. The name of the town, Helena, came from the daughter of Sylvanus Phillips.

This historical marker about the history of the Helena area stands at the Arkansas Welcome Center near the abandoned M&NA grade just south of downtown Helena. Photo by Barton Jennings.

Helena was made the county seat in 1830, the same year that Sylvanus Phillips died. A post office opened in 1831 and trade on the Mississippi River led to the Town of Helena being incorporated in 1833. It is now recognized as the second-oldest incorporated city in Arkansas, incorporated as a city in 1856. Because of its position, it attracted a number of merchants, bankers, and steamboat owners. This led Helena to resemble the many river towns up and down the river with expensive houses on the ridges, large warehouses and docks along the river, and the typical taverns, brothels, and housing for the working class.

During the Civil War, Helena was a key blockade point on the Mississippi River and Union forces occupied the town in 1862. From here, campaigns against Vicksburg and Little Rock were planned and supported. Because of this, the capture of Helena and then the defeat of Confederate forces attempting to retake the town on July 4, 1863, have been listed as one of the three critical Union victories, along with Gettysburg and Vicksburg, that are considered the turning point of the Civil War. One point of pride for locals during the war was that seven Confederate generals were from the Helena area. Among these was Patrick Cleburne, a famous local businessman. Cleburne, two other generals, and many veterans are buried in the Confederate section of Maple Hill Cemetery in Helena.

Because of the presence of Union forces, Helena was an early target for runaway slaves. So many slaves showed up and were given their freedom that two black regiments were formed at Helena. In 2011, Helena's Freedom Park was designated by the National Parks Service as a site on the National Underground Railroad Network to Freedom, the first site in the state of Arkansas to receive that designation. There are a number of other reminders of the Civil War era. The remains of four Union batteries are still visible, with Battery C being restored. A replica of Fort Curtis has also been built to explain the city's Civil War history.

After the war, Helena recovered quickly due to its location on the Mississippi River. It gained a reputation as a major cotton town, and a place where almost every evil could be obtained with ease. Mark Twain visited and wrote about Helena, stating that "Helena occupies one of the prettiest situations on the Mississippi" in his book *Life on the Mississippi*. He also wrote that Helena was "exceptionally productive" and "the commercial center of a broad and prosperous region."

The late 1800s and early 1900s saw railroads arrive and a move away from the river to other modes of transportation. Industry, especially those related to timber, located on the edge of town, creating communities such as West Helena. However, the Eighteenth Amendment and its prohibition of alcoholic beverages closed many of the businesses related to barrel making. During January 1927, Helena opened a new $400,000 river terminal, hoping to expand shipping. Shortly afterwards, a second assault against Helena was the Mississippi River Flood of 1927. The Depression hit before the town recovered, a second flood in 1937 did more damage, and railroads that served the town were lost over the next decade or two. With the timber gone, Helena reverted back to a large farm town, moving cotton, fertilizer, and other farm crops.

The 1927 flood was a major event in Helena. While some levees already existed, major work was conducted to prevent a repeat of the 1927 event. Railroads followed the larger levee, which is now also used as a walking trail. Near the Missouri Pacific station, the tracks belonged to the MP. Further north and near the ferry slip, the tracks like this belonged to the Yazoo & Mississippi Valley (IC) and could be used by the M&NA. Photo by Barton Jennings.

Helena was the location of the first broadcast of *King Biscuit Time*, a show dedicated to Southern blues music. First aired on November 21, 1941, the show is still on the air on the original KFFA. It is the longest-running daily American radio broadcast in history, and has won numerous broadcasting awards. The show is broadcast live from the studio at the Delta Cultural Center and visitors are encouraged. World War II provided some economic boost for the community, especially with the car parts and box manufacturing companies. Shortly after the war ended in 1946, the school systems of Helena and West Helena were merged.

Like many southern cities, the 1950-1970s were hard as industry and the economy changed, civil rights and school desegregation were pushed, and many workers moved away for better jobs. The century of segregated communities and the history of conflict between Helena and West Helena led to years of efforts to try to consolidate the cities. Finally, on January 1, 2006, the two merged creating the city of Helena-West Helena, Arkansas. In 2010, the combined population was 12,282.

In 1990, Union Pacific was the only rail carrier serving the Helena area. Many companies had their own switch locomotives, such as this Baldwin diesel used by 5 Rivers. Photo by Barton Jennings.

The Helena-West Helena area has been the hometown of a number of famous people. For example, John Hanks Alexander, the first African-American officer to hold a regular command position, and the second African-American graduate of the U.S. Military Academy, is from here. Country Music Hall of Famer Conway Twitty once lived here. Baseball stars Alex Johnson and Ellis Valentine claim the area as home. Finally, the first African-American president of the Board of Commissioners of Cook County, Illinois, John Stroger Jr., came from Helena.

Delta Cultural Center

Located in the Missouri Pacific depot and a series of nearby storefronts on Cherry Street is the Delta Cultural Center. This is another must stop for any exploration of the area. The center provides an opportunity to wander this former passenger depot and freight house. The displays in the Missouri Pacific depot include items about area railroads, industry, farming, the Civil War, and the 1927 Flood. A noted feature is the bell from Illinois Central's *Pelican* ferryboat.

Attached to the station is Missouri Pacific caboose 13461, which can be toured. This caboose was built at the Sedalia (Missouri) shops of Missouri Pacific in 1950. Originally numbered 1196, it was one of 180 welded cabooses built by the railroad. The caboose was modernized in the late 1960s. When Missouri Pacific became a part of Union Pacific, the caboose became a member of class CA-21. The caboose was finally retired on April 1, 1987, and donated to Helena during May 1989.

Helena Street Railway Company

Helena was an early home of a streetcar system. The first system was chartered on March 8, 1887, as The Citizens Street Railway Company. The original shop was at the southwest corner of Cherry Street and Phillips Street, now the north end of the Delta Cultural Center. The system originally operated up Cherry Street through the business district, and then connected with the neighborhoods to the north. The *Whipple's Electric, Gas and Street Railway Financial Reference Directory* (1890) reported on the Helena Street Railway Company, which had just taken over The Citizens Street Railway Company, by stating that the route was 3.5 miles long and used standard-gauge track. The operation had eight two-horse cars and forty horses.

As an effort to extend the system, the Interurban Railway Company began building an electric trolley line between Helena and West Helena. Almost immediately, the West Helena Company bought both the Helena Street Railway and the Interurban Railway and extended the system through a deep cut through Crowley's Ridge to West Helena. Within a few years, there were plans being proposed to extend the line far beyond West Helena. *The Contractor* of November 15, 1912, stated that "The Helena Street & Interurban Railroad Co. is reported to be making surveys on its extension from Helena to West Helena and to Marianna." A report on December 1, 1912, stated that "the Marianna Electric Ry. Co. is reported chartered to build electric railway from Marianna to Helena." The Hornor family, responsible for much of the early development of West Helena, was listed as the officers.

The 1914 *McGraw Electric Railway Manual* stated that the Interurban Railway Company connected Helena and West Helena with 5.2 miles of track, 18 motor and 16 other cars. The repair shops were shown to be in West Helena, the general offices in Helena, and that Beech Crest Park in West Helena was owned by the system. Beech Crest Park, located along Crowley's Ridge on the east side of West Helena, often featured moving pictures, trails, picnics, fairs, and other events. E. C. Hornor was president and J. S. Hornor was secretary and treasurer of the companies.

The route of the streetcar in Helena started at a turning wye on Bisco Street about one-quarter mile south of Louisiana Street. The streetcar headed north and then turned east on Louisiana for one block to Chickasaw. The line went two blocks north on Chickasaw and then east on Missouri to Cherry Street. Here it served the Missouri Pacific station and then went north past the Yazoo & Mississippi Valley – Missouri & North Arkansas station. At Porter Street, the line turned west to College, turned north to Perry, and then west again. The interurban part of the line closely followed today's Business Highway 49 to West Helena. The route went west down Plaza Street and the seven-bay shop was located where today's municipal building stands at the northwest corner of Plaza and 1st Streets. The line turned using a loop at Washington Street further to the west. The streetcar system finally shut down on August 5, 1933, and was replaced by the buses of the Twin City Transit Company.

The Missouri Pacific Railroads

Besides the electric interurban railroad, there were four different steam railroads that once served Helena. From the west, the first two were the Arkansas Central Railway, later the Arkansas Midland Railroad, and the Iron Mountain & Helena. Then there was the Missouri & North Arkansas, also from the west. The final railroad was the Yazoo & Mississippi Valley from the east, crossing the Mississippi River to reach Helena.

Heber Springs (AR) to Helena (AR)

The Iron Mountain & Helena was the first railroad at Helena. It and the Arkansas Midland both later became a part of Missouri Pacific. The Arkansas Midland route was abandoned during the 1930s, and the Iron Mountain route became part of Union Pacific in 1982. In 1992, the line from Lexa to Helena was turned over to the Arkansas Midland Railroad, owned by the Pinsley Railroad Corporation. In late 2014, Pinsley sold their Arkansas railroads to Genesee & Wyoming. The Helena line was embargoed on March 31st the following year because it failed a track inspection. By November, local efforts resulted in the line being rebuilt and opened again.

In 1896, the Arkansas Midland had a 5-stall roundhouse, machine shop, turntable, blacksmith shop, and other facilities on the northwest corner of Phillips and Franklin in Helena. This railroad arrived at the roundhouse from the south with a rail line up Franklin, serving the W. D. Reeves Planing Mill less than two blocks to the south. The Arkansas Midland passenger and freight depot was near the Mississippi River on the southeast corner of Natchez Street and Missouri (also known as Caroline) Street. Across the tracks to the east was the Helena Ice Company and the Berton & Johnson cotton sheds. To the southwest of the station was the Helena Mill of the Arkansas Cotton Oil Company. From the station, an industrial lead headed south to serve the Planters Compress and Storage Company, Planters Cotton Gin, Kaiser Lumber Company, and the Helena Box Factory. To the west of this industrial area was the R. McCoy Lumber Company, which had its own logging railroad that connected with the Mississippi River. Just to the south was the Straub Brick Company. North of the station on the river bank near Rightor Street was a ramp to connect with a rail ferry.

The Iron Mountain & Helena had for many years its own depot located at Louisiana and Yazoo Streets. However, when the Arkansas Midland was acquired, the company consolidated in the Natchez and Missouri Streets depot.

The St. Louis, Iron Mountain & Southern (Missouri Pacific) station, built in 1915, still stands and is used by the Delta Cultural Center as a museum about the region. The station included both passenger and freight sections, as well as office space on the second floor. Photo by Sarah Jennings.

As shown by this 1918 Sanborn map, the Missouri Pacific passenger station at Helena was surrounded by tracks, with the MP tracks to the east and the M&NA tracks to the west in Natchez Street.

Sanborn Fire Insurance Map from Helena, Phillips County, Arkansas. Sanborn Map Company, Oct, 1918. Library of Congress, Geography and Map Division. https://www.loc.gov/item/sanborn00265_007/. Page 22 of 38.

In 1915, the old Arkansas Midland station was replaced with a new red brick building with limestone accents. Today listed on the National Register of Historic Places, the two-story building is described as having been built with "detailing from the Craftsman period as well as subtle Classical Revival influences." The station was built with a two-story northern section, with upstairs offices designed as the regional headquarters for the St. Louis, Iron Mountain & Southern. The southern end served as a one-story freight house. Originally, the freight and baggage sections were separated by a breezeway which was enclosed early in the building's existence. In the 1940s, Missouri Pacific ran 5 passenger trains in and out of Helena each day, and they also ran a "doodlebug" from Helena to Memphis every day.

One of these trains was the regionally famous *Delta Eagle*. The *Delta Eagle* was the Missouri Pacific's first diesel-powered streamlined train serving Arkansas. The train featured a unique consist using a diesel locomotive which was built with a baggage section at the rear, plus two coaches. The train initially operated between Memphis and Tallulah, Louisiana, but was cut to Helena to McGehee on October 27, 1954. The train last operated on February 27, 1960.

In 1918, Missouri Pacific also had a separate freight depot located just south of the intersection of Yazoo and Louisiana Streets. Neither of these streets still exist. Yazoo is now named Frank Frost Street, and Louisiana was located one block south of Arkansas. The depot no longer stands, but the land it sat on is now unused, and is located immediately west of the two stub tracks southwest of Scoular.

Today, the former Missouri Pacific station is known simply as The Train Depot and serves as part of the Delta Cultural Center. It includes displays on the Civil War, the Great Mississippi Flood of 1927, and other area histories.

Missouri & North Arkansas and the Yazoo & Mississippi Valley

The fourth railroad was the Louisiana, New Orleans & Texas Railroad, which used a transfer boat (ferry) to bring cars across the Mississippi River starting in 1889. The trackage in Arkansas was technically the Louisville, New Orleans & Texas Railway Company of Arkansas. The Interstate Commerce Commission stated that the railroad consisted of a terminal yard in Helena, a total of 0.895 miles of track.

The foundation of the old Yazoo & Mississippi Valley track scale can still be found along the levee at the east end of York Street. Photo by Barton Jennings.

The railroad was later the Yazoo & Mississippi Valley (Y&MV), and then the Illinois Central Railroad in 1946. The Yazoo & Mississippi Valley was the primary partner with the Missouri & North Arkansas, and served Helena using the *Pelican* from 1930 to 1971. The transfer boat could hold 15 to 20 railcars on two tracks. The end of ferry service became official with a March 23, 1973, ruling of the Interstate Commerce Commission.

The Missouri & North Arkansas Railroad Company came to Helena in 1906 and operated until 1946. When it was building towards Helena, it received a great deal of encouragement from the Helena area, and the company actually acquired options on real estate all the way to Pensacola, Florida. Later, the Helena & Northwestern Railway operated the line from 1949 until 1951. After that, the line was abandoned and tracks removed, except for a few isolated industrial tracks that were kept to protect a few rail shippers.

The remains of a number of tracks used by the M&NA still exist in Helena, including these in an alley near the former freighthouse. Photo by Barton Jennings.

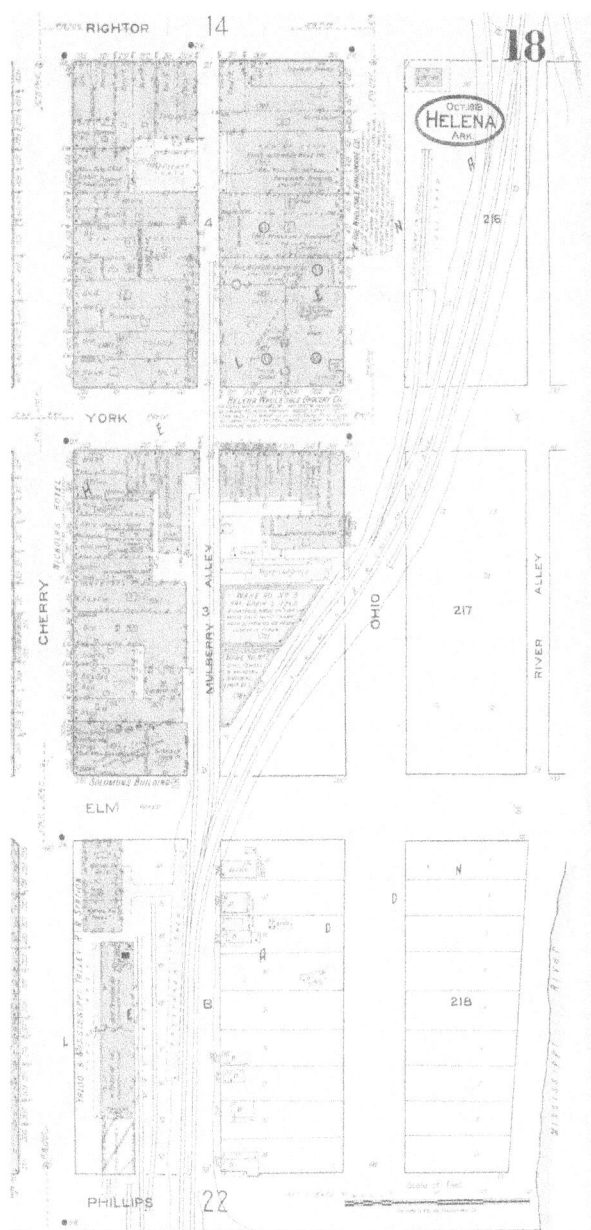

Sanborn Fire Insurance Map from Helena, Phillips County, Arkansas. Sanborn Map Company, Oct, 1918. Library of Congress, Geography and Map Division. https://www.loc.gov/item/sanborn00265_007/. Page 18 of 38.

The M&NA and Y&MV shared passenger station and freight house facilities in Helena, located on Cherry Street several blocks north of the Missouri Pacific station. In 1936, Mixed Train #212 had a departure time of 10:00am. Southbound #211 was scheduled to arrive at Helena at 4:30pm.

In Helena, the Missouri & North Arkansas and the Yazoo & Mississippi Valley/Illinois Central had a number of joint operations, including tracks and buildings. This included a station and freight house on the east side of Cherry Street in the 200 block. Just north of the Y&MV/M&NA station were several tracks that ran down back alleys to serve customers. The tracks can still be followed east of Cherry Street, where a line down Mulberry Alley served the Helena Wholesale Grocer Company on York Street, and even further north to several cotton warehouses, an icehouse, and other wholesale companies. Most of these buildings have been gone for years.

This old warehouse still stands with abandoned tracks in the neighboring street, but it was in the area that fell under the rules of the Yazoo & Mississippi Valley. Photo by Barton Jennings.

Heber Springs (AR) to Helena (AR)

The agreement between the two railroads clearly showed who had responsibility for what parts of the railroad network. The Yazoo & Mississippi Valley water tower (a 16' x 19' 26,000-gallon tank connected to the city water system) was the most important part of the whole agreement. All references in the agreements use the tower, with Y&MV rules governing east of the tower and M&NA rules west of the tower. This use of M&NA and Y&MV was continued in the timetables of both railroads until 1946, long after both had changed their names.

A 1918 Sanborn map showed the water tower to be on Natchez Street, about a block south of Arkansas. Heading south, the joint M&NA/Y&MV track ran down the center of Natchez. Almost immediately, there was a diamond with the Missouri Pacific, just about where The Scoular Company office and scale is today. At the time, immediately to the west was a seed and meal warehouse of the large Union Seed & Fertilizer Company complex. Heading further south, the M&NA and Y&MV had a junction, with the Y&MV track heading on south and the M&NA mainline curving off to the southwest. Just south of this junction was the Y&MV water tank, located at the north end of what Sanborn called the Y&MV "Train Supply Station." From the north, these buildings included an office, a blacksmith shop, a store house, a sand dryer, and a coal bin. All were located on the west shoulder of Natchez Street, about where the Scoular elevator bins stand today.

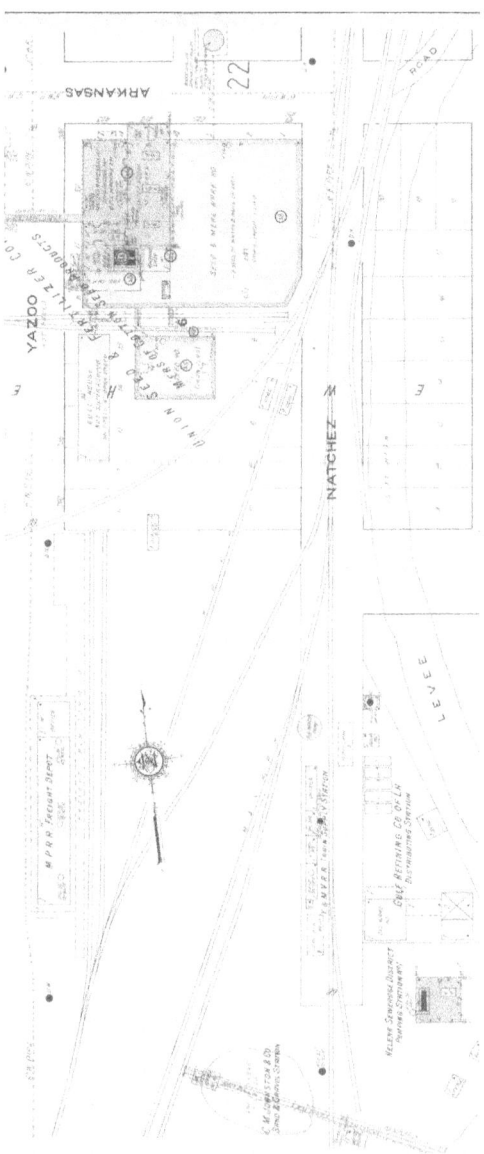

Sanborn Fire Insurance Map from Helena, Phillips County, Arkansas. Sanborn Map Company, Oct, 1918. Library of Congress, Geography and Map Division. https://www.loc.gov/item/sanborn00265_007/. Page 24 of 38.

Heber Springs (AR) to Helena (AR)

Even though older terms were used, with the creation of the Missouri & Arkansas Railway, the trackage rights agreement was renewed on October 18, 1935. According to Interstate Commerce Commission records, the M&A was allowed to operate over 0.56 miles of the Louisville, New Orleans & Texas Railway Company of Arkansas (LNO&T) mainline, plus 2.0 miles of yards and sidings at Helena. The LNO&T obtained the right to use 1000 feet of track west of the M&A outer yard. In addition, the M&A and the LNO&T agreed to continue to use the Louisville, New Orleans & Texas passenger and freight stations, yards, and team tracks.

Speeds in Helena were slow as 5 mph was the speed limit for all Y&MV yard tracks. An interesting speed restriction on the Missouri & Arkansas trackage was found in a 1941 Illinois Central timetable. It lists a 5 mph speed limit for M&NA bridge #358, the "Spider Web Bridge."

During the late 1920s, this was the second largest interchange point on the M&NA. During the period 1926-1928, the M&NA delivered 6924 cars to the Y&MV and received 2463 cars, out of a total of 36,863 and 35,095 cars. This was 19% of the outbound traffic and 7% of the inbound traffic. For 1949, the Illinois Central reported doing more than one million dollars worth of business in Helena. The Helena & Northwestern was clearly mentioned as a connecting line. In 1950, the IC sold to the H&NW former IC Office Car #11. It had earlier been rebuilt into cafe-sleeper #3902 and named "Cottonland." Before shipment to the H&NW, it was stripped down and sold as a shell.

The Yazoo & Mississippi Valley became the Illinois Central by 1951. The Illinois Central stopped coming to Helena in 1973 and its tracks were sold to Missouri Pacific.

M&NA/Y&MV Passenger Depot and Freight House

There were once great plans for the Missouri & North Arkansas at Helena. A number of people related to the railroad created the Helena Terminal Railway, chartered on May 5, 1909, with the goal of building a belt around the city, as well as a grand union passenger station. The two railroads had many of the same corporate officers, but the belt line and station were never built. Instead, the M&NA built their own route around the south end of Crowley's Ridge, including a small yard and shop complex, as well as many spur tracks to reach various industries. There were also announced plans to build a station on the corner of Ohio and Market Streets, just north of downtown Helena. Various reports from 1910 and 1911 state that the station would cost $25,000 and be "the finest in the state." The May 3, 1911, issue of *Engineering-Contracting* stated the location was being used by the Newman Coal & Ice Company. However, just as the Helena Terminal Railway was never built, the same can be said for the M&NA station.

One of the earliest signs of agreements between the M&NA and the Yazoo & Mississippi Valley was the 1917 construction of a joint depot and freight house. This was the second depot in the area, as the Yazoo & Mississippi Valley Railroad had built a combination passenger and freight depot before 1900 on the southeast corner of Cherry and Elm, now a parking lot. In 1917, a two-story passenger depot was built at Cherry and Elm, while a freight depot and railway express office was built immediately to the south. The second floor of the passenger depot was used for offices by both the Yazoo & Mississippi Valley and the Missouri & North Arkansas. The telegraph call was always "HU" for the Helena depot.

The former joint freight house, used by the M&NA and the Yazoo & Mississippi Valley, still stands and now houses KIPP Delta Public Schools. Photo by Barton Jennings.

A plan of the station from the era provides a description of the complex. The passenger station was at the north end. The public area was described as having the "waiting room white" to the north, the ticket office in the center, and the "waiting room Negro" on the south end. Further to the south was the freight house. It was broken into three parts, with the north end used as the outbound freight house, the southern part as the inbound freight house, and an open paved platform just south of the building.

After the M&NA abandonment, the station offices were consolidated to allow rental of office space in the depot. The depot was torn down in 1962, but the freight house still stands on the east side of Cherry Street. Today it is used as classroom space for KIPP Delta Public Schools, a series of six charter schools in Helena, Blytheville, and Forrest City, Arkansas. The schools specialize in preparing under-served students for a pathway to college. The classrooms are amazing and still include the original large freight doors and many of the other building details.

KIPP Delta Public Schools has done a wonderful job of restoring the M&NA/Y&MV freight house. While the building is used for classrooms, the structure has been well preserved with many parts, such as the sliding freight doors, restored and operational. Photo by Barton Jennings.

About the Author

For almost three decades, Barton Jennings has been organizing charter passenger trains and writing the route descriptions, both for planning purposes and for the enjoyment of the passengers. These trips have been from coast to coast, often covering operations that haven't seen a passenger train in decades. In addition, he has written a number of articles about various railroads for rail hobby magazines. His basement has several rooms full of books, timetables and other documents about this and other railroads – important research items from a time long before today's internet. This book on the Missouri & North Arkansas Railroad is part of this effort to preserve railroad history.

Bart was born in Northwest Arkansas and still has strong ties to the area, having lived in Berryville. He still regularly visits the area, including seeing friends who have parts of the old Missouri & North Arkansas grade on their property. While working for Union Pacific, he often covered the Helena area, adding knowledge about this part of the M&NA. He has been fortunate to get to know many of those who have known and researched the railroad, and has long shared ideas and information. Today, Bart Jennings, after years working in the railroad industry, is a professor of supply chain management and teaches transportation operations. He also still teaches workshops for the railroad industry, a way to stay in touch with the industry he loves.

This book is an outgrowth of all of these experiences and previous writings about the Missouri & North Arkansas. It is unique in that the historic Missouri & North Arkansas Railroad essentially ended on September 20, 1946, when management finished removing foreign cars after the announcement of a strike by operating employees. By this time, the M&NA had already failed and the Missouri & Arkansas Railway had taken over for a final dozen years. Most of the railroad was abandoned, but small parts remained, operated by smaller railroads that also soon failed. Today, several miles of tourist railroad, a few buildings and bridges, and lots of miles of grade are all that are left.

This route description was begun in the 1970s as remains of the railroad's history were explored. Much of the information comes from internal railroad records, government and public records, and conversations with old and new friends. The information from the Missouri and North Arkansas Research Group, and the assistance of the Boone County Historical & Railroad Society, cannot be overstated. It is hoped that you enjoy your adventure with the Missouri & North Arkansas Railroad. Hopefully this book will be of assistance in some ways – *Missouri & North Arkansas Railroad: History Through the Miles*.

The author at Wheatley. Photo by Sarah Jennings.

www.ingramcontent.com/pod-product-compliance
Lightning Source LLC
Chambersburg PA
CBHW052007070526
44584CB00016B/1654